Eddie Dean

The Golden Cowboy

Eddie Dean

The Golden Cowboy

By Stephen Fratallone

Published in the USA by:
BearManor Media
P O Box 71426
Albany, Georgia 31708
www.bearmanormedia.com

ISBN   978-1-59393-780-5 (paperback)

Printed in the United States of America.

Book & cover design by Darlene and Dan Swanson of Van-garde Imagery, Inc.

Contents

Dedication

For the Glosup Family with much respect
and admiration, and for Ursula, my dear mother, and for
Stephen and Rachel, my beloved children, with love. ~ S. F.

Foreword

To write about Eddie Dean, who in my mind, was the most talented individual I have ever known, would be in itself a Herculean task. Eddie Dean was a singer, songwriter, artist, sculptor, sportsman, actor, carver, hunter, philosopher, legend, husband, and father. He was my idol. He was my hero. But more importantly, I was so blessed to have him as *my* dad.

He expressed himself so well through a variety of mediums. He was so full of life, dedicated to family, to history, to humanity, and to his profession. He was the guy to "ride the river with." Everyone I know loved this man for the person he was, as well as for his talent and fabulous singing voice. For example, when Eddie Dean sang "Old Man River," the goose bumps that came as a result were so big you needed a bigger shirt.

The Glosup Family is so fortunate to have Stephen Fratallone to write Dad's biography so well. The research was very thorough and fantastic. I know more about my family history than ever before. I conveyed my feelings to him about this numerous times and commended him on his knowledge of history and his ability to convert all this information into easy-to-read and interesting prose. Thank you, Stephen.

My sister, Donna, and I were truly blessed when my dad and my mother, Dearest (his rock), fell in love and created us. Donna would also have loved to have written about Dad if she were still living. She, with Dearest and Dad, will enjoy looking at their history together compiled so aptly by Stephen.

It is my hope that you will enjoy as I have, reading *Eddie Dean: The Golden Cowboy* again and again for the beautiful memories it brings.

Edgar Glosup Jr., Shingle Springs, CA, 2014

Acknowledgments

Putting together a book requires a great deal of time and team effort, especially when writing a biography. Needless to say, extensive research has to be conducted and gathered on the subject matter in question before even a sentence can be written.

While the author receives the credit for writing the book, of course, there are many individuals behind the scenes who contribute to insure that what the reader holds in his or her hands is a high-quality, honest, accurate, informative, and entertaining finished product.

I wish to publicly give a loud shout of thanks to the following individuals for their assistance in helping to make this "labor of love" possible:

To the late Eddie Dean, "The Golden Cowboy," without you, there wouldn't be any story! Thank you and your late wife, Dearest, for having the wisdom and foresight to save everything—well, *almost* everything—pertaining to your life and career, especially many of your photos, movies, recordings, and newspaper clippings as well as taped and transcribed interviews. Such light has helped to illuminate your amazing story much easier. My only regret is not being able to know you while you were alive so you and I could have worked together on writing your story. It had always been your wish to tell your story "like it is." I hope my humble efforts on these pages did just that, and would have pleased you.

To Ed Glosup Jr., Eddie Dean's son, for being such an enthusiastic supporter and cheerleader for this project when I first brought to your attention the idea of writing a book about your dad in early February 2012. Your graciousness, patience, guidance, and the amount of knowledge and material that you possess about your dad's life is simply amazing and such a blessing! I can well see why he is your hero. Working alongside you helped to make this book project not only a breeze, but exciting. I felt that I was sharing a part in Eddie's life right there with you. Thank you bunches!

To the late Donna Lee Knorr, Eddie Dean's daughter, who tried to get the ball rolling back in 1982 with the idea of doing a book about her father. Due to her failing health issues, the project fell temporarily by the wayside. Through her initial efforts, she helped to lay a solid foundation concerning her famous father's early life by taking it upon herself to record and transcribe interviews she conducted on her dad. All quotes by Eddie Dean notated in this book are derived directly from audio tape interviews and from transcribed interviews.

Her pioneering work along with the able assistance of her husband and writer, Ted Knorr, is invaluable to this project and is much appreciated. Now, more than thirty-three years later, her vision of a book about the life and times of her father, Eddie Dean, has finally materialized. It is this writer's sincere hope that such a book, and the effort put forth in creating it, would be pleasing to her.

To Joel Klein, my friend, encourager, and fellow Eddie Dean fan, who from the moment I presented my idea to you about writing this book, you were elated. You eagerly offered me help and assistance wherever possible by pointing me in directions where I could maximize potential resources for the successful completion of this project. Thank you! You are truly a good friend.

To Marilyn Tuttle, Joe Parker, and Boyd Magers, many thanks for your willingness to share your thoughts and recollections with me about Eddie Dean. Your comments and anecdotes helped to give color and shading to this project.

Finally, to you Western film and music fans that want to read something more in-depth about Eddie Dean, thank you for reading this tome. May you enjoy getting acquainted or reacquainted, whatever the case may be, with "The Golden Cowboy."

Stephen Fratallone, Chico, CA, 2014

Introduction

E ddie Dean can always be seen riding the trail in those grand ol' "clean" B-Western films in which the good guys always won and the bad guys always lost. It's not always like that these days. In fact, many would argue that the moral compass of American society since the latter third of the twentieth century has gone down the tubes. In an age of pluralistic relativism, good is now considered bad and bad is what will land you a lucrative "tell all" book deal or even perhaps your own talk show on television.

Dishonesty, self-centeredness, lewdness, and disrespectful behaviors tempered by the disillusionment of situational ethics are, sadly, the "new" values being forged into the fabric of our society today.

Eddie's films always had a good moral to them. It's something most films of every genre severely lack today. Our culture desperately longs for and looks for those heroes who have the integrity to live out those good morals both on and off the screen. Eddie was such a hero. He lived what has been commonly referred to as "The Cowboy Code."

The genesis for this "Cowboy Code" originated with Gene Autry as a way to instill in his many young fans what the American cowboy came to represent. Its precepts were to be respected and individually assimilated in a young person's life as part of his or her character development. Other cowboys, such as Roy Rogers and Hopalong Cassidy, had their own particular codes as well, but all conveyed similar standards of conduct.

This "Cowboy Code of Honor"[1] stated that:

1. A cowboy never takes unfair advantage—even of an enemy.

2. A cowboy never betrays a trust. He never goes back on his word.

3. A cowboy always tells the truth.

4. A cowboy is kind and gentle to small children, old folks, and animals.

5. A cowboy is free from racial and religious intolerance.

6. A cowboy is always helpful when someone is in trouble.

7. A cowboy is always a good worker.

8. A cowboy respects womanhood, his parents and his nation's laws.

9. A cowboy is clean about his person in thought, word, and deed.

10. A cowboy is a Patriot.

If any anyone thinks that the "Cowboy Code" is frivolous or outdated, think again. In 2011, the Montana State Senate passed a bill to adopt "The Code of the West"[2] from the book *Cowboy Ethics*[3] and make it the official Montana Code. The book was written by James Owen calling attention to the Enron and Wall Street scandals and to look at what we had become as a society and individuals.

Owen came up with his "Code of the West" that's similar to the "Cowboy Code" calling for a return to common sense principles and to a higher standard of moral and ethical grounding.

Eddie's films, like those of his contemporaries, were based on a formula of action, comedy, and music. Their films were predictable. There is some comfort that can be found in predictability. Even though things may look bleak or seemingly hopeless as the drama unfolds, you *always* knew that

Eddie was going to triumph in the end. Every one of those "horse operas" had that basic format to them. That format never deviated from one singing cowboy movie to the other.

Eddie Dean was what I call a "blue collar" singing cowboy. He was an iconoclast of sorts. While the bigger name leading B-Western heroes all wore white hats, Eddie wore both white and black hats, depending on his films. He felt that a good guy could wear a black hat, and he proved it. So did other silver screen cowboy heroes such as Tex Ritter, Hopalong Cassidy, Al "Lash" La Rue, and "Wild Bill" Elliot, for example.

While the more celebrated singing cowboys such as Gene Autry and Roy Rogers wore more elaborate outfits and rode handsome steeds who were arrayed in stunning gear and saddles and who seemed more intelligent than most humans, Eddie presented himself as a "no frills" kind of guy. Yes, he was smartly dressed, usual wearing his trademark "bib" Western shirt with his bandana knotted under the collar, but his on-screen wardrobe was nothing considered too ostentatious.

Eddie also rode a number of horses in his films – four to be exact – four beautiful looking creatures to be sure, but they were never featured doing any amazing stunts or coming to the rescue of their owners when the chips were down. Despite the lack of such theatrics, Eddie's horses did, however, receive billing before the film's other co-stars, which seemed more in line with protocol of the time.

And then there was Eddie's voice, that magnificent, "golden voice" that stood alone in a class all by itself, that superlatives could not do any justice. Many Western stars thought Eddie was one of the best if not *the* best singer of all the singing cowboys.

Gene Autry told Eddie on a number of occasions that if Eddie had come out to Hollywood three years before he did, Autry would never have had a chance (at stardom).

Roy Rogers echoed a similar sentiment every time he would introduce Eddie to an audience when he said, "Every time I hear Eddie Dean sing, I'm glad I have Trigger."

My friend, Craig Cronbaugh, a former news editor for a small rural newspaper in Iowa, hit the nail on the head when he wrote a commentary a few years ago about the irreplaceable "golden stars" who had recently passed on. Certainly Eddie Dean fits in that category. "Our golden entertainers became part of our heritage," Cronbaugh wrote. "They reflected our lives.

They made us laugh and kept us entertained during the Great Depression, both world wars, the Korean conflict and the war in Vietnam. These famous people are the ones who were around when our twentieth century mediums of radio, television, and motion picture productions were getting started. In a sense, these 'golden stars' *were* the industry. I am very thankful we have film, videotape, and various audio recording methods. This allows us all, young and old, to enjoy, once again, the golden stars."[4]

On a personal note, I am ecstatic and thankful that film and recordings of one such "golden star," Eddie Dean, are available for us to enjoy over and over again. I hope you will agree.

May this book you are holding in your hands about the life and times of Eddie Dean be something you can enjoy over and over again as well. So, saddle up, Partners, as we ride down the trail to visit Eddie Dean, "The Golden Cowboy."

1

The Glosups and the Vandergriffs

It was once widely believed throughout folklore that the seventh son of a seventh son was someone special, someone unique. Such a child was thought to be endowed with certain notable talent, special powers or abilities, unusual intelligence, or even extraordinary fortunes. The number seven, with its significance to this particular birth order, was regarded as a sacred and magical number among many ancient peoples, particularly the Hebrews, Assyrians, and Arabians. This fascination with the number seven still holds a place of special interest even today in the modern world.[1]

The ancient belief about the seventh son of a seventh son has meritorious distinction when it comes to singing cowboy star Eddie Dean. To say that he was special or gifted in many ways would be an understatement. His notable talents – and there were many – lay indisputably in his musical artistry as a natural and versatile singer blessed with what many have considered to be a "golden singing voice." His ability to capture the hearts of his listeners with his compositional prowess and compelling vocals endeared him to many, both professionals and non-professionals alike.

Such abilities beckoned him, as a natural progression, to seek his fortune in the entertainment arena through the medium of recordings, radio, motion pictures, and live performances. As a screen actor, he kept viewers on the edge of their seats with his fast-action Western dramas, while instilling time-honored values that, in the long run, the good guys win over the bad guys.

On a personal level, Eddie was a well-grounded individual who didn't take himself or his "stardom" too seriously and yet who was keenly aware of his priorities as a loving and devoted husband and father of two, which helped to dispel the notion that all Hollywood marriages are fickle and disposable.

In addition, he loved to bless other people by excelling in other creative outlets, such as oil painting, wood carving, leather work, and guitar making.

Yes, the number seven had played out with some prominence in Eddie Dean's life. He was indeed born the seventh son of a seventh son of a seventh son in the seventh month, in the seventh year of the twentieth century. He wavered from having a perfect streak of sevens by two days; being born on the ninth of July instead of the seventh.

Setting numerology aside, it was a joyous and blessed event for James and Eva Glosup when their youngest of seven boys and the eighth of their nine children, Edgar Dean Glosup, was born on Tuesday, July 9, 1907, on their small farm in rural Posey, Texas, in north central Hopkins County, about eighty-five miles northeast of Dallas and twelve miles northwest of Sulphur Springs, the county seat. Eddie stated years later that he was named after acclaimed American literary author Edgar Allan Poe.

There was some discrepancy concerning Eddie's middle name. Early on he was referred to as Edgar Dillard Glosup, believing he was named after his maternal grandfather, Thomas Dillard Vandergriff. However, according to Eddie, the name of Dillard was never confirmed as his true middle name. So he went through life by his given name of Edgar Dean Glosup.[2]

Eddie's future fame, curiously enough, was first prophesied by his mother.[3] When he was about four years old, he was playing near the front of the house on the family farm building a railroad track from old telephone wire and train cars out of small boxes along with wheels for the trains from the spoons his mother had discarded. As he was playing, he said he suddenly got notably frustrated about something. His mother, who was nearby, heard him and came over and asked her toddler son what was the matter.

"I just can't seem to get it done today, Mama," young Eddie said.

"Don't worry about it, son," his mother lovely reassured him. "Someday, thousands and thousands of people will know who you are."

Eddie looked around and replied, "Mama, we are out here in the country. The nearest town is a mile away. How will anyone know who I am?"

"You just remember, I know."

The other Glosup children were Rufus Alvin, known as Alvin (1895); Thomas Franklin, known as Frank (1897); Daisy Mae (1899); Virgil, (1902); James Clifton, known as Jimmie (1904); and the baby of the family, Frances Lorene, known as Lorene (1917).[4] Two boys died in infancy: one in the birth order between Alvin and Frank named Johnny, who died at age two in 1898; and the other, an unnamed stillborn, between Jimmie and Eddie. What made Eddie's birth extra joyous and special for his parents was he came immediately after the death of a brother; he was a child that lived.

Both of Eddie's parents and their families were true pioneers in every sense of the word and epitomized that spirit in how they lived. Life wasn't always easy but they made do with what they had, and what they didn't have, they got creative.

Eddie's father, James Franklin Glosup, was born on January 19, 1868, and was himself a seventh son of a seventh son and the second youngest child of twelve siblings, hailing from Jackson, Alabama, a crossroad hamlet along the Tombigbee River about seventy miles north of Mobile. Jackson was founded in 1816, and after going through a few name changes over the years, the town eventually settled on its current name, after President Andrew Jackson.

Very little is known about Eddie's paternal grandparents. James' father, Joel B. Glosup, was born on August 8, 1811, a seventh son in his family. His mother, Julien Shelton Glosup, was born on March 3, 1828. The couple were married on March 21, 1843. Joel was thirty-two years old at the time, while Julien was fifteen. While there was a seventeen-year difference between them in their ages, such nuptial arrangements weren't unusual in that day. Grandpa Joel died in 1889, at age seventy-eight.

James had two older brothers whom he never met. The oldest, Clinton Bradshaw Glosup, born on November 22, 1843, grew up in Lauderdale County, Alabama,[5] located at the northwest corner of the state bordering Tennessee and Mississippi. He was killed while fighting for the Confederate cause in the Civil War. He was a private in the 35th Alabama Infantry Regiment, Company A.

The 35th Alabama Infantry Regiment was organized at Lagrange, AL, on March 12, 1862, with about 750 men recruited from Franklin, Lauderdale, Lawrence, Limestone, and Madison counties. Ordered to Corinth, LA, it was there they brigaded under General John C. Breckinridge. The regiment followed that officer to Louisiana and took part in the attack on Baton Rouge (August 5, 1862), with four killed and twenty-one wounded. It was part of the force with which General Earl Van Dorn assaulted Corinth (October 3-4, 1862). Casualties were heavy for the Confederates (over 4,800). It is believe that Clinton Glosup died in the battle of Corinth.[6]

James' other older brother, Frederick Hardin Glosup, the sixth child born, died in January 1860. He was six years old. Cause of death unknown.

James' remaining siblings were Sampson Shelton Glosup, born September 16, 1845. Sampson was blind and died before the turn of the century. Story has it that he loved to entertain the youngsters by taking his walking cane and making different sounds of birds and animals by shaking his cane on the floor.

Hardly anything is known about James' brother, Martin Van Buren Glosup, named after America's eighth president, who was born on November 25, 1847; and Mary Emaline, James' oldest sister and the fourth of the Glosup children, born on February 18, 1849; Isabella Glosup, born in 1851; and Elizabeth Glosup, who died in 1874, four months after her eighteenth birthday; cause also unknown.

Rounding out the Glosup brood were Henry Clay Glosup, born on November 9, 1858; Frances Glosup, born on April 20, 1861, just eight days after the outbreak of the Civil War; Elizabeth Jane Glosup, born in 1865; and Joel "J. B." Glosup, born on May 5, 1869.

The Glosups, who were of English, Scottish, and German descent from the Black Forrest region of Germany, were farmers, having made a meager living in Alabama growing cotton and corn. In the early 1880s, Texas ran ads and placed articles in southern newspapers to attract settlers to Texas. Most new settlers during this time were farmers.

Feeling that this would be a wonderful opportunity to forge a better life for themselves, Joel and Julien Glosup – now both in their senior years – and their children decided to pull up roots and make the 650-mile trek from Jackson to settle in Decatur, Texas, outside of Fort Worth. James was fourteen years old at the time.

It took the family over six weeks to travel that distance by horse and wagon through fairly rough and somewhat dangerous territory. Often times they had to work together to build make-shift bridges that had washed out in order to cross rivers.[7]

James, who was a thin-framed man sporting facial features similar to that of screen actor Percy Killbride of "Pa Kettle" fame, minus of course, the ever-present derby that he wore, would later tell Eddie with awe how he rode the first train from Fort Worth to Decatur, a forty-five-mile exertion, and observed an incident that was to fade into history, never to be seen again. While on that train ride, he saw a huge drive of Texas longhorns. Their enormous horns clicking together could be heard for a great distance and the sun glinting on their horns gave the impression of a vast lake.[8]

Not long after moving to Decatur, James' parents died. The Glosup siblings were able to purchase land in Posey where the entire family settled in, surrounding each other on neighboring farms. Posey wasn't the Garden of Eden, but land there was workable and sold for a good price, something along the lines of about a dollar an acre.

The area was first settled by Aden Posey around 1846. After the Civil War a small community grew up around a gristmill operated by a man named Jones. A two-room public school was in operation around the turn of the century. A post office was established in 1902 under the name Reuben but was renamed Posey four months later in honor of Aden Posey. The post office was discontinued in 1906, and the mail was sent to nearby Peerless.[9]

At its height between 1910 and 1920, Posey had a cotton gin, a school, two stores, a blacksmith shop, and a Baptist church. The cotton gin burned in 1925 and was not rebuilt. In the mid-1930s the community had the church, the school, two stores, and a number of scattered houses. The population in 1940 was twenty. The school was consolidated in the early 1940s with North Hopkins School. In the early 1960s Posey still had a church, a cemetery, and a few houses. In the late 1980s it was a dispersed rural community.[10]

The remainder of James' siblings all took stock in helping to farm the Posey area where the arid climate made it ideal to grow cotton, corn, oats, and beans, while raising chickens, hogs and quite a few head of cattle, mostly milking cows.

Joel Glosup, James' younger brother by over a year, with his wife, Eleanor, settled on the adjacent farm less than a mile away. Known by the family as "J. B.," Joel depended on James to handle many of the practical day-to-day business dealings concerning the family farms.

"Uncle Joel looked to Papa to take care of everything," Eddie said. "He could hardly live without living next to Papa. He just thought that nobody could do things like my dad could."

Some of Eddie's earliest recollections occurred when he was three years old that involved his Uncle Joel and Aunt Eleanor. The first recollection had to do with him walking with his uncle and aunt back to their home three-quarters-of-a-mile away. He started to cry because his little legs couldn't keep pace with those of the two adults. Sensing her young nephew's frustration, Eleanor picked Eddie up and carried him rest of the way.

"As young as I was, I immediately felt that somebody besides my mama really cared for me," Eddie said. "It had a profoundly positive impact on me."

The other memory involved Eddie and a young calf that was born a month earlier on the Glosup Farm. Young Eddie wanted to ride the calf so he asked his mother if she thought his papa would mind if he rode the calf. His mother told him that she thought his dad wouldn't mind. In fact, Evie helped her son find a rope and formed a half-hitch over the calf's mouth to be used as a halter.

"I learned to ride that little calf," Eddie said. "It was the first time I rode an animal of any kind. I rode it to Uncle Joel's and Aunt Eleanor's home so I didn't have to walk there again until I got older."

Another brother of James, Henry Clay Glosup, was a blacksmith. He forged the plowshares, horse shoes and other metal work that needed tending for the family. As a kid, Eddie said he used to help his Uncle Henry run the forge.

James' sister, Frances, and her husband, Bud Sledge, who also farmed and ranched, lived close at hand as well. Eddie fondly remembers that his Uncle Bud had a mustache so long that "he placed it over each ear which made him look like he had mutton chops." Eddie also stated that he really loved his Aunt Frances, as she was the only one of his dad's sisters that he had ever known.

Eddie's mother, Eva Alice Vandergriff Glosup, known as "Evie," was born on January 7, 1878, about forty miles south of Nashville, Tennessee, the second of six children to Thomas Dillard and Sophie Jane Hathaway Vandergriff.

The Vandergriff Family, farmers of Dutch lineage, also decided to create a new life for themselves in Texas. So at age six, Evie and her family packed up their belongings and said farewell to "The Volunteer State" to say hello to "The Lone Star State," traveling through the relatively harsh terrain by oxcart driven by a pair of oxen. The family settled in New Boston about eighty miles northeast of Sulphur Springs, near the Arkansas and then-Oklahoma Territory borders. The area was ripe for agricultural pursuits with its rich bottom lands, fertile soil, and abundant forests of shore leaf pine, cedar and white oak.

When he was little, an inquisitive Eddie once asked his mother how the bits were put in the oxen's mouths in order to guide them as they made their way to Texas.

"Honey," she replied, "we didn't put a bit in their mouths. My papa and brothers just used a halter and a line and they would walk alongside the oxen with a whip. They taught those oxen to be that way and once they became trained, they were very gentle and they did what you wanted them to do by just snapping the whip."

That very same yoke that the oxen were hitched to during the Vandergriffs' trek from Tennessee to Texas hung for many years on the joists in the tool house on the farm in Posey. As a child, Eddie admired it with loving covetousness and said that he wanted to have that oxen yoke someday for his own. Unfortunately, he never did.

"I don't know whatever happened to it or who got it, but I never did," he said years later. "I love history and that yoke was part of history. It represented a spirit of fortitude and tenacity in my pioneer family. For Mama's family to come so far from Tennessee and Papa's family to come all the way from Alabama in those days is beyond comprehension. I would often wonder how they ever made it."

Thomas Dillard Vandergriff, the family patriarch born in 1851, was a distinguished looking gentleman with curly hair who sported a white beard and mustache. He walked with a crippled leg that never healed correctly as a result of being kicked by a mule in the shins years earlier.

Thomas couldn't read, write, or do arithmetic until he married his wife, Sophie Jane Hathaway Vandergriff, in 1871. Sophie Jane, born in 1855, claimed to be a direct descendent of English royalty stemming as far back as the Elizabethan period of the late sixteenth century.[11]

Thomas was also handy with a rifle.

One of Eddie's earliest recollections he said, came at age three when his grandfather would take him hunting for bullfrogs and that Thomas would never miss his intended targets.

Much to young Eddie's delight, Grandpa Thomas also loved showing off his marksmanship skills for his young grandson by shooting empty .22 caliber short-shell casings off a post from about 20 paces away.

"I guess I was kind of his pet," he said.

Evie's other siblings on the farm included two brothers, James J. Vandergriff, who was a blacksmith by trade and went on to own the area cotton gin and general store, and Sheeley Vandergriff, who was nearly blind, but was according to Eddie, "as fine a fiddler as you ever heard in your life," playing anything from breakdowns to schottiesches; and two sisters: Daisy Vandergriff and her husband, John Orr; and Willie May Vandergriff.

It isn't clear exactly where or how James Glosup and Evie Vanderg-riff met but it was more than likely it was through an area church social or grange social. There was, however, a ten-year difference between them in their ages. In 1893, at the tender age of fifteen, Eva Alice Vandergriff became Mrs. James Franklin Glosup.

Evie was a large woman who had beautiful teeth that accentuated her infectious smile. She could hold her own in doing the work of a man if it was necessary, which she did often. Eddie stated that there were a number of times when he'd seen her help his dad pick up a 500-pound or 600-pound hog to hang it up and dress it out.

"It's unbelievable how these old pioneers made it," he said.

In addition to pitching in doing the occasional "man's work" around the farm, Evie was the principal domestic for the Glosup household. She did the washing, the sewing, the cooking, the baking, and the canning that kept her family on the go. She insisted that every member of her family eat well because they all worked hard.

Her only vice, if it can be called that, was to regularly use a pinch of snuff placed between her teeth while chewing on a piece of hackberry wood, a popular habit of native Tennesseans.

Intrigued by what Evie always put between her teeth, a then-four-year-old Eddie once asked his mother if he could try some of her snuff and sur-prisingly, she granted his request.

"Mama fixed some up for me, gave it to me and had me chew my tooth-brush," Eddie said. "At first I thought it would make me sick, but it didn't. It didn't bother me at all, but I never got any more snuff."

James was a stern yet God-fearing man; a Baptist Christian in denomi-nation. Although his formal schooling ended when he finished the seventh grade, he became well-educated on his own, reading whatever books or other printed literature he was able to find. In many respects he was a type of Renaissance man. In addition to farming and ranching, he also taught music as a side line. He was a fine singer who directed the country church choir. He was skilled in carpentry and was a wiz with numbers as well.

"Papa could take a carpenter square and cut every piece of lumber before it was put up and almost fabricate it like they do today," Eddie recalled. "He'd have somebody cut the lines where he'd mark and they would fit. He was good at mathematics, too. If someone told him to multiply three numbers by three numbers he could give the answer before anyone could figure it out on paper."

Besides building his one-story three-bedroom farm house with dining room, living room, fireplace, along with barn and silo on his 190-acre farm, James' carpentry skills were also welcomed by his neighbors in helping to build extra stories on their houses and by helping to rebuild the grain elevator for the area farmers. He went on to build the first Baptist church in Posey, as well as the first one-room school there, the same school that Eddie attended.

Prior to the school being built, many of the young people in the Posey area couldn't read or write, and therefore, went without any basic formal education. Once the school was built, however, these young men and women, many of whom were in their late teens and early twenties, were then able to attend school, some for the very first time, for a few hours a day after completing their early-morning farm chores.[12]

Such reality wasn't far removed as what was portrayed by the character of Jethro Bodine, the handsome and strapping but naive and simple-minded twenty-something nephew of Jed Clampett on the television sit-com, *The Beverly Hillbillies*, who boasted about having completed the fifth grade. In the minds of uneducated mountain folk, such matriculation was admired with high regard.

The large one-room school house had two teachers: a female teacher for the younger children and a male teacher who taught the older minor-age and adult-age students.

The other teacher at that school was Alvin, Eddie's oldest brother, who at the ripe old age of nineteen, was also the school's principal. Alvin was the first of the Glosup children to secure a formal education for himself. And it was Alvin who gave his youngest brother his first taste of corporal punishment.

Eddie explains: "I was about four years old and this one day I went out to use the outhouse which was about a hundred yards way from the school.

While I was out there, my Cousin Darrel, Uncle Joel's boy, who was fifteen, came out from the latrine smoking a cigarette, which was against school rules. He wanted me to take a drag off his cigarette and I didn't want to, fearing that I might get sick. I yielded to his pressure and I took a puff. When I returned to the room, my teacher said to me, 'Let me smell your breath.' She smelled the smoke of that cigarette on my breath and made me stay after school. My brother Alvin then gave me the whipping of my life on my bottom with his belt! He then had me stand in the corner. I thought it was unfair as I didn't think my 'punishment' fit the 'crime.' Years later Alvin told me he felt guilty about the incident and said that he felt compelled to do what he did because he couldn't show favoritism. He apologized to me and said he hoped he hadn't hurt me too badly."

In a more celebratory school setting, six-year-old Eddie was involved in a school play for the community organized by his older brother Frank. During the play, Eddie recited a sentimental poem he had composed called "Going Back to Grandpa's," about the frequent visits he would make to his grandparents' home, who lived just three-quarters-of-a-mile away. Needless to say, the audience was so moved by his sweet recitation, there wasn't a dry-eye in the place.

"It was a pretty poem," Eddie recalled. "I thought so much of my grandparents. They were such warm people. I would go anytime to visit them, mostly by myself."

When homework needed to be done, Eddie would complete his assignments by finding a comfortable spot in front of the large brick fireplace in the living room. The lighting was brighter there as oppose to sitting at a table illuminated by a small coal oil lamp. He would also lay down on the hearth in front of the fireplace to relax by doing his drawings.

Boredom and idleness weren't words found in the common vernacular associated with life on a farm. There was always *something* to do and always *something* that needed attending. Maintaining a farm required the use of every available body that could work. Each member of the Glosup family, from the parents right down to the youngest child, had particular chores for which they were held accountable. Eddie was acclimated to farm life very early, at around age four.

Every morning at four, in the darkness of the new day, rain or shine, family members stumbled out of bed, got dressed, and trekked out to the barn to feed the horses and cattle, cleaned out their stalls, and milked the cow—all by hand, thank you very much. Evie would stay behind in the kitchen to prepare breakfast.

As the chores in the barn neared completion, the tantalizing aroma of Evie's breakfast delights of hot biscuits and eggs with cornbread and ribbon cane syrup along with homemade jellies filled the air, making the family farmhands salivate with hungry anticipation.

Before coming into the dining room to break bread, Eddie and family would wash up outside using an old pan filled with water from a cistern that was immediately built next to the house.

Fifteen-year-old Brother Frank helped to dig out the current eighteen-foot-deep cistern, which was bricked in like a jug.

Eddie recalled when Frank was working laying the brick walls half-way down the cistern, a loose brick fell on his head and knocked him out. Fortunately for Frank, Papa James was nearby to climb down the well on a rope to rescue him.

The cistern held water that would run off the house. Two or three perch fish were kept inside it to help keep the water clean. In time, the fish would eventually get black from being in that water. As a result, the cistern needed to be periodically cleaned out.

Evie would also hang jugs of fresh cow's milk from a rope in the cistern's water in order to keep the milk cool.

After breakfast was eaten, there was more work still to be done. The older children fed or "slapped the hogs," cleaned out their pens, while the younger children fed the chickens and gathered their eggs that were laid in the hen house. The middle aged children went out to help work in the fields.

Eddie remembers very vividly when he was seven years old, getting a taste of working in the fields during the late summer months picking cotton. He would get there just at sunrise to begin the long and arduous day of picking "King Cotton" in the grueling Texas heat.

"There was a certain pride among farmers and especially with kids like me that the quicker you could do a man's day's work the better you felt about yourself," he said. "I think it helped us to grow up faster."

Eddie claimed that it was during his time working in the fields that he first began to hear music in his head; beautiful music played by a large orchestra. At first, he thought it was probably something he had inadvertently conjured up in his mind as a pleasant way to deal with the tedious yet physically-demanding task of picking cotton, but soon he was hearing such music everywhere he went and in everything he did.

"I didn't know where the music came from," Eddie confessed. "I could always hear this tremendous orchestra and I thought that someday I would direct a great orchestra and write great music. I always sensed hearing this music had something to do with my future."[13]

Since the Glosups had a fair number of children, they developed a system by which as the older children left the farm to go out on their own, the younger siblings were expected to step up to do whatever needed to be done. It was very evident that every member of the family worked hard to make a living and all the Glosup children had great respect for their parents.

By the time oldest son Alvin went off to join the Navy during World War I, son number two Frank had become an excellent horseman and a fine roper. In fact, Frank had developed such equine skills that he could drive and plow a team of mules without the use of bridles. People in the area would come from miles around to see.

Brother Frank went on to became a Baptist minister, serving at First Baptist Church in Duncanville, Oklahoma. He later served as a Baptist missionary for Indian Reservations in Oklahoma. He married Rose Hooten and they had three children: two sons, Durwood and Frank, Jr. and a daughter, Eva Marie. Frank, Jr. and Eva Marie both passed away early in life.

Brother Virgil didn't stay long on the farm, leaving at age fourteen to work for the railroad. Virgil was called "Buster" before he was officially named Virgil. He went on to become Chief Engineer for the Chicago and North Western Railroad based in Chicago. He later married his wife, Ruth, and together they had three daughters: Mary Jo, Betty, and Barbara.

While Jimmie almost stayed on the farm as long as Eddie did, he was regarded as sort of the family pet, whose foibles were more readily overlooked than those of the other Glosup children.

The farm can be a double-edged sword: it can bestow blessings with the fruits of nature's bounty as well as be the recipient of nature's harshness. The occasional Texas tornadoes that would rip through the prairie lands were a powerfully destructive and deadly force of nature that could annihilate a large farm in a matter of a few brief moments. Some tornadoes could actually build to cataclysmic capacity as the one so memorably depicted in the film classic, *The Wizard of Oz*. For the safety of family members during such a perilous event, every farm had a storm cellar built.

The Glosup boys helped Papa James build their own storm cellar that was eight feet deep, and was bricked in order to keep the temperature inside it very cool all year round. A small hole was dug to the top surface for ventilation. James built shelves inside the storm cellar to store canned fruits and vegetables should the need to remain longer in it surpassed a few hours. Entrance to the storm cellar, built about thirty yards away from the house, was by way of a heavy wooden door galvanized with corrugated tin and secured inside by three different bolts with timber beams for sturdiness. Tornadoes are so powerful they were known to even tear off the most heavily fortified portals.

When not protecting its inhabitants from the devastating effects of tornadoes, the storm cellar also acted as a "root cellar," a place where food items such as eggs, potatoes, fruits, and vegetables would be stored in a cool environment to retard spoilage.

Area farmers cultivated mutual cooperation with each other by developing a "Good Neighbor" attitude long before the term became part of U.S. foreign policy. Neighbors helped each other in times of need. If a there was a storm coming and one neighbor got behind storing grain, other neighbors who were caught up would go and help out. According to Eddie, sometimes there would be forty to fifty people working.

"That's just the way they used to do it," he said. "The same way with branding and dipping cattle. You had to dip cattle in a tick-killing compound at a certain time and if someone needed help doing that, the neighbors would go help them. To me, it was a wonderful attitude those old timers had."

Other items that farming neighbors shared with each other was the telephone, or more specifically, the "party line" of the telephone. While the telephone had been around since Alexander Graham Bell first patented the invention in 1876, it took thirty-six years for this "voice box of communication" to make its way to the farming-ranching community of Posey, Texas. When the telephone finally did come to Posey, its inhabitants welcomed the new technology with open arms. Papa James and the neighboring farmers worked to cut poles for the telephone wires, put up the cross bars and insulator, and helped to string the wires from pole to pole. The telephone switchboard, which allowed for the formation of telephone exchanges, was stationed in the Glosup home.

Six-year-old Eddie, who also wore the hat of the part-time area telephone operator, ran the switchboard on Sunday afternoons after church while his folks took a horse and buggy ride to visit neighbors. Plugging the wires into the various sockets on the switchboard so callers could get "connected" with each other, young Eddie would often listen in on "party line" calls as a way to pass the time. Needless to say, he was privy to a good deal of local and unnecessary gossip.

Other jobs Eddie did around the farm included filling the silos with hay so the cattle could eat dry hay during the winter months. The silos helped to keep the hay from becoming moist and fermented in the cold, moist weather, thus keeping the cattle from getting intoxicated.

Sorghum cane was previously stored in those silos prior to being squeezed in to making sorghum syrup, a sweeter used on hot biscuits, pancakes, and other hot cereals.

As time went on, various improvements in and around Posey were initiated. One such improvement was roads, helping to make shipping grain and cattle to from market easier and faster. Papa James was appointed the first road commissioner in the Posey area. A large grader for those roads was kept on the Glosup farm.

Nine-year-old Eddie proved to be a big help to his dad in this endeavor as well as to the community by driving a team of two horses and two mules in tandem while James ran the grader with its big, powerful blades and large wheels.

While the community in and around Posey came together not only in the bad times, they always made it a point to come together in the good times as well to celebrate life in all its abundance They took pride in their regular "singing conventions" which featured local talent. This was not some ho-hum talent show sponsored by a weekly afternoon ladies garden club. No, these events showcased the *crème de la crème* of home spun musicians and singers who boasted exceptional talent, albeit, untrained talent, who breathed the very essence and soul of country living into their musical offerings.

In was at these events as well as at Saturday evening informal get-togethers at the Glosup Farm and at Sunday church services, that Eddie was first exposed to music.

Not only was food in abundant supply on the farm, but music as well. As a family, the Glosups would often entertain themselves with old-fashioned "sing-a-longs" by singing church hymns and other Gospel tunes accompanied by sister Daisy Mae who played the pump organ.

"When people came over to our place they'd bring their guitars and fiddles and we'd start singing and have a lot of fun," Eddie said. "Anytime you have music in the family it's a great communicator. Most people are too busy watching somebody else do it now, watching the pros."

As Eddie grew to adolescence, people soon recognized that he had an usually fine singing voice. They would often say to his father, "Jim, that kid of yours sure can sing."

These types of sincere words of encouragement only whetted Eddie's appetite to become more serious about singing than he had. Farm life was tough and was more often than not, a financially non-profitable profession, as honorable as the work may be. Eddie didn't relish the idea being a "tiller of the soil" for the rest of life, after witnessing his father's lifelong financial insecurity.

With the advent of radio and phonograph records becoming more popular at the conclusion of World War I, Eddie was more exposed to various tastes of music outside of his small farm-based world. He liked what he heard, knowing that if given an opportunity, he could make his mark by doing equally as well or even better with his God-given musical gifts.

When the time came, he set out to begin pursuing his goals, unintentionally at first but rather, through a series of chance encounters with the right people at the right time.

2

How Ya Gonna Keep 'Em Down On The Farm?

A popular 1919 Tin Pan Alley song about American troops returning from World War I asked "How Ya Gonna Keep 'Em Down on the Farm, After They've Seen Paree?" In fact, many returning dough boys did not remain "down on the farm;" there was a great migration of youth from farms to nearby towns and smaller cities.

Such migration had much to do with the saga of the American farmer with its re-occurring theme of attempts at keeping one step ahead of their creditors. Money problems and farming always seemed to go hand-in-hand. With all the hard work that went into farming and very little to show for it, American farmers by enlarge, were usually always heavily in debt to the banks for one reason or another. They were either borrowing money for improvements on the farm or borrowing money to compensate due to crop failure, always with the hope that next season's crops will bring them through. More often than not, it never did.[1]

The Glosups weren't any different. For most of his life, James Glosup was, in the words of Eddie, "always broke." That seemed to change during World War I, when the United States was a critical supplier to other Allied nations, as many European farmers were in the army. The rapid expansion of the farms coupled with the diffusion of trucks and Model T cars, and the tractor, allowed the agricultural market to expand to an unprecedented size.

James Glosup reaped a brief moment of prosperity for he and his family during this time, but the small gains they did make didn't allow them to get ahead financially. There was always some debt that needed to be paid off. However, with the end of the war European soldiers returned to their farms and market for American exports shrank. Both farmers and economists had not foreseen the drop in demand for American goods. The abundant harvest coupled with falling demand left an excess of crops and not enough profit to pay for expenditures. The downturn was only very brief, as was the entire post-World War I recession in North America.[2]

It was during this time that Eddie also helped his father farm an extra hundred acres of land in order to make a living.

"Things were really bad as it was a sad part of our life at home," Eddie recalled. "We worked our heads off and there wasn't any valued in it. We went broke and the only things we had to eat were what we grew."

The brief recession along with a local misunderstanding over land boundaries was all that was needed to finally bring James to his Waterloo, thus causing him to sell his family farm in Posey and to move twelve miles southeast to Sulphur Springs in Hopkins County.

It seems that there was some discrepancy over the original survey records between the Glosup Farm and the farm belonging to its neighbor, Joshua Hendrickson. According to the initial survey, Hendrickson had mistakenly posted fencing that encroached eight feet over onto Glosup land. James requested Hendrickson to re-post eight feet back, of which he obliged.

When James sold the farm to his brother-in-law, John Orr, Orr had the land resurveyed. The results confirmed that the original survey was indeed correct. However, the new survey also revealed that there was more acreage to the farm than what was initially thought. As a consequence, James had to make up the loss on those resurveyed acres, which totaled $1,000.[3]

Orr never offered to divide the newly discovered acreage with James which would have allowed his brother-in-law to retain some personal as well as financial dignity. Orr's attitude over this business deal was one of cold indifference.

Eddie remembered his uncle saying, "Well, I'm sorry, Jim, that's the way it is, you know. You need to make good on your financial responsibility and move on and to forget about your mistake."

According to Eddie, the situation created a strained relationship between his father and uncle that never healed.

"Uncle John was really cold about the situation," Eddie said. "We all loved Aunt Daisy and we all felt bad about what happened. Because of it, Dad's relationship with Uncle John cooled off a lot."

With the move to Sulphur Springs, twelve-year-old Eddie emigrated to a much larger agricultural community and matriculated to better schools. By 1920, Sulphur Springs, with a square-mile radius of eighteen miles, reported a population of 5,558, which made it the largest town in Hopkins County. [4]

Sulphur Springs received its name from the springs of sulphur water that were abundant in the area before the arrival of the settlers. During that time, Native American tribes, originally the Caddo Indians, who were later displaced by the Cherokees, frequently set up temporary camps around the springs. When the first settlers arrived in the late 1830s, most of them used the land around the springs for setting up their camps as well. [5]

The village became a city in 1854 when the first post office was established. The city's name was originally Bright Star. Mail to and from the city was delivered by the Pony Express.

On May 18, 1871, the county seat of Hopkins County was moved from Tarrant to Sulphur Springs. The name "Bright Star" was removed from the postal directory.

The dairy industry has always been a major component of the local economy in Sulphur Springs. Known as the "Diary Capital of Texas," Sulphur Springs is home to the Southwest Dairy Museum which features artifacts on the history of the dairy industry.

As of 2013, Sulphur Springs boasted a population of over 16,000.[6]

James Glosup was able to purchase a small farm, about 150 acres, in which the family grew cotton, oats, wheat, and hay. In 1880, there were seventy-four farms operating in Hopkins County. By 1920, the Glosup farm was one of just forty-four in the area.[7]

While most of the Glosup sons had moved on and were finding their own way in life, Eddie helped his father in keeping the farm going.

While James and Evie always hoped that their sons would continue the generational lineage of farming, they also wanted all their children to have an education. He and Evie insisted that they attend school.

Eddie attended the local ward school, one of the rural Kindergarten through eighth grade grammar schools located in a specific section or zone in Sulphur Springs. Mondays through Fridays Eddie walked or rode his bicycle on the three-and-a-half miles of dusty dirt roads each way to and from the farm. Eddie was also granted permission by each principal throughout the remainder of his educational career for him to miss the first and last month of school each year due to his need to be on the farm to help his father with harvesting chores.

Upon entering the ninth grade at the newly built, two-story, all brick, Sulphur Springs High School, Eddie rode his horse to school during that same three-and-a-half-mile trek from home until the equine beast's behaviors created a "messy" dilemma in which Eddie had to cease riding the animal to class. Not even divine intervention from attending mandatory Monday morning chapel services at school would help defer the inevitable

"After I tied my horse to the hitching rail outside the school building, it would do its business and Mr. Bass, the principal, received some heated complaints about it from our school custodian," Eddie recalled. "My horse also tore down the hitching post and that's when I was told I couldn't ride my horse to school any longer."[8]

Since he couldn't ride his horse to school, Eddie decided he would run to and from school instead. As a result of all the running he did, Eddie became interested in joining the school's track team. The seven-mile round trip run proved to be excellent conditioning for him so that he easily made the school track team, competing in the 220-yard dash and as the "anchor" of the four-man 440-yard relay team.

By his senior year in high school, Eddie took second place in the 220 at the Texas District Track Meet in Greenville. He qualified to attend the State meet in Austin but didn't go because he couldn't financially afford it.

"In those days, I had to pay my own way to attend the State meet and my family just didn't have the money to help me go," Eddie lamented. "I was disappointed."

However, Eddie found other extracurricular activities while in high school to keep him busy and to showcase his abilities. With his penchant for art, his natural yet untrained talents were put to good use in his senior year as art editor of *The Hi Lander*, the school's annual. He was responsible for assembling all the photo layouts, drawing all illustrations, and saw to it that the annual was printed correctly.

Mr. Bass saw promising signs in Eddie of becoming a fine artist and sculptor. He encouraged the high school pupil to exhibit his drawings whenever possible. One year, Eddie carried off high honors for a landscape drawing he had entered in a Sulphur Springs art contest.

In addition, Eddie was elected class Reporter during his junior year for the school's newspaper, *Hi-Life*, after the initial elected Reporter, George French, and his family unexpectedly moved from Sulphur Springs. Eddie was also a regular contributor of original poetry for the school newspaper.

To say that Eddie was a stand out among the Sulphur Springs High School associated student body of 261, and especially among his own sixty-two-member junior class, would be an understatement. His other high school activities that school year included being a very "spirited" assistant leader on the school's forty-member Wildcat pep squad, a member of the Junior Halloween Party Committee, and a sought after musical participant for numerous school and community-related events.

When it came to singing, Eddie's peers and the ten-member high school faculty knew of no other teen that was better. Eddie's vocal talents graced the Junior Class Christmas Party in December 1925, held at a fellow class-mate's home, in which he sang a very moving rendition of "Silent Night."[9]

Eddie and brother Jimmie teamed up with other upper-class students to take part in *The Moonlight Cabaret Minstrel*, a variety show that was held in the early spring of 1926 and which received rave reviews from the community at large.

Eddie also joined forces with Jimmie and his fellow senior classmates, Grady King, known as "Smilin'," and Oscar Lee Crain, known as "Kinky" (referring to the texture of his hair), to form the "Brothers Quartet." Officially, they were referred to as just the "High School Quartet." The Glosup Boys and King had been singing together for the past three years with Virgil, Eddie's and Jimmie's older brother, who rounded out the original foursome. After Virgil moved on, Crain was asked to fill in the empty slot.

Crain was a senior transfer student from Cumby, Texas, located fifteen miles west of Sulphur Springs which boasted a population at that time of approximately 900. Cumby High School was also a rival school in inter-varsity athletic competition.

King was also very active as a teen in the Sulphur Springs Municipal Band, comprised largely of Sulphur Springs High School musicians. He later went on to play bass professionally in Ted Fio Rio's band in California.

The vocal group participated in most school and community-sponsored shows and were well-received every time they performed. Their repertoire included a variety of music ranging from Gospel to Pop, from sentimental to barbershop quartet.

In the 1926 edition of the *Hi-Lander*, superlatives seem to do the Quartet no justice. An entire page of the annual had the following to say about them:

"Probably no High School has a male quartet of which it is as proud as we are of ours. Not many schools can boast of the genius we have found in these four: Crain, King, Jim and Edgar Glosup. The quartet furnished a half hour of jollity for the entire school on the afternoon of December 23 (1925) with fiddler Johnny Paul, and accordionist Ken Coopern, just when the holiday animation was running riot, but no one wanted the curtain to close the program as soon as it did, though its drop marked the beginning of a few days vacation. Their encores were innumerable. Crain was the only new member this year. He came to us from Cumby and we've enjoyed him. King and the Glosups were old members, but with a permanently established reputation in Sulphur High. We doubt if the vacancies left by their departure will ever be filled."

Eddie's musical talents were also recognized during this period by his church as he was appointed choir director at First Baptist Church of Sulphur Springs at the ripe old age of sixteen. He conducted choir practice faithfully every Wednesday evening while continuing to develop his own singing skills by performing occasional solos with the choir. This experience, he would later say, helped to instill in him more of an interest in and an appreciation for music.

During his junior and senior years in high school, Eddie served as local president of the Baptist Young People's Union of America (BYPUA), the denomination's national youth organization. He even taught twelfth grade Sunday School. When First Baptist Church needed repainting, Eddie and his older brother, Virgil, were one of the first young people to volunteer their services as well as one of the bravest. They were the only two who stepped forward to paint the high ceiling in the sanctuary á la Michelangelo: on wooden scaffolding while lying on their backs.

While Eddie's high school career was stellar, brother Jimmie, nicknamed "Jimmie Darden" by his classmates, also had a pronounced presence at his Alma mater. In addition to singing in the High School Quartet, he was cast in the school play, Microbe of Love, a comedy, and he also playedfootball in his sophomore year and was a member of the school's track team for three years.

In fact, Eddie credits his older brother with providing him with stability and grounding during his early years in high school.

"I was always had closer relationship with my brother Jimmie than the rest of my brothers since we were closer in age, held similar interests, and we shared a lot of experiences together and would share professional experiences together as we got older," Eddie recalled. "After he graduated in 1926,

I felt a void in my senior year of high school realizing that nothing remains the same and that we all move on."

Throughout the 1920s radio was quickly becoming a very popular home entertainment device in America. Families could listen to world and local news as well as some their favorite musical entertainers right in the comfort of their homes.

The first radio the Glosups ever had was built by son Alvin who studied electronics while serving in the Navy. It was a small crystal set in which stations were tuned in properly by moving a small wire around on the enclosed crystal in the radio casing. Whatever little free time the family did have to listen to the radio, they were able to pick up programming from local regional stations in Ft. Worth and Dallas as well as the larger mid-west stations such as WSL in Chicago.

In addition to the local Gospel and Country music in his area, Eddie was influenced by some of the more popular singers of his day that broadcast over radio, such as Vernon Dalhart, Peg Moreland, and later, Jimmie Rodgers.

Vernon Dalhart was a popular American singer and songwriter of the early decades of the twentieth century who proved to be a major influence in the field of Country music.

Dalhart's 1924 recording of "The Wreck of the Old 97," a classic American railroad ballad about the derailment of Southern Railway *Fast Mail* train No. 97 near Danville, Virginia, became a runaway hit, becoming the first Southern song to become a national success.

Dalhart's recording of "The Prisoner's Song" was a No. 1 hit for twelve weeks in 1925-1926. He recorded under a host of pseudonyms given to him by recording managers. It is the considered opinion of musicologist and discographers that Dalhart had the most recordings of any person in history.[10]

Peg Moreland, or "Pegleg" Moreland as he was also referred to, was a male singer from Texas known as "King of the Little Ditty." He was called "Peg" due to the fact that he used a wooden leg in the style of Long John Silver. He picked a guitar and sang folk songs, mostly humorous folk songs.

He was a regular on the *Early Birds Show* on WFAA in Dallas, Texas, in the 1940s and also he made personal appearances at local fairs.[11]

Listening to and watching Moreland perform planted the seed in Eddie to someday take up the guitar, when he was able to afford one.

Jimmie Rodgers, known as "The Blue Yodeler," was recognized most widely for his rhythmic yodeling. Among the first Country music superstars and pioneers, he was the first figure inducted into the Country Music Hall of Fame and is fondly referred to as the "Father of Country Music."[12] His combination of blues and hillbilly styles also made him an early influence of rock and roll, and he was also part of the first group of musicians inducted into the Rock and Roll Hall of Fame.

Among the most noteworthy of his recordings were his series of "Blue Yodels," recorded between 1927 and 1933, in which he drew from Appalachian hill ballads, black spirituals, rural blues, and white pop music.

Rodgers worked on the railroad from the age of fourteen, learning the blues from black workers on his crew. At twenty-four, he contracted tuberculosis and was forced to quit his job. Over time his tuberculosis worsened and he died in May 1933, at age thirty-five.

In June 1927, Eddie graduated Sulphur Spring High School. After he turned twenty the following month, Eddie left home in search of work to help pay off the $1,000 debt his father owed on the farm due to crop failures from bad weather that year and lack of irrigation capabilities.

"For farmers in the South, we felt the Depression before it actually hit and I knew I had to go out on my own and try to do something to help ease the financial burden," Eddie said. "I kind of felt as if I was abandoning my folks. When I told my parents what I should do, they agreed that I should do something on my own."

Eddie decided to contact his eldest brother in Dallas in order to seek his fortune in "Big D." His father drove him in the family's old Model-T Ford to the bus station in Greenville, about thirty miles west of Sulphur Springs. In an emotional farewell, James and Eddie stopped together at the steps of the courthouse to say their goodbye's. After a tearful hug, James reached into his pocket and pulled out the last $3 he had in the whole world and gave $2 to his son for expenses.

After his father left, Eddie figured that he could save what little amount money he had plus the additional $2 his father had just given him on travel expenses by hitch-hiking to Dallas. After walking a few miles out of town, two men driving a dark colored automobile gave Eddie a ride to his destination.

Eddie's stayed the first few nights in Dallas with his brother Rufus Alvin and his wife, Cory, in their apartment. Their apartment was adjoined to another with each bathroom facing back-to-back from each other. Half way through dinner on the first evening, a loud noise came from the other tenet's bathroom. The noise startled Eddie. He jumped out of chair and he exclaimed, "What in the world was that?"

Laughing at her brother-in-law's reaction, Cory said, "Boy, Eddie, you sure are a country boy! That's the next store neighbor flushing his toilet."

Eddie sheepishly admitted that he had never before heard a toilet flush.

"That's the truth," he said. "Even at school we didn't have toilets. We had outhouses."

Eddie then boarded at the local YMCA, where the rooms were clean and cheap, at a cost of $6 a week. He soon found employment in the warehouse section at the *Dallas News*, courtesy of Earl Wilson, a fifth cousin, who also worked there.

Eddie's job was to pick up a stack of newspapers three feet high that had just come off the printing press and carry them forty feet to a table where inserts would be placed in the newspapers.

"It was one of the hardest jobs I ever had," he said later on. "I didn't like it at all."

Union problems arose during this time compounding Eddie's dislike for his job and which made working at the newspaper very difficult and at times, dangerous. Numerous fights periodically broke out over union-related situations. Even Eddie got embroiled in one such fight.

After a few days working at the newspaper, he saw two good size men attack his cousin, Earl Wilson. Wanting to help protect his cousin, Eddie jumped in the fight. Eddie got scuffed up pretty good in the brawl succumbing to a hurtful punch to the left side of his jaw by one of the thugs during his cowardly retreat from the scene.

The police soon arrived and took Eddie and Wilson into protective custody up to the top floor of the famed Adolphus Hotel on Commerce Street at North Akard Street. The cousins were sequestered together in a locked room for three days and nights while guards were posted outside their hotel room door.

After the third day, the Grand Jury of Dallas came to their room to interview them about what had transpired. Eddie and Wilson soon found out that the two roughnecks they tangled with belonged to the union. The thugs were trying to "persuade" Wilson to join the union, of which he had not yet joined.

"It was an experience," Eddie said about the affair. "I couldn't believe that people would do things like this because of an organization. I was always taught there were other ways to settle things, like discussion; not by fighting and hurting others. I was an innocent bystander trying to protect my cousin. That's all I did."

Not wanting to be embroiled in any further union conflicts, Eddie quit his job at the *Dallas News* after one week's stay.

Eddie's brother, Rufus Alvin, got him a job as a machinist with the Austin Bridge Company, a company that fabricated and installed steel truss bridges since 1889. Rufus was then-secretary to the company president.

"My brother, Rufus, was one of the fastest typists I ever knew and a fabulous camera man to boot," Eddie said. "He did all the advertisements for the Austin Bridge Company that appeared in various magazines."

Rufus Alvin later became director of the YMCA in Houston, Texas. He and Cory later became parents to a daughter, Sonja. He died in 1960.

"I loved my brother, Alvin, dearly," Eddie said. "Even though he was my oldest brother, he was also one of my best friends."

Eddie apprenticed for six months under Erik Harmon, a tough taskmaster from Germany, who insisted that his workers give attention to detail by adhering to a commitment to excellence in their work. Eddie's brother, Virgil, had also worked at one time under Harmon's fastidious eye.

Eddie worked six days a week earning $36 a week. He would often work double shifts from 7 a. m. to 11 p. m. in order to send as much money home as he could. His duties included using a lathe to drill holes in 300-pound tungsten steel beams. Every hole that was drilled had to be precise, according to exact specifications, as the bolts that would hold these beams in place had to fit perfectly.

"Mr. Harmon was a tough boss but I learned discipline from him," Eddie said. "So my time at the Austin Bridge Company was good experience even though it wasn't the type of job I wanted to do."

What Eddie really wanted to do was sing. Music was quickly holding more than just a casual interest for him. He was hearing that beautiful music in his head and feeling it in his heart more intensely now than he had as a child. The music was becoming more frequent, focused, and directed. It was, in a mystical way, developing into a "oneness" that would prove indivisible to the young Edgar Dean Glosup.

Eddie knew he would sound better with musical accompaniment, having his mind set on playing a guitar while he sang. So he went out looking for one. On one particular Sunday afternoon he had passed a pawn shop and hanging in the store window was an old Stellar acoustic guitar. Stellar guitars are noted for being finely crafted instruments sold at affordable prices. The guitar cost $6. Eddie had $7 in his pocket and happily walked out of that pawn shop that Sunday afternoon with a "new" instrument.

Eddie then teamed up with his cousin Arnold Vandergriff, the son of Sheeley Vandergriff, his uncle, the blind fiddle player, to learn how to play the guitar. Cousin Arnold initially taught Eddie some of the basic chords on the guitar. After a few lessons, Eddie quickly caught on and for the most part, became self-taught on the stringed instrument.

Whenever the opportunity would present itself, Eddie would periodically sing during lunch breaks at work for his fellow workers. His musical offerings were so appreciated that he was dubbed "The Canary."

"I was told many times by the guys I worked with that I shouldn't be working in a shop like this, that I should be in show business," Eddie said.

Such kudos only affirmed Eddie's resolve to make music more of a priority in his life; to strive toward making a livelihood from it. However, until a time that such an opportunity should present itself, Eddie continued to work diligently and hard at the Austin Bridge Company, faithfully sending most of his weekly pay checks home to his parents.

Eddie's dream of making a livelihood from music took one step closer to becoming reality one Sunday morning. As he walked out of the Dallas YMCA, he reconnected with Otis Deaton, a music teacher who taught Eddie a few years earlier the concept of singing from "shape" notes. Shape notes are a music notation designed to facilitate congregational and community singing. Shapes were added to the note heads in written music to help singers find pitches within major and minor scales without the use of more complex information found in key signatures on the staff. The notation became a popular teaching device in American singing schools.[14]

During a two-week period every summer while the crops were all laid by, the community hosted a singing school in which vocal coaches would come to town to teach the youth of the area how to sing, with Deaton being one of these visiting vocal instructors. The community paid for this instruction, which included lessons in voice, harmony, and sight reading.

These vocal coaches didn't make much money, but according to Eddie, "all of them were excellent musicians who could successfully teach the concept of music and singing in a relatively short period of time. Once a person got the idea where notes went in relation to each other, the starting point became irrelevant and any song could be sung in any key." In fact, Eddie said that attending these singing schools helped to instill in him a greater desire to sing.

Deaton, who sported a full head of curly hair and was marked with a hawk nose, went on to compose such noted Gospel songs as "He Is the Lily of the Valley," "Jesus Walks the Way Before Me," "We'll Keep Telling the Story," "There Will Come a Day of Days," and his most noted work, "Give the World a Smile," which became the theme song for the Stamps Quartet and the first Gospel song to become a gold record.[15] Deaton was impressed early on with Eddie's singing voice.

That chance meeting of the two men outside the Dallas YMCA that Sunday morning would prove fortuitous for Eddie. When Deaton asked Eddie what he was doing in Dallas, Eddie told him.

"How would you like to sing for a living?" Deaton asked.

"When do I start?" Eddie replied enthusiastically.

"Tomorrow."

Eddie immediately quit his job at the Austin Bridge Company and joined Deaton to be part of a quartet who sang Southern Gospel music. The musical foursome was called the Vaughan Quartet, named after its benefactor, James David Vaughan.

Hailed as the founder of Southern Gospel Music, James David Vaughan was a musical pioneer noted for his school of music and for the Gospel music publishing company that bears his name. He sponsored a traveling Gospel quartet to advertise and sell his songbooks resulting in the birth of the Southern Gospel Music industry.

Vaughan broadcast Southern Gospel music over one of Tennessee's first radio stations, WOAN, a station he founded in 1922 and continued to operate until 1930. He also founded Vaughan Phonograph Records, the first record company in the South. Vaughan died in 1941 at age seventy-seven.

On the last weekend in July, to commemorate Vaughan's birthday, is the James D. Vaughan Quartet Festival, featuring four-part harmony of quartets. Proceeds from the festival go to benefit the James D. Vaughan Museum in Lawrenceburg.

The Vaughan Quartet consisted of Deaton who sang the top tenor part in addition to playing piano for the group; Theo Casey, bass; Henry Long, baritone; and Eddie who sang the tenor lead. Eddie possessed a two-octave vocal range in which he could also sing bass parts.

The Vaughan Quartet worked for the James David Vaughan Company selling the current year's *Gospel Music Book,* written in shape notes. Each member of the Quartet earned $5 a day for living expenses and ten cents for each book that they sold. The book cost thirty-five cents.

They traveled for six months throughout the dusty country roads of east and north Texas and Oklahoma in a 1917 black, four-cylinder, Willys Knight two-door automobile. They would give concerts at schools and community auditoriums, and just about anywhere people would listen long enough in attempts to sell those music books.

If the Quartet was in between concert dates and they happened to travel through a small town and saw a school, they would stop in to talk with the principal asking if they could do a show for the students in an "impromptu" assembly in the hopes of doing a bigger show that evening.

"We'd do a straight mini-concert for the students at their assembly and we'd ask them to tell their folks to come back to the school auditorium that night for a big ninety-minute concert, "Eddie said. "We'd pack the place and we were able to sell a lot of books that way."

While the majority of the Quartet's repertoire consisted of scared music, of course, some comedy songs as well as popular and concert music were also added to the mix. Each member would be featured on two or three solo pieces. Eddie's featured selections included "The Lord's Prayer," and "Barefoot Days" and "On the Party Line," a pair of Peg Moreland tunes. He would also sing such classics as "Chloe," "Old Man River," "Danny Boy," and its variation piece called "O Mary Dear," made famous by John McCormack, the celebrated Irish-tenor.

"John McCormack was a big record seller in those days and I learned "O Mary Dear" from his recording," Eddie recalled. "It's the same exact melody as "Danny Boy," although it's more of a love song. I sang it to let people know that there was another version to 'Danny Boy.'"

Traveling from place to place in their Willys Knight car was anything but comfortable or luxurious. The four "traveling troubadours" braved fair the elements of nature as best they could from extreme cold in West Texas without benefit of heat in the car with only the side curtains that locked with buttons to keep the frosty, biting wind from pummeling them to blinding sand storms. Eddie related one such experience:

"We ran into a sand storm one night in West Texas and I'm not exaggerating, we couldn't see twenty feet ahead of us with the headlights on! It was just like running into a big cliff. We stopped and we could faintly see a picket fence along the side and knew there must be a house there somewhere. We found the house and we could see a light inside. We knocked on the door and asked for shelter and the family of six who lived there welcomed us in. The wife even fed us. They put us up for the night. This is the honest to God truth, when we woke up in the morning there was at least a half-inch of sand on the bed. Our noses were full of old, dirty sand. It was unbelievable. I got out of bed and looked back to see the sand begin to drift onto where I had laid and it just looked like talcum powder. To the people who lived there they were used to it, and didn't seem to bother them. Before we left that morning, the wife cooked us a beautiful breakfast and how she ever did it with all that sand, I don't know."

In another escapade, Eddie was propositioned for spontaneous matrimony by an unlikely individual. During the Quartet's travels through Oklahoma, they performed at a church in a small town along the Red River just north of Wichita Falls, Texas. A very attractive young Cherokee maiden named Marie Lynn, attended the concert and was so smitten with Eddie that she approached him afterward and told him, "I love you. Marry me. My father owns a lot of land on the Oklahoma side of the Red River. If you marry me my father will give us seventy-five horses, one hundred fifty head of cattle, twenty-five mules, and a house to live in."

"I couldn't believe what I was hearing," Eddie said in an interview years later. "This was absolutely crazy. The last thing on my mind at that point was marriage. I told her I'd have to think about it and that I would let her know."

The flame of hopeful marital union with Eddie burned bright in Marie Lynn's heart for a year, then fizzled out. While Eddie was in Chicago, she wrote him a letter stating that she had waited for him for a whole year and that she wasn't going to wait any longer. She was going to marry a Choctaw Indian.

"I don't know how she knew where to write me, but I was sure glad that was the end of that 'romance,'" Eddie waxed philosophically.

While concluding a tour with the Vaughan Quartet through Arkansas, Eddie met up with Virgil Stamps who hired him to sing with his trio for the remaining few months of their tour.

Virgil Oliver "V. O." Stamps has been recognized as the first person to popularize southern-style Gospel singing across America. Though he was a noted singer, writer, publisher, and pioneer recording artist, his greatest accomplishment was spreading Gospel music through the then-new medium of radio.

For several years his company counted many salaried quartets and more than a hundred affiliated quartets on radio stations nationwide. The Stamps Quartet remains an internationally respected Gospel aggregation today.

Stamps worked for the Vaughan Music Company as a quartet singer and field representative from 1915 until1924. In 1915, he composed his first song, entitled "The Man Behind the Plow."

Stamps launched out on his own in 1924 and founded the V. O. Stamps Music Company in Jacksonville, Texas. In that year, the first session of the V. O. Stamps School of Music was held, with a faculty that included Thomas Benton, C. C. Stafford, R. B. Vaughan, and Otis Deaton. In 1925, he published *Harbor Bells*, his first song book.

Two years later, Stamps merged the company with J. R. Baxter, Jr. to form the Stamps-Baxter Music and Printing Company based in Dallas. Through his leadership and promotion, the company became by the late 1930s, the most successful publisher of shape-note songbooks in America.

Stamps organized a personal quartet in which he sang bass. He was a pioneer in the use of radio for promoting Southern Gospel music and quartet singing. Dallas radio station KRLD gave the quartet a daily show in 1936, after a large response from their radio performance at the Texas Centennial Exposition.

Stamps also wrote the music and melody for the famous Gospel song, "When the Saints Go Marching In," in 1937, while Luther G. Presley wrote the lyrics. Other songs written by V. O. Stamps include "Love Is the Key," "Singing on My Way," and "I Am Going."[16]

Stamps died in 1940 at age forty-eight. He was inducted into the Southern Gospel Music Hall of Fame in 1997.

Stamps also offered Eddie slightly more money than what Vaughan had been paying and so he became the newest member of the Stamps Trio. The trio consisted of Stamps, bass; Marshall Yandell, middle tenor, who also played piano; and Eddie who sang the top tenor parts. Each trio member sang solos and followed a similar musical repertoire for performances as that of the Vaughan Quartet.

"We had quite a trio," Eddie recalled. "Marshall would open the show playing the piano while singing. V. O. would then come on to sing a few selections in his deep bass voice. I would come out last and after my selections, V. O. and Marshall would come back and we'd do our trio numbers. I remember Marshall Yandell as one of the greatest sight-readers I ever knew. You could hand him a piece of sheet music and he'd read it like an instrument on the first try; lyrics, the music, and chromatics. He was that good."[17]

The Stamps Trio concluded their brief tour in Dallas, and that's where Eddie and Stamps parted company. Stamps was so taken with Eddie's musical abilities, he asked him to teach music and voice at the Stamps School of Music. However, Eddie turned him down.

While singing on the road with Gospel groups was fun and taught Eddie much about an audience, it wasn't profitable. Eddie realized that he wasn't making the money he thought he could in order to send home to his parents. He still wanted to sing for a living and believed he could do just that, but he also knew he had to look elsewhere to find his breaks.

He had previously sought singing jobs at various Dallas radio stations but was turned down because he was told they "don't use singers like that" at the stations.

Realizing that the Dallas area afforded little opportunity for an aspiring artist, Eddie set his sights north to the "Windy City," Chicago, the hub of the Midwest, where the unknown awaited him but also where Country music was more of a marketable commodity.

Above: Eddie Dean at about a year-old posing for a photo with brother Jimmie, age 4.

Below: The Glosup Family farm house in Posey, Texas, ca. 1911. Eddie Dean is the small child standing in the front to the right of James Glosup, his father.

Above: Eddie's parents, James and Evie Glosup,
on the farm in Sulphur Springs, Texas, ca. 1934.

Below: Jimmie (left) and Eddie (right) with Evie Glosup,
their mother, in Sulphur Springs, Texas, ca. 1934.

Above: The Glosup Family in Sulphur Springs, Texas, ca. 1934. Pictured in the back row, are left to right: Uncle Joel Glosup; his wife, Aunt Lena Glosup; her mother, Grandma Facing; Eva Alice Glosup; Frances Lorene Glosup; and James Franklin Glosup. Pictured in the front row are, left to right: an unidentified cousin; Edgar Dean Glosup (Eddie Dean); and James Clifton Glosup (Jimmie Dean).

Above: James Glosup and Evie Glosup with Frances Lorene Glosup, their youngest daughter, and family dog, in Sulphur Springs, Texas, ca. 1933.

Above: A pair of photos of 18-year-old junior Edgar Dean Glosup from the 1926 Sulphur Springs High School yearbook, *The Hi-Lander.*

Above: Class of 1926 senior photos from *The Hi-Lander* of Jimmie Glosup, Eddie's brother (left); Grady King (center) and Oscar Lee Crain (right). During their senior year at Sulphur Springs High School, these three young men joined Eddie to form the highly acclaimed "High School Quartet."

Above: Jimmie and Eddie Glosup's Alma mater: Sulphur Springs High School in 1926. The school had a 261-member student body taught by ten full-time faculty.

Below: Twenty-year-old Eddie Glosup in 1927 decked out in his tweed suit just around the time he left home from Sulphur Springs to seek work in Dallas to help pay his parents' farm debts.

Southern Gospel music benefactors James David Vaughan, above, and
Virgil Oliver "V. O." Stamps, below, helped to give Eddie his first
professional singing experiences.

3

That Toddlin' Town

When Eddie first stepped foot onto the streets of Chicago in 1928, he was entering an entirely different world from whence he grew up during his first two decades of life. The "Windy City," with a population of nearly three million, was already the economic, cultural, and entertainment industry hub of the Midwest.

Throughout 1920s America, "The Roaring Twenties" or "The Jazz Age" as it was later called, was a time of hedonistic mindset in the aftermath of the disillusionment of World War I. It was a season when prosperity reigned in the larger cities and politicians promised a "chicken in every pot." It was a period where the liberation of women had its genesis with being granted voting rights in the shadow of the newly ratified Nineteenth Amendment to the Constitution. A new breed of women emerged called "flappers" who wore short skirts, bobbed their hair, listened to jazz music, and flaunted their disdain for what was then considered acceptable behavior. Flappers were seen as brash for wearing excessive makeup, drinking, smoking, treating sex in a casual manner, driving automobiles and otherwise flouting social and sexual norms. It was also the era of Prohibition, that failed "noble experiment," in which the sale, manufacture, and transportation of alcohol was outlawed. Chicago epitomized the center of Prohibition, complete with speakeasies, bootleggers, and notorious gangsters, of which Al Capone was its ruling potentate.

Liquor was recognized as the new "liquid gold" in the city, raking in millions of dollars each year for Capone and his cronies, who had organized an elaborate smuggling ring that brought the high-demand commodity for his thirsty customers into the U.S. virtually undetected from Canada and other foreign countries.

A gentleman's magazine at the time featured an article on bootlegging, stating:[1]

> "The sale of dissipation is not only a great business; it is among the few greatest businesses of Chicago. The leading branch of it . . . is the sale of alcoholic liquor . . . The liquor interests are vastly more extended in Chicago than any other [city]. There are 7,300 licensed liquor sellers in Chicago, and in addition about a thousand places where liquor is sold illegally. The only business which approaches it in number of establishments . . . is the grocery trade, which has about 5,200. The city spends at least half as much for what it drinks as for what it eats . . . ."

Chicago was also the destination of a great flux of all races from the South who had come north to seek better economic fortune and artistic expression. Chicago was *the* Jazz Mecca of America during this period yet surprisingly, it also hosted a thriving, robust, and loyal Country music haven years before Nashville would lay claim to such honors.

Chicago was vastly different than the "Lone Star State." Eddie's trek to that "toddlin' town" came complements of his brother, Virgil, who provided his younger sibling with his free railroad pass. Virgil started working for the Chicago and North Western Railroad as a teenager. Working for the railroad provided a good, stable living for Virgil, who eventually worked his way up the ranks to become the Chief Engineer for the Chicago and North Western Railroad based in Chicago. One of the benefits of working for the railroad was that employees were provided their own free travel pass to ride anywhere the railway operated.

The Chicago and North Western Railway (C&NW) of Illinois and Wisconsin was the successor of the old Chicago-Milwaukee Railway. A number of smaller independent railroads in that bi-state area merged in 1863 to form the Chicago-Milwaukee Railway. An additional merger twenty years later of the CMR with other lesser known Wisconsin railways was absorbed into the C&NW. Over the years, the C&NW became one of the largest railroads in America as a result of more mergers with other railroads. The company was then purchased by Union Pacific Railroad in 1995, and dissolved shortly thereafter.[2]

When Eddie decided to make his move to go to Chicago, V. O. Stamps gave him enough money to go back home to Sulphur Springs to let his parents know of his intentions. After receiving his parents' blessings, Eddie had enough money left over to take him to Kansas City, Missouri, where he caught the train to Chicago on his brother's railroad pass.

"As I was boarding the train for Chicago, the conductor looked at me kind of skeptically and said, 'You sure are a young engineer!'" Eddie recalled. "I was nervous that he wouldn't let me on the train, but he accepted the pass and I was on my way."

When Eddie arrived in Chicago he had three cents to his name and was met at the train station by Virgil. Eddie stayed with his older brother at his apartment along with Virgil's three roommates: for a total of five Texas boys sharing one large apartment splitting the monthly $35 rent, as well as the housekeeping chores.

Eddie soon "beat the bushes," as he called it, looking for any job he could find to put a few dollars in his pocket in order to help carry his own financial weight with his brother and fellow roommates.

"I didn't want to mooch on my brother and my roommates," Eddie said. "I didn't think it was the right thing to do."

A few weeks later, Eddie went to audition for a singing job at radio WLS, the largest radio station in Chicago and in the Midwest. Owned by the Sears-Roebuck and Company, the station first began broadcasting in April 1924. The station's call letters, WLS, written out in lightning bolt script as its logo, stood for "**World's Largest Store**," a moniker the giant retailer and catalog merchant worked hard to earn and of which it liked to make known in its advertisements.[3]

Originally, the main focus of WLS was farm and civic programming interspersed with popular music, comedies and radio serials. The station proudly boasted of its mission statement: "WLS was conceived in your interests, is operated in your behalf, and is dedicated to your service. It is your station."[4]

Eddie auditioned for Ford Rush, the station's head announcer, and Glenn Rowell, WLS' Studio Director, who also headed up the station's music department. The duo was also a very popular musical comedy team on WLS known as "Big Ford and Little Glenn."

Rush and Rowell recognized Eddie's talent and took an immediate interest in the young singer. They tried their utmost best to get him a job at the station but their attempts were overruled by WLS management who reasoned that the station had enough performers on its payroll at the present time.

Despite his initial rejection, Eddie was soon befriended by two other Chicago-based radio performers. They had heard him sing and wanted to help him get his foot in the door as an entertainer. "Cousin" Herald Goodman and his partner, Freddie Owens (his real name was Freddie Yeatzel), known to their radio audience as "The Orange Brothers," hosted their own County music show at radio WMMB, located on the "Windy City's" South Side. Goodman later debuted as an actor in his one-and-only film appearance playing himself in the 1941 Monogram Pictures release of *Saddle Mountain Roundup* starring Ray "Crash" Corrigan, John "Dusty" King, and Max Terhune, better known as "The Range Busters." He also wrote a twelve-page booklet of the same name containing songs, pictures, and stories of the Southwest. Both Goodman and Yeatzel persuaded the station to put Eddie on the air during an open fifteen-minute time slot.

"I took out my old Stellar guitar and started singing just about every song I could think of," Eddie recalled. "I was nervous as it was my first time on radio, but I thought I sang pretty well. I was just hoping that something good would come out of the experience."

Something good did come out of the experience. Three days later, a very elated Herald Goodman telephoned Eddie to tell him that the radio station wanted him back to do another fifteen-minute show. Eddie was ecstatic when he heard the news. Maybe this was the break of which he had been hoping.

In the days immediately following his on-air debut, Eddie had received a substantial amount of mail from radio listeners expressing their pleasure with the young Texan's way with a song. So the station invited him back for a reprise.

However, the mail that Eddie received indicated that the audience did not understand or grasp his last name. Every piece of those written expressions of adulation addressed to him bore witness to that fact with the misspelling of his last name on the envelopes. It was a miracle in and of itself that the station's publicity department and mail room were able to figure out to whom those letters were addressed.

"My last name, Glosup, is kind of an unusual name, and people would spell it every different way imaginable," Eddie said. "I had gotten used to it."

Eddie's tenure at WMMB was short-lived as his second appearance at the station, although equally successful as his first, proved to be his last. Organizational budget restraints would once again deny him acceptance for employment with that particular entertainment venue.

Possessing a tenacious and resilient spirit by not allowing such setbacks to deter him from what he wanted to do, Eddie kept pressing forward. Goodman and Yeatzel took Eddie under their wings trying everything they could to help him get a job in Chicago. One of the first things they did was to encourage Eddie to change his name to one which would be shorter and easier to spell and pronounce. The three friends huddled together at a local restaurant to brainstorm stage name options, with Goodman writing down any and all possible considerations on a piece of paper. A few sheets of paper later, Eddie initially came up with a name he liked.

"I chose the name of Eddie Stone based on the name of one my favorite actors at the time, Lewis Stone," Eddie said.

Stone, who was nominated for the Academy Award for Best Actor in

1929 for *The Patriot*, would later play his most famous role as Judge James Hardy in the Mickey Rooney *Andy Hardy* series.

"Cousin Herald said the name I had chosen was a good name, but it's a Jewish name. I asked him, 'So, what's wrong with that?' He replied, 'You don't look like a Jew!' The three of us had a good laugh over that because Herald and Freddie were both Jewish."

Eddie finally settled on a stage name compromised of his first two names: Eddie Dean. And so with one short breath the young singer bade *adieu* to Edgar Dean Glosup, while saying hello to Eddie Dean, future star of stage, screen, radio, and recordings![5]

"I actually settled on the name Eddie Dean because at that time I was only thinking of how it would look and fit on theater marquees," Eddie said with a chuckle. "I never dreamed of going into pictures at that time. Back then, people in the entertainment business didn't have hard-to-pronounce, or bland-sounding, or really ethnic-sounding names. If someone had an unusual name it was changed. These days, it seems, the more arresting the name, the more appealing it is. Take Arnold Dorsey, for example. He is a fine singer but after he changed his professional name to Englebert Humperdinck, his recordings began to take off. Look at Arnold Schwarzenegger. If he had been acting in the late 1920s, he would have had to change his name."

Eddie never officially changed his name to Eddie Dean. He always kept his birth name for personal and legal reasons.

The Orange Brothers then referred Eddie to WBBM, the sister radio station to WMMB, for an audition. Broadcasting commercially since 1924, WBBM was owned by Leslie and Ralph Atlass, of the Mallory Battery Company of Lincoln, Illinois. The radio station's call letters stood for "World's Best Battery Maker." In later years, an alternate meaning, "We Broadcast Better Music," was created. WBBM became a Columbia Broadcasting Company (CBS) affiliate since 1928.[6]

Once again with guitar in hand, Eddie sang his heart out to win for himself a fifteen-minute daily radio show starting the following day.

Eddie's first broadcast as Eddie Dean on WBBM turned out wonderfully well. Too wonderfully well, in fact, to suit the station's program manager. Eddie explains:

"After I was off the air, the program manager called me into his office and gave me hell. 'What is this about?' he wanted to know. 'How can you come to this radio station and have this many people call in? I got forty calls about you. Nobody's ever gotten that many calls on this station.'

"I told him I didn't know he was talking about, which I honestly didn't. He accused me of setting things up to have people call in during my broadcast saying how wonderful I was. 'I still don't know what you mean,' I told him. 'I'm a Texas kid. I don't know anyone here in Chicago. I just sang my songs. That's all I did.' Well, he didn't believe me and he practically ran me out of the station. I guess you can say I had my fifteen minutes of notoriety after all. (laughs) I told 'Cousin' Herald and Freddie about what happened and both guys just about flipped their lids."

Eddie decided to take matters into his own hands, so to speak, by going to the radio station across the street from the famed Wrigley Building on North Michigan Avenue to talk with the studio manager about getting a job. The station was starting up a newly formed network called the National Broadcasting Company (NBC). Eddie thought he could land a radio job by getting in on the "ground floor," so to speak, of an up-and-coming company.

The manager told Eddie that he couldn't use him as a singer at the moment but asked if he would consider engaging himself in a special yet advantageous cultural project that would no doubt be very fulfilling for Eddie both personally and professionally and which would have the potential of making both the station and he a lot of money. He asked Eddie if he would travel throughout the South to search out and listen to the old folk songs of those regions, commonly referred to as authentic "hillbilly music," and to collect them by writing down the music and words so they could be complied and published in to book form. American folk singer and radio entertainer Bradley Kincaid, himself a prolific composer of Folk and Country music, had recently done just that, publishing his first edition of his 1928 songbook called *My Favorite Mountain Ballads*, which sold more than 100,000 copies.[7]

Eddie told the manager he would love to do the project provided he would be backed financially by the network as he didn't have any money for travel and other expenses. The manager declined to bankroll Eddie on the project, so Eddie's potential career as an aspiring musicologist regrettably ended before it ever began.

Eddie then received word from Goodman and Yeatzel that the duo had set up an audition for him with bandleader Wayne King who was currently playing at the famed Aragon Ballroom on the North Side of Chicago. The 28-year-old King, who a year earlier left the saxophone section of the illustrious Paul Whiteman Orchestra to form his own outfit, would come to be known as "The Waltz King" because much of his most popular music involved waltzes.

Eddie sang several numbers for the distinguished-looking yet personable bandleader during the audition, but when finished, walked away without getting what he wanted: a job.

"King told me he liked how I sang but that he didn't need a male vocalist. He wanted a female singer," Eddie said. "He also said that he didn't want anyone to overshadow him on his own show. When I assured him that I wouldn't do that to him, he wouldn't hear of it. I thanked him for his time and I left."

With that particular kind of rejection, Eddie quickly realized that his philosophical understanding of the entertainment business was so vastly different than that of the reality of the perceived threat to over-inflated egos of veteran performers.

"I was always taught it was the show itself that was the most important thing, not the individual," Eddie said. "It didn't matter who you had on the show. As long as the show is good, even if it's your own show, you still get the credit. Mr. King didn't think that way."

For Eddie, the show still went on, as he tried to make a break for himself any way he could. Once again, through the benevolent intervention of the Orange Brothers, Eddie was able to get a four-week stint singing at the Triangle Café, frequented occasionally by crime boss Al Capone, over on the ethnically diverse West Side of Chicago.

In his attempt to make a good visual impression for his audition, Eddie took the initiative to wash his one and only, albeit, dirty suit in the bathtub at his apartment. He didn't have the money to get it professionally cleaned, nor could he have gotten it cleaned that quickly anyway even if he did have the money. He spent four hours on the afternoon of his audition with an iron drying his suit, stretching it and pressing it to where it looked decent.

Eddie performed a nightly floor show singing popular songs of the day along with a smattering of cowboy songs while accompanying himself on his old Stellar guitar.

Working in a nightclub setting was a new experience for the young Texan and under the tutelage of some of the other café performers, they showed him how to walk up to customers' tables during his performance to retrieve tips. It was the tips in which the performers earned most of their money.

"If the customer liked your performance, they would have their thumb on top of the table with their palm under the table in order to slip money in your hand as you walked by," Eddie explained. "That way they didn't want others to know what they gave you, maybe for fear of embarrassment, I don't know. Anyway, that's just how they did it. I was fortunate in making quite a few dollars in tips which helped me get along in Chicago."

After the Triangle Café engagement ended, Eddie was pointed in the direction of auditioning for another singing job through the seemingly endless professional contacts provided by "Cousin" Herald Goodman and Freddie Yeatzel.

"These guys were two of the best friends I ever had," Eddie said affectionately about Goodman and Yeatzel. "They were always looking out for me."

They told Eddie to see Ernie Young, a producer of stage shows at fairs, who operated his famed "Ernie Young Revue" based out of Chicago. Young's Revue included singers, dancers, comedians, acrobatic acts, musicians, and at times, "freak show-type" wonders.

Eddie's audition with Young started off on the wrong foot. He misunderstood that the try out was to take place at a location four blocks north from his apartment, when in reality the location where the stellar producer was holding auditions was *forty* blocks away. Not having any money for car fare, Eddie walked the entire distance to the appointed meeting, much to the consternation of Young who insisted that members of his troupe as well as aspiring troupe members be on time for all rehearsals and performances, including *auditions!*

Tired and a bit winded from his seemingly endless walk along the "concrete prairie" of the North Side, Eddie sincerely apologized for his tardiness and quickly regrouped and sang a few songs to win the audition, thereby overcoming any negative first impressions Young may have harbored of him.

The thirty-member company plus crew left a few days later traveling by train to begin their mid-summer to late fall season of providing entertainment at state and county fairs throughout the Midwest and selected parts of the Southwest. Their first date was San Antonio, Texas.

Eddie teamed up to form a singing duo with another troupe member; a fine-looking young man from Glasgow, Scotland, with a big tenor voice named Johnny Sloan. Sloan, who was three years Eddie's senior, was short in stature with dark hair who spoke with a thick Scottish brogue, and who was classically trained to sing in operetta style. As opposites as they may have appeared, the pair of singers immediately hit it off and became good friends, working up a very compelling and captivating routine while on the train ride down to San Antonio. Throughout their association together, Eddie eventually taught Johnny how to sing Country Western music.

The Revue's first performance was just a "stone's throw away," Eddie said, from the famed Alamo, where on March 6, 1836, after a thirteen-day siege, nearly 200 defenders of Texas freedom died in battle against the invading Mexican army of over 1,500 soldiers. The Alamo came to symbolize a heroic struggle against impossible odds; a place where men made the ultimate sacrifice for freedom. To this very day, the Alamo remains hallowed ground and the bastion of Texas liberty. Even Eddie was profoundly moved by seeing the historical site for the very first time.

"Growing up in Texas, we learned about Texas history before we learned about U.S. history," Eddie explained. "I wept when I walked on the grounds of the Alamo. I'm not sorry for doing that because all the people who died there fought for Texas freedom. It was an emotional moment for me knowing that these men were killed for my sake and for all Texans."

The Ernie Young Revue was an instant hit with San Antonians in its debut while the team of Dean and Sloan brought down the house with their musical act which featured their jaunty and giddy version of the Scottish ditty, "Roamin' in the Gloamin'," composed and popularized by famed Scottish entertainer Sir Harry Lauder years earlier.

While at the Revue's stop in San Antonio, Eddie discovered his partner had issues with alcohol.

"Johnny always carried a flask of bootleg whiskey with him in his suitcase," Eddie said. "But I never saw him drunk during a performance, that I will say. He was professional about that. After our show in San Antonio we stayed in a hotel that evening before taking the train the following day to our next destination. Johnny was drinking heavily and said he couldn't sleep. In his drunken state he wanted me to sock him on the chin to be knocked out so he could sleep. I didn't want to do it, but he kept pleading with me to do it. Just to shut him up, I hit him with a right cross that sent him across the room onto his bed. I tucked him under the bed covers fully clothed. The next morning he woke up complaining about a sore jaw and asked me what had happened. When I told him, he never asked me to hit him again."

In another incident just prior to tour's end, Eddie said Sloan was inebriated in the hotel room they shared and in an illogical act of spite and defiance, pulled the flask of bootleg whiskey out from his hip pocket, turned facing Eddie and raised the flask in a salute and said, "Here's to you, you S. O. B." Instead of drinking the homemade moonshine, he poured its contents in an open drawer of the dresser.

"I didn't know what that was all about," Eddie recalled with a laugh. "Johnny must have been really drunk to actually know what he was doing. He would never have wasted whiskey like that."

The Revue was enthusiastically received everywhere they played, resulting in another successful season. It's closing show was held in early October in the village of Walthill, Nebraska, near the Missouri River just south of Sioux City, Iowa, next to the Winnebago Indian Reservation. The following day the train took the newly disbanded troupe back to Chicago where Eddie and Johnny found themselves out of work.

Eddie and Johnny rented an apartment together in Chicago as both men struggled to find work in the entertainment arena wherever they could. When such jobs were hard to come by, Eddie even went so far as to wash dishes at a local restaurant in order to, as he put it, "just to stay alive. "

During this interim period, Eddie also worked at trying to improve his singing act by including a tap dancing routine in order to be more "marketable." He had incorporated a little of it during the last few weeks of touring with the Ernie Young Revue. The Ehrhardt Brothers, Ben and Gus, dancers who were also touring with the Revue, taught Eddie how to do some basic tap dancing steps.

"I wanted to entertain people and I had to work out to where I could really get a job," Eddie said. "I got some tap shoes and a rope. Will Rogers was big at the time and he was a master ropes man and always did rope tricks in his act. I figured if he could do it, so could I. I came up with the idea that I could sing a little, dance a little and do some fancy rope tricks as a way of trying to build myself a Vaudeville act. Not surprisingly, nothing happened. (laughs)"

Eddie's passion and enthusiasm for professional self-improvement was commendable but it didn't sit very well at times with the elderly lady who lived directly below him in the same apartment building who found his practicing intrusively disturbing. After numerous complaints to the landlord, Eddie was told he needed to find some other place to practice his "hoofing" routines.

In the mean time, roommate Johnny Sloan thought about contacting Earl May, who owned May Seed and Nursery Company, in Shenandoah, Iowa, on the chance of he and Eddie getting a job. Shenandoah, a town of four square miles, is located in the lower southwest part of the "Hawkeye State" near the Iowa-Missouri border about sixty miles southeast of the Omaha, Nebraska.

In addition to his seed company, May also owned radio station KMA in Shenandoah, which began operation in 1925. The following year, May won *Radio Digest* gold cup for bring voted "World's Most Popular Radio Announcer" by over 452,000 people throughout the United States. KMA operated on a slogan of **"Keep Millions Advised."**[8]

As of 2013, KMA radio as well as the Earl May Seed and Nursery Company are still in existence and continues to operate as a family-owned business being an important economic staple in the community of approximately 5,500. May's granddaughter, Betty Jean Shaw, is the current head of the company.[9]

Before before joining the Ernie Young Revue, Sloan sang with the Lyceum Company, an organization that worked to foster the spread of knowledge through various educational and cultural activities including the fine arts. The Lyceum Company traveled through Shenandoah and Sloan made an appearance on KMA.

May was so impressed with Sloan's singing that he told the young Scot that if he ever needed a job, he should call him and that he can come to work at KMA.

"When Johnny shared this news with me, I told him to make the call," Eddie said. "We were in pretty desperate circumstances. We owed rent on the room and were out of food. Anything was worth a try."

So Sloan put in a collect call to May to see if the radio owner would be true to his word. He was.

In fact, May's word was good as gold. Sloan also put in a good word for Eddie, and May hired him sight unseen.

"Get on a train and come down," May told the boys.

"We can't, Mr. May. We're broke," Sloan told his new boss. "We haven't any money."

"Well, I'll send you the money."

May wired the money and Eddie and Johnny boarded the train the following day to make the 500-mile trek from Chicago to Shenandoah with just the clothes on their backs and their trusty guitars.

"We left all of our baggage and all of our wardrobe, our tuxedos, and other clothing items for different shows, everything, with the land lady as good will that we'd eventually pay her," Eddie said. "She was nice about it."

When the boys arrived in Shenandoah, May was surprised to see them without luggage and wanted to know what happened to their bags. When the nursery giant was told of their hard-luck story, he immediately put Eddie and Johnny back on the train to Chicago with round trip fare and enough money to square away their debt with the land lady. Returning to Shenandoah with all their luggage and wardrobe in hand, the vocal duo had an apartment ready and waiting for them at the hotel compliments of their new employer.

Eddie and Johnny immediately went to work at KMA whose studio theater in the one-floor building seated about 200 people. The theater ceiling was painted in blue accented with white stars giving the appearance of an open evening sky. Its ambiance was such that one wouldn't think of being in a radio station attending a broadcast but rather, being entertained in a small, yet stylish music hall.

The new singing team was well-received by the KMA listening audience. May also took an immediate liking to Eddie and loved to hear his new find sing such tunes as "Berry Pickin' Time," one of Eddie's most requested songs which hailed from the "Peg" Moreland canon. Much of Eddie's repertoire of solo material came from his time spent in Dallas, which he dusted off and presented with fresh, new spins to the KMA audience.

Eddie's salary at KMA was $75 a week. Every Saturday afternoon May would call Eddie into his office and say, "Eddie, hold out your hand." He would then slowly and carefully count out seventy-five gold one-dollar coins and concluded the counting ritual with the words, "Now, Eddie, I want you to save a little, spend a little, and give a little away."

"Mr. May was the nicest and kindest man," Eddie said. "His goodness and kindness left a lasting impression on me. Working for him was a real joy. I really appreciated his weekly comment to me as he paid me my salary. It's a beautiful sentiment and when you think about it, it makes a lot of sense. It's a wonderful philosophy to live by. Many years later, I wrote and recorded a song about his words called 'Save a Little, Spend a Little, Give a Little Away.' It was also recorded by Michael Parks, a fine actor and singer who is a good friend of mine."

Things were going pretty smoothly for the boys until one day an efficiency expert from Chicago came to the radio station at the behest of May to check out how the studio was operating. Accompanying him on the inspection tour was a large gallon jug of bootleg wine. The efficiency expert also stayed during his two-day visit at the same hotel where Eddie and Johnny lived.

Sloan was out running some errands that afternoon while Eddie stayed at the hotel and was invited to the efficiency expert's room for a chat concerning his role at the radio station. The boys were not scheduled to do a show together until later that evening.

At the conclusion of the informal meeting, Eddie's host offered him some of his bootleg wine to drink. Eddie accepted and took a sip of the homemade fruit of the vine as a token of respect and of the man's hospitality. He then left to go to one of the local restaurants near the hotel to eat a hearty chicken dinner before going on the air.

Moments after placing his dinner order, Eddie suddenly doubled over with violent stomach cramps.

"That wine made me sick," Eddie recalled. "I took a sip of it even though I seldom drink. I don't know what was in that stuff but it made me sicker than dog."

After stepping outside the restaurant to vomit, Eddie gained enough strength and composure to walk the two short blocks back to the apartment and crawled into bed to ride out the storm until it passed. Sloan went to the station that evening and sang alone, covering for his ill partner.

On his walk home from the station, Sloan experienced a frightening situation that no one should ever have to experience. As he stopped in front of one of the stores on Main Street to get out of the breeze in order to light a cigarette, a man dressed in a suit standing nearby in the shadows told Sloan to stop what he was doing and to come to him. Fearing that the man was a robber, Sloan started to run away. The man shouted for Sloan to stop and began firing his gun at the singer as he gave chase.

Sloan ran back to the apartment wildly banging on the door and yelling hysterically for Eddie to let him in. Upon being let inside the apartment, Sloan frantically told his partner to lock the door because someone was after him.

A few moments later there was pounding on the apartment door from a man claiming to be a police officer and demanding to be let inside. Eddie peered through the keyhole and yelled back that he didn't believe that he was a police officer because he wasn't wearing a uniform and warned him to get away from the door or he'd shoot him with his gun. Eddie didn't own a gun, as it was a bluff on Eddie's part in an attempt to scare away the would-be intruder.

The next morning, four police officers came to Eddie's and Johnny's room and brought them to the town court house just in time for them to appear before the local magistrate. The boys were accused of evading a police officer and Johnny, in particular, for suspicion of attempted burglary.

"I listened to Johnny explain his story to the judge," Eddie said. "Then the judge wanted to hear my side of the story. I candidly told him that I'd run too, if someone in plain clothes was shooting at me. It was then that I learned that the policeman who shot at and chased Johnny thought Johnny looked suspicious standing in front of that store at night and thought he was about to burglar it. The judge then said, 'This court will refer this case to the District Court in Clarinda.' The next day we went to court in Clarinda. The district court judge heard the case. The case against us was dropped and we were released and the judge issued an order that all police officers in Shenandoah be clothed in uniform. So Johnny and I helped to get police officers in Shenandoah to wear uniforms."

What Eddie and Johnny experienced didn't affect their good standing with Earl May or with the KMA listeners. Everyone realized that what had happened was a big misunderstanding.

Eddie and Johnny stayed with May for almost a year. As 1929 would soon be drawing to a close in a month and a new decade of uncertainty approached brought on by the Great Depression a few months earlier, Sloan received a call from Earl Williams, the program director of station WNAX in Yankton, South Dakota, offering the singer a job.

The Yankton area was home to clusters of various European ethnic groups and the station management had heard about Sloan because he came from Scotland. They needed a singer who could represent Scotland by singing many of the native songs of the old country for its Scottish radio listeners.

Sloan told WNAX management that both he and Eddie work together as a team and asked if he could bring him along. Management agreed. After some careful thought and deliberation, the boys accepted the offer.

"Because Johnny was responsible for me getting the job in Shenandoah, I thought it would be fair to him if I went to WNAX even though Mr. May offered to double my salary and pay me $300 to stay," Eddie said. "Mr. May told me if I wanted to go that he would understand. He wasn't going to stand in my way. It was a difficult decision for me to make because Mr. May treated us so well."

So the partners caught the train to make the 220-mile trip to Yankton, South Dakota, in the winter of 1929, with temperatures welcoming them at a chilling -30°.

Yankton, with its nine-square-mile radius, was named for the Yankton tribe of Nakota (Sioux) Native Americans. Known as the "Mother City of the Dakota's" for being one of the first established cities in the Dakota Territories, Yankton is located in the southeast corner of the state along the Missouri River bordering Nebraska, its neighbor to the south.

When Eddie and Johnny arrived in Yankton the town had a population of 6, 072. In 2010, the population had risen to 14, 500.[10]

WNAX was one of the early broadcast stations going on the air in 1922. The call letters represented "North American radio eXperiment." The station was purchased in 1926 by Deloss Butler "D. B." Gurney, who owned Gurney's Seed and Nursery Company, the largest nursery in the general area. The station became known as "WNAX: The Voice of the House of Gurney in Yankton." Due to the flat landscape of the Upper Great Plains the station's powerful signals covered a five-state area.

After a brief period in D. B.'s home, the studio was moved to the third floor of the seed house, the headquarters of the Gurney Seed and Nursery Company. The station was used to promote Gurney products and services, making Gurney's a household name.[11]

J. B.'s. son, John Chandler "Chan" Gurney, was the programmer for the station. A native of Yankton, he was a sergeant in the U. S. Army during World War I and later became a U. S. Senator (Republican) serving from 1939 to 1951, serving as chairman of the U. S. Senate Committee on Armed Services. After Gurney's death in 1985, the City of Yankton renamed its airport the Chan Gurney Municipal Airport in his honor.

With the addition of broadcasting live talent and folksy commentary, WNAX's attracted thousands of listeners and sold millions of Gurney seeds and trees and other farm supplies as well a vast array of other commercial items ranging from grocery, to gasoline and automobile products.

In 1983, a fire destroyed the main WNAX building. Lost in the inferno were the station's historic live recordings, as well as thousands of records that were destroyed.

In addition to their singing act which they did a number of shows per day, Eddie and Johnny broadcast commercials, public service announcements and reported local news. They were soon sponsored under the auspices of the WNAX-brand of coffee called Sunshine Coffee and were known professionally as "The Sunshine Coffee Boys."

The boys sang all types of songs on their program. They were on a music publisher's mailing list and they frequently were sent sheet music of all the latest songs. As a result, there was never a lack of potential material that could be utilized on a day's program. In fact, Eddie and Johnny would often "wing it" by featuring a new song that arrived in the mail to them that very day!

"We'd go on the air and I'd say 'Well, here's a song we just got in today's mail. We haven't looked at it yet, so let's see what's it like," Eddie said. "And we'd sing it right on the air. Some of the songs were pretty good. A lot of it was pop music. We'd get a lot of things from the M. M. Cole Publishing Company and we'd use a lot of their music. We used to get letters from Mr. Cole thanking us for it."

While Eddie knew the job at WNAX was fulfilling a desire for him to perform professionally, little did he know that the time he would spend there would provided him the springboard for greater changes in his life both professionally and personally.

Above: A professional publicity photo of budding singer/entertainer
Eddie Dean with his Stellar guitar while working with the
Ernie Young Revue based out of Chicago.

Above: Eddie Dean with Johnny Sloan, his Scottish singing partner.

Above: The original home of WNAX in Yankton, South Dakota, was on the third floor of the Gurney Feed and Nursery Company seed house.

Below: During the early 1930s WNAX moved to a more modern venue.

4

Sunshine Coffee and The Dean Brothers

After spending almost a year together at WNAX, the Dean and Sloan singing team parted company. Sloan's departure came as the result of having been bitten by the love bug. Not long after his arrival in Yankton, Sloan began dating Mary Nelson, a member of the Nelson Family, a Danish musical clan comprised of Papa Nelson, his son, and his three daughters. The group was a popular act on WNAX.

"Johnny came to me this one day and told me he was leaving to get married and that he was moving back to Chicago," Eddie said. "His announcement to me didn't come as a total surprise. Once I saw that he and Mary were pretty serious about each other, I knew our days as a team were numbered."

Like Eddie's brother, Alvin, Sloan went on to work for the YMCA and retired from professional singing. The only singing he did after that was in church. Eddie said the last time he saw Sloan was in 1977.[1] He was still working for the YMCA in Chicago at the time.

Hoping that he wouldn't be out of a job due to his partner's exodus, Eddie asked Chan Gurney, the station's program manager, if he could stay on as a single act. Gurney consented.

Eddie's solo career at WNAX lasted five full days. The day after Sloan and his bride left Yankton for Chicago, Eddie received a letter from his father informing him that brother Jimmie, who had been working with brother Virgil on the railroad in Chicago, was out of work and needed a job. Papa James also asked his youngest son if he could get his older brother to work together with him at the radio station.

Eddie talked with Gurney about bringing his brother on board to work with him as a singing team. Gurney was cool to the idea and told Eddie, "What you have been doing is enough. We don't need anybody else. Just do what you have been doing. Besides, we can't pay him."

"But he's my brother and he needs a job," Eddie insisted. "He's an excellent singer. You won't go wrong if you hire him."

After some diplomatic persuasion, Eddie finally talked his boss into letting *him* hire his brother, splitting his salary with Jimmie down the middle.

"Offering to pay Jimmie half my salary was the only way management was going to let my brother come work at the station," Eddie said. "I didn't mind. Jimmie was a fine brother. I respected him, too. I didn't have to think twice about splitting my salary with him because of what he did for our mama when we lived on the farm in Posey. When Mama got severely sick, Papa was worried as to how we would get a hold of the doctor. Jimmie, who was thirteen, rode three miles on his horse in the dead of night during the pouring rain wearing a slicker and brought the doctor, riding double on his horse, to our place to treat her. He stayed up all night and then took the doctor back home in the morning again riding double on his horse. I was nine years old at the time and I thought that was such a selfless act. It had such an impact on me about my brother. When it came to Jimmie needing a job I didn't care if he took all the money."

Jimmie himself couldn't be particular about the pay arrangements either. He at least would be earning an income, which he welcomed with open arms. South Dakota in 1930 was feeling the tough economic effects of the Great Depression. Climate changes were also beginning to take its toll on the prairie farmers with harvest failures due to lack of rainfall coupled with over-cultivation of farmland. By 1935, the notorious Dust Bowl would invade the "Black Hills State," burying prime farm land and communities in deep mounds of desert-like sand causing a large exodus of residents to relocate, thereby decreasing the state's population by seven percent by the end of the decade.[2]

With Jimmie's arrival at WNAX, he and Eddie were once again a team; a team that Eddie savored with great delight. He always loved singing with his older brother. Harmonically, they blended beautifully together. This would be the first time since their high school days that the two Glosup boys sang together in a public/professional arena.

One of the first things Jimmie did was to drop the Glosup surname, changing his professional name to Jimmie Dean as a way of keeping in uniformity with Eddie. The pair would be known as "The Dean Brothers: Jimmie and Eddie." Since Jimmie was the elder sibling, Eddie deferred top billing to him as a sign of respect. It was also a sound business move since Eddie knew that Jimmie's pride of working for his younger brother could potentially be a sticky issue in their professional and personal relationship.

The "sticky issue" that Eddie tried to avoid eventually came to a head in an ugly way a few years later after Jimmie had gotten married. Jimmie's wife, Ruth, made it an issue.

"Ruth couldn't get along with me sort of being the leader of the team," Eddie said. "We had a little family problem that way, but overall, things worked itself out and it was resolved."

Eddie and Jimmie roomed together in the same boarding house in Yankton where Eddie and Johnny Sloan stayed. The boarding house was owned by an vivacious elderly lady who also supplemented her income by making her own bootleg whiskey.

This presented some challenges for Eddie in terms of keeping vigilance over his older brother since Jimmie liked to drink, more times than not, to the excess. The bootleg whiskey made by their landlady provided Jimmie easy access to the illegal brew, which exasperated his life-long battle with alcoholism.

The Dean Brothers became the second manifestation of "The Sunshine Coffee Boys" as well as the most popular. The two spokespersons for the caffeine beverage helped to increase sales and in so doing they received lots of fan mail. They were quickly becoming local celebrities. They even had publicity photos taken of them standing next to sacks of WNAX Sunshine Coffee that were printed on postcards and mailed to all fans who wrote to them and was signed, "Harmoniously Yours, Eddie and Jimmie Coffee Boys."

Not only did the boys just entertain by singing duets together because they were under the auspices of Sunshine Coffee sponsorship, Eddie also took it upon himself to *study* coffee as a way of being more authentic with their presentation. It was he who did all the commercials for the coffee product.

"I wanted to know all there was to know about coffee," Eddie said. "I knew where it came from, how the coffee beans were grown, and how it was made, so when I talked about it over the air, I knew what I was talking about. I was trying to be efficient."

The Dean Brothers started their work day going on the air at 5:30 a. m. for Sunshine Coffee. They would do five thirty-minute Sunshine Coffee shows per day, with remaining air times at mid-morning, late morning, early afternoon, and with their last show ending at 4:30 p. m.

Jimmie never did any solo work. His only participation was singing duets with his brother. Eddie, on the other hand, was also involved with other programming at WNAX. He hosted a thirty-minute daily children's show and was known as "Uncle Eddie" in which he told stories while music would be played in the background through the use of a microphone that was held in front of the speaker to a record player.

He also did a fifteen-minute daily musical show with Randy Ryan, one of the announcers at the radio station, for Gurney Rose Bushes. Ryan and Eddie wrote a theme song for the show about the rose bushes they were selling. In between musical selections, the pair would also engage in some lighthearted banter which would always segue into Eddie putting in a plug for his sponsor's rose bushes.

When not doing any shows, Eddie would also fill in his day where needed by reading the latest news casts or doing commercials on a variety of products.

By this time, in addition to playing guitar, Eddie also became proficient at playing the violin and mandolin as a way to broaden his musical appeal and to add color and contrast to the Dean Brothers' act.

Eddie himself became so popular with listeners at WNAX that even his speaking voice was recognizable by those in the outlying farming communities. Eddie explains:

"I went out pheasant hunting and I walked onto a field where this older gentleman was plowing. He had a radio in his cultivator that was tuned to WNAX. We chatted for a bit about the game situation in the area. I didn't tell this old timer who I was, but right in the middle of our conversation he said, 'You're Eddie Dean!' We never met before but he knew my voice. It just brought home to me how really powerful a medium radio was in those days."

Various smaller musical aggregations would also occasionally broadcast at the station, such as a group called the "Little Symphony Orchestra," which performed neo-classical repertoire. In fact, Chan Gurney's wife was so taken with Eddie's musical abilities on the violin that she wanted him to sit in with this group for a broadcast, thinking that having a staff member from the station perform with them would add some respectability to the proceedings. Eddie obliged playing the second violin part, and playing it well.

In addition to the Dean Brothers, other musical acts were popular regulars on WNAX. For almost ten years beginning in 1927, the twenty-four-year-old accordion-playing Lawrence Welk and his nine-piece Novelty Orchestra was the station's house band broadcasting about three times a week. Long before he was known for his "Champagne Music," Welk toured the Midwest specializing in polkas, waltzes, schottisches, and novelty instrumentation.

Welk's pianist, "Spider" Webb, who in 1928 composed "Spiked Beer," the band's notable ragtime-style piece, was also hired to play solo keyboard for broadcast. He would play the piano so hard at times that he broke the instrument's wires!

"We'd always get a laugh out of that," Eddie recalled.

Other listener favorites over the WNAX airwaves included the Nelson Family Band, and John Jensen, a young man crippled from the effects of polio who played guitar and sang folk songs. He also played the harmonica to accompany his singing.

"The station was busy all the time," Eddie said.

The station was so busy that even individuals of notoriety would occasionally pass through its portals. One such individual was James Cash "J. C." Penney, the entrepreneur and founder of the J. C. Penney retail stores. Penney was in town to help raise continuous funds for the Mount Rushmore National Memorial that was currently being constructed in the Black Hills on the west side of the state. The project, which began in 1927, was designed to represent the first 150 years of American history with sixty-foot sculptured bas relief likenesses of presidents George Washington, Thomas Jefferson, Theodore Roosevelt, and Abraham Lincoln carved into the granite rock of Mount Rushmore.[3]

WNAX management was on board with such a venture and had its station staff members create shows on the radio to help raise money for the project.

"When I got to the station early one morning to do my show," Eddie recalled, "I was on the elevator going to the third floor of the Gurney Seed Building and on the elevator was J. C. Penney. I recognized him from his picture that was hung in the J. C. Penney store in Yankton. I was pretty amazed that he was at the station so early at five in the morning. I introduced myself to him. 'I heard you yesterday over the radio,' he said. 'I enjoyed your music very much. It's good to see you.' Mr. Penney was a very nice gentleman even though our encounter with each other lasted just a few moments."

Later that same afternoon, Gutzon Borglum, the Danish-American sculptor commissioned to sculpt the Mount Rushmore project (in collaboration with his son, Lincoln Borglum), came to the WNAX studio to talk with D. B. Gurney. During a break, Eddie had a chance to introduce himself to the senior Borglum and to show him a wooden pipe in which he carved out a very striking likeness of Abraham Lincoln. One of Eddie's hidden pastimes and talents was painting and intricate wood carving.

"I showed Mr. Borglum my Abe Lincoln pipe and he was very impressed," Eddie said. "He told me, 'Quit singing and help me build Mount Rushmore, please.' That was quite a compliment coming from a man of such respected stature. He was very personable, too.

"I went on to ask him, 'Mr. Borglum, how do you figure where to blast in order to prepare the hill for your sculpture?' He said, 'I made a drawing of the figures and then I confer with my chief engineer who handles the dynamite to discuss how much rock I need to cut out.' As one sculptor (of sorts) to another, I was really fascinated by what he had to say."

While in Yankton, and separate from what he and Jimmie were doing together on radio, Eddie moonlighted by forming an eight-piece band comprised of string instruments, accordion, percussion, one brass, and one clarinet. They toured the general Northern Plain States area of the Dakotas, Minnesota, Nebraska, and Iowa playing for various dances. Their band book consisted of numerous Pop, Country, and Ethic tunes reflective through such musical styles as polkas, waltzes, and tarantellas. Eddie was the leader of this band and in many ways his aggregation mirrored the repertoire of the Welk Orchestra at the time.

Both Eddie's and Jimmie's radio personality status helped to elevate the band to enthusiastic acceptance among the folk living in those outlining rural communities.

"You sure learn about the people when you do as much traveling as we did," Eddie recalled. "See, up in that country in those days, you'd have a town maybe of all Swedish people, and in another town they'd nearly be all Norwegian, another would be all German, and another nearly all Bohemian, and Irish, and so on. The band would play those tunes that were associated with a particular ethnic group. The band played them beautifully.

"We'd do many of those old traditional dances. You'd be standing up on stage and see the people dancing and it looked like a beautifully rehearsed show. Sometimes both the men and women would come to these dances dressed in their native costumes; some very beautiful costumes, too. It was really something to see. These dances a lot of times would be held in a large hall or armory that would hold a few thousand people. We'd pack them in, too, just like Lawrence Welk did. "

Many of these dances were not held on just weekend evenings but also on week nights. A good number of these dance dates were located about a 200-mile or so radius from Yankton. Driving at night on gravel roads in a four-cylinder automobile with a 40-horse-power engine was, needless to say, quite an experience.

In fact, Eddie was making good money working for the radio station prior to forming this band that he was able to purchase his first automobile: a black 1930 Ford Model A Deluxe Tudor Sedan for $468. His car became one of the two vehicles used to transport the band and its equipment to and from engagements.

Eddie, Jimmie, and crew developed a rigorous routine that helped to increase the percentages that they would make the scheduled dance on time. Within minutes after completing their last radio show for the day at 4:30 p. m., the Sunshine Coffee Boys packed up their instruments and headed out from the station to the automobiles where the remaining band members were already packed and waiting to move out.

The band would play for a four-hour dance ending at 1 a. m., and they would quickly pack up and get on the road so that their leader and his brother could get back to the radio station by 5:30 to start another day's broadcast.

"A lot of times we didn't get any sleep," Eddie said, "or we slept when we could on the car ride back to Yankton while taking turns driving. I remember one time I didn't get to bed for eight days! I slept a little in the car and I just made it back in time to take a quick shower, then go the air."

In addition to performing, each band member was assigned to certain duties since they didn't have the benefit of a full-time manager or booking agency so they and they alone were responsible for their own care and welfare. This included transportation, band set up and tear down, selling and taking admission tickets at the door.

"I was running the band," Eddie said. "Jimmie sold the tickets along with another band member who would take tickets at the door. One band member wanted to do the bookings so we let him. The band members would split among themselves half the take of a night's receipts, which in those days added up to pretty good money."

Eddie recalled playing for a dance at the armory in Luverne, Minnesota, a 120-mile jaunt from Yankton. The band took in $1,800 that night and arrived back in Yankton just in time for Eddie and Jimmie to do their 5:30 morning show, despite having to drive through a few unexpected and out-of-the-way detours on the return trek.

While traveling to their intended destinations, the boys would always take their shotguns with them in case an opportunity would present itself to bag a pheasant or duck. The band had just finished playing a Friday night dance at the Corn Palace, in Mitchell, South Dakota, a 100-mile journey from Yankton. The Corn Palace is renown as an unusual tourist spot for its uniquely designed corn murals. In its over 125-year existence, it has played host to dances, basketball tournaments, university graduation ceremonies, stage shows, and industrial exhibits. The Palace each year is redecorated with naturally colored corn and other grains with natural grasses to retain its pride as "the agricultural showplace of the world."[4]

Since Eddie and Jimmie didn't have to be at the radio station until Monday morning, the band was able to take somewhat extended tours during the weekends. While in Mitchell, the musicians stayed overnight at the home of a widow who was an acquaintance with one of the members of the band. Eddie and the widow talked briefly before retiring for the night. She told him that she had a small silver pistol that had belonged to her late husband and that she wanted Eddie to have it. Eddie graciously accepted the gift.

The following night, the band was scheduled to play at a large dance hall near a lake outside the town of De Smet. During the relatively short drive there, Jimmie wanted to try out the silver pistol. He was driving 55 mph on the dirt highway when he spotted a rooster up ahead. Guiding the steering wheel of the car with his right hand, and with the pistol in the other, Jimmie stuck his left arm out the window, fired a round at the rooster as it fluttered away, and shot it dead, right through its head.

A band member in the back seat of car couldn't believe anyone could shoot a gun that well.

"There's nothing to it," Jimmie replied back nonchalantly.

When the boys arrived at the dance hall, the building was dark, boarded up, and abandoned. There wasn't a soul to be found anywhere. Eddie explained what happened next:

"When we got there, we were unaware that the place was closed up for quite some time. Obviously, it was a booking mishap. As we were checking the place out, a door was left open and in the back of the dance hall there was an old shooting gallery that must have been left over some time ago from a carnival. All the parts were rusted so that the rabbits, deer, ducks, and other animal targets you would shoot at couldn't move. We decided that since we were there, we'd have some fun and use the shooting gallery to get in some target practice. We located an old generator that was nearby that worked, giving us light.

"Since Jimmie bedazzled us with his shooting skills earlier on the road, we all figured that he would shoot gunshot embroidery patterns on those stationary targets. Do you know that rascal couldn't hit any of those targets? Nope, not a one. That incident earlier with the rooster was just a fluke. He killed that bird on just plain dumb luck!" (laughs)

While the lifestyle Eddie was leading between his work at the radio station and leading the band was successful as well as hectic, he nevertheless loved what he was doing. However, it wouldn't be long before new opportunities would be calling themselves to the attention of the young Texan via a chance meeting with a certain "someone" that would radically forever change his life for the better.

5

Dearest, Eddie's Truly Fair

That "someone" who would radically change Eddie's life forever came in a 5-foot 2-inch body named Lorene St. Clair Donnelly, who was also known as "Dearest." Eddie was introduced to Lorene through Fleming Allen, a mutual friend.

Lorene was born on October 4, 1912, on the family farm in Volin, South Dakota, about sixteen miles northeast of Yankton. Volin hadn't grown much within the past one hundred years as the recent population count was at 161.[1] She was the daughter of John Henry Donnelly, born July 29, 1870, a staunch Irish Roman Catholic who originally hailed from Platteville, Wisconsin, and who died on November 13, 1922, at age 52, and Bessie Marie St. Clair Peterson (sometimes spelled Pederson according to some official documents) who was born in Norway in 1881. It was said that Mama Donnelly's family tree can be traced back in Norway to about 400 A.D.

"I didn't realize until afterward that I was married to such an important person." Eddie once quipped jokingly about his wife's lineage.

Lorene was the youngest of four children – three daughters and a son - born to the Donnelly's. Papa Donnelly, was forty-one years old and Mama Donnelly was thirty-one when Lorene was born. Lorene's older siblings were, in birth order, Vernon, Dottie, and Fern.

Lorene graduated from Yankton High School in 1930. As a teen, she worked part-time taking tickets at the local movie theater in Yankton before being employed for some time at the Dakota Radio Shop in Yankton. It was at the movie theater that Allen knew Lorene, as Allen was the theater's organist.

Eddie was in perpetual motion while at WNAX with his radio duties and the band and Allen thought that Eddie could benefit from Lorene's company, since he observed that they seem to have a lot in common with each other. What turned out to be a common denominator in their relationship was their instant mutual attraction, a chemistry that was so evident when they were in each other's company.

Love bloomed quickly between Eddie and Lorene, and after a year's courtship, Lorene accepted Eddie's proposal of marriage, with a wedding date yet to be determined.

With over a year-and-a-half of faithful and outstanding entertainment service to WNAX, Eddie and Jimmie were given a tip by Earl Williams, the station manager at WNAX, on a better paying singing job that would expand their music and talents elsewhere in the hopes of furthering their careers. They were enticed away from their hectic life style in late August 1931, through an advertising agency that hired the boys as a migrant specialty act to advertise a variety of products particular to specific radio stations throughout the Midwest. The sponsors of these products paid the Dean Brothers' salary while buying time on the radio station for them to perform by endorsing their products. The pay was much better than staying at WNAX and moonlighting by working the eight-piece band. The down side of this new job was that the time spent in each city would be temporary; lasting on an average of three to four months.

The first boss Eddie and Jimmie worked for during this new arrangement was Joe Nichols, the program manager for radio WIBW in Topeka, Kansas. Nichols, a former sergeant in the Army, ran the station like he did with the soldiers that were under him in the military: with precision, efficiency, and fairness. He even looked much like the typical drill sergeant as portrayed in films, but he also possessed a caring heart.

WIBW was owned by U.S. Senator Arthur Capper (R), the former publisher of the *Topeka Daily Capital*. While serving in the Senate from 1919 to 1949, Capper chaired committees on agriculture and forestry and was even featured on the cover of *Time* magazine in 1926. In 1927, he purchased WIBW, among the first radio stations in the state. Capper died in December 1951, at age eighty-six.[2]

After the Dean Brothers' first week at the station, Nichols noticed that Eddie just didn't have the enthusiasm in his speaking voice, the twinkle in his eyes, or the vibrancy in his step, even though he and Jimmie sang wonderfully together over the air and put on a good show for radio listeners. In short, Eddie just looked down.

Nichols approached Eddie and said that he didn't look very happy and asked if the singer liked working at WIBW.

"I like it here just fine," Eddie replied to Nichols. "I know that I'm not as happy as I should be. I left my bride-to-be back in Yankton. I promised her that I would come and get her as soon as possible but I didn't know how to ask you for the time off to go and get her."

"You take all the time you need to go bring her back here," Nichols said. "You'll get your salary just the same."

An elated and thankful Eddie shouted "Yippee!" He ran to the nearest phone and called Dearest letting her know he would be on his way to Yankton within the hour.

"I gassed up my old sedan and drove the 325 miles from Topeka to Yankton," Eddie said. "By the time I arrived the next morning, Dearest had everything all ready. The following day, we were married."

The day of the blessed nuptials took place at 9:30 a. m. on September 11, 1931, a beautiful fall Friday morning. At the Sacred Heart Roman Catholic Church in Yankton, Monsignor Lawrence Link, a German-born priest who spoke English with a very thick German accent, officiated. Since Eddie wasn't a Roman Catholic, he was granted special dispensation to marry Dearest, a devout Catholic, by Bishop Bernard Joseph Mahoney of the Diocese of Sioux Falls. Serving as Eddie's Best Man was Earl Williams. Dearest's Maid of Honor was Fern D. Donnelly, her sister, from Yankton.

It was a small wedding attended by the immediate members of the Donnelly Family and a few mutual friends of the bride and groom. None of Eddie's immediate family attended the wedding due to the immediacy of the affair and the great distance involved in traveling to it.

Shortly after saying, "I do," the twenty-four-year-old Eddie and his new eighteen-year-old bride left the church to make their way back to Topeka so Eddie could resume work.

They spent their first night together as husband and wife in Shenandoah, Iowa, at the very same hotel where Eddie and Johnny Sloan lived when both of them worked for Earl May at KMA. Eddie was still fondly remembered by the town's locals who resided at the hotel and he was given a warm reception when they saw him.

"I want you to all meet my bride," Eddie said proudly as he presented Lorene to his former neighbors.

"Aw, Eddie, you sure can pick 'em young, can't ya?" replied someone with a playfully teasing voice, igniting hearty laughter from the small crowd of well-wishers gathered in the hotel lobby.

The newlyweds then went to the KMA station to visit with Earl May, who was thrilled to see his former employee again and to meet the new Mrs. Glosup. He graciously insisted that he host dinner for them at his home that evening. Eddie and Lorene accepted. The Glosups and the Mays had a wonderful and relaxing evening together spending those few hours getting acquainted and reacquainted.

The next morning, Eddie and Lorene drove the remaining 150 miles to Topeka, arriving at their apartment by mid-afternoon. Dearest wasted no time in the days ahead adding her "personal touch" to their love nest. She proved to Eddie to be a patient, loving and understanding wife as well as an exceptional homemaker.

About a month in to their stay in Topeka, Eddie was able to take a few days leave from the station so he took Lorene and drove down to Sulphur Springs, Texas, to visit his folks so they could meet his new bride.

"Mama and Papa welcomed Dearest with open arms," Eddie said. "They both thought I had the right gal."

In Topeka, as they were in Yankton, it didn't take long for Eddie and Jimmie to became very popular over WIBM. Their on-the-air musical offerings were so compelling that sales on the farm and ranch products they were advertising were the best they had ever been. Sales on certain products often doubled thanks to the Dean Brothers. In short, they made money for their sponsors.

The boys had such tremendous professional success that their stay in Topeka lasted almost two full years. They even had complete musical control over the material they used.

During this time, Eddie and Lorene took the opportunity to begin raising a family. The crowning climax to that successful endeavor came eleven months after their arrival to Topeka with the birth of their first child born on August 9, 1932, a girl named Donna Lee Glosup. Actually, Donna Lee's name was a play on the words of Lorene's maiden name of Donnelly.

Before she could walk, Donna Lee amazed everyone around her by talking; uttering few words that are normally impossible for children eleven-months old to do, according to Eddie.

Even Jimmie found Topeka to be a haven for romance during this period as he married Ruth Houghton, who hailed from nearby Lawrence.

Life was good for Eddie and family while in Topeka. Eddie also took up painting again as a therapeutic form of relaxation. A woman named Haddie Rusterson, who resided in the same apartment complex, had lost both of her arms below the elbows from a cotton gin accident years ago. She watched Eddie paint and was inspired by his artistic ability. She, too, wanted to try painting, which she did by using her feet. Eddie coached her on how to mix the paint on the paint board and she learned on her own how to hold the brushes between her toes.

"She was amazing!" Eddie recalled about this woman. "She was determined to learn how to paint. She did well, too. I'm always taken back as to how the human body can adapt."

Eddie and Lorene also engaged in the process of creating another addition to their family. In October 1933, Eddie's and Jimmie's stay in Topeka ran its course and they had to move on. Their next destination was at radio station KCKN in Kansas City, Missouri, a mere sixty-five-mile jaunt east.

The Dean Brothers stayed at KCKN for four months. While there on December 31, 1933, Eddie and Lorene welcomed Eddie Dean Glosup Jr. into the family. They wanted to use Eddie's professional name for their son's first and middle name.

Years later, when Eddie was doing musical shows, he traveled through Kansas City. Dearest, Donna, and Eddie Jr. accompanied him on tour. The family stopped at St. Luke's Hospital where Eddie Jr. was born. The younger Eddie, who was about seven years old at the time, took the opportunity of proudly boasting to the nursing staff at the front desk that he was born in that hospital, garnering an enthusiastic response from the cute way he said it.

As Donna and Eddie Jr. became of age, they attended Catholic schools, as a result of a promise Eddie made to Dearest prior to marriage.

"I believe Catholic schools gave the most complete and comprehensive education for kids at that time," Eddie said. "I'm a very lucky man to have brilliant children. They are the treasures of my life. Both Dearest and I tried to bring up our kids the best we could, even though I was gone a lot. I couldn't have found a woman as good to me as my Dearest. She accepted me as a person, as an artist, as a musician, and as an actor. She has stuck by me in my work and has supported me. She was encouraging me by always telling me, 'You can do it. You can do it.'"

Lorene was "christened" Dearest years later by her two children, Donna Lee and Eddie Jr. after seeing the movie in which the leading lady was dubbed "Dearest." Both Donna Lee and Eddie Jr. liked the name so much they started calling their mother it. From then on, Lorene St. Clair Donnelly was known affectionately by everyone as "Dearest."

While in Kansas City, the Dean Brothers continued what they called "bicycling." The term had to do with "bicycling" or going to different, yet smaller radio stations in the general outlying area to do shows while representing various sponsors.[3] For example, the Brothers would start off their radio day at the "mother station" in Kansas City at 5 a. m. under the auspices of "Crazy Water Crystals." By mid-morning they would be at another station doing a show at 11 a. m. for "Harness Bill's Kalash Farm Equipment" so that the farmers could hear it while taking a short lunch break after completing their morning chores.

By mid-afternoon, they would head out to do another show for early evening at another station for different a sponsor such as "Purina Dog Chow." The "bicycling" would repeat itself the following day.

The Brothers were in constant motion, so to speak, but they were young, energetic and focused, as the hectic pace of their work didn't seem to affect them at all.

After their contract expired in Kansas City, the Dean Brothers plus their families, moved to their next job assignment in Minneapolis, Minnesota, for three months. It was there that Eddie heard for the first time a young and exciting sports announcer broadcasting a Chicago Cubs baseball game via telegraph reports over WHO radio in Des Moines, Iowa. That young sports announcer was twenty-three-year-old Ronald Reagan, who later became a popular motion picture actor, Governor of California, and finally America's fortieth President from 1981 to 1989.

"Reagan made the radio listener feel that he was actually right there at the game itself," Eddie said.

From Minneapolis the Dean Brothers and their families trekked to their next job at radio station KMMJ in Clay Center, Nebraska, about 150 miles southwest of Omaha. The station was established by the Johnson Company to promote its nationally known "Old Trusty" poultry incubators and brooders which it manufactured in Clay Center. The boys' short stay in Clay Center was unfortunately marred by personality conflicts with management.

The head of advertising on the products that were sold on the air didn't like Jimmie Dean for some reason, and according to Eddie, this man tried to break up the singing duo so that Eddie could be hired on as a solo act.

"I didn't know what the real story was on this guy but for some reason he didn't like Jimmie or wanted him around," Eddie recalled. "Jimmie was a likeable guy. We were employed by the advertising company as a duo act. We had a contract. There was no way I was going to let him break up our act."

A short time later, the advertising head ended up firing the Dean Brothers because according to Eddie, "I wouldn't let him fire Jimmie."

Now suddenly faced without a job or money, and with no place to go, Eddie confessed that he didn't know what to do. He knew that he had to make a decision quickly as he had a wife and two small children to support. He knew he could always return to Yankton as he had a standing job offer any time he wanted from the manager of WNAX. But Yankton was farther away at that moment than what he liked.

Eddie remembered that Earl Williams, the Best Man at his wedding, and his wife, lived in Omaha. Williams was let go from WNAX soon after Eddie and Dearest were married and he and his wife relocated to Omaha where he found a good job working at a hardware store. Eddie thought that Williams could lead him and Jimmie to a possible job.

Before driving to Omaha, Eddie fed his family on what little money he had left in his pockets: just enough to buy one hamburger and some milk. When Eddie and family arrived in Omaha, Williams took them in to stay in his home.

The next day, Williams took both Eddie and Jimmie with him to the hardware store where he worked to meet the store's advertising manager. As fate would have it, the advertising manager was same person who had recently fired Eddie and Jimmie in Clay Center. His area of supervision extended into Omaha.

Fortunately for the Dean Brothers, there was an opening for their musical act and salesmanship abilities at radio stations WOW and WAAW in Omaha, so the ad manager rehired the singing duo.

"Jimmie and I were grateful to be working again, but the advertising manager who fired us did us dirty," Eddie said. "I told him when he rehired us that since he fired us without any notice, we're going to leave him without any notice should we get another job. He took my comment with a grain of salt as he didn't believe that Jimmie and I could get hired any place else."

Eddie and Jimmie did two late afternoon radio shows, first at WOW, with its call letters standing for **W**indow **O**ver the **W**orld, and then at WAAW, the latter holding the distinction of being Nebraska's first radio station, established in 1922. The Brothers had thirty minutes from the conclusion of their show at WOW to get across the busy main street to the top floor of the 20-story WAAW building to do their second show. There were numerous times when Eddie and Jimmie arrived in front of the microphone at WAAW with literally seconds to spare prior to going on the air. It was exciting but nerve racking at times.

After working a few months in Omaha, Eddie received a telephone call from Fleming Allen who was a songwriter and program manager at WLS in Chicago offering the boys a chance to audition for the very popular radio show, The *National Barn Dance*.

"Fleming called me with the news just as Jimmie and I finished our show at WOW," Eddie recalled. "I was excited about the offer and I asked him when he wanted us. He told me as soon as we both could get there. That was good enough for me. I told Fleming that we'd be there. I then told Jimmie that we would leave for Chicago after we finished our next show at WAAW. That was pretty bold of me as we would only be going to Chicago to audition. We didn't have a job yet at WLS, but I knew we'd get it."

True to the promise he made to the advertising manager who rehired he and his brother, Eddie did not give notice of the Dean Brothers' impending departure. At the conclusion of their radio show on WOW, Eddie said goodbye and thanked their loyal listeners and proudly announced that he and Jimmie were heading for Chicago.

As Eddie and Jimmie opened the door to leave the WOW studio, with Eddie carrying his fiddle underneath one arm and his guitar underneath the other and with Jimmie carrying his guitar and the duo's bag of music and in a hurry to get to the other station to do their final show, there standing in the middle of the doorway was this imposing figure; a six-foot, three-inch hulk of a man. He was heavyweight boxing champ, Max Baer, a native of Omaha. A week earlier on June 14, 1934, Baer won the World Heavyweight Championship after scoring a Technical Knock Out over the massive, 275-pound Primo Canera, the then-reigning World Heavyweight Champion and native son of Italy. Baer was in his hometown to celebrate his victory.

"Boy, you guys sounded great!" Baer enthusiastically told Eddie and Jimmie.

Not wanting to be rude, Eddie and Jimmie thanked Baer for the compliment and gave the Champ a few minutes of time before they had to politely excuse themselves to go back to work.

"Years later, I got to work with Max's son, Max Baer, Jr. on two episodes of *The Beverly Hillbillies*," Eddie said. "He played the character of Jethro Bodine, the good-looking, strapping, twenty-six-year-old bumpkin who was the nephew of millionaire Jed Clampett. I was contracted to be on the show as a police sergeant who loved to yodel but needed training. Actress Bea Benaderet, as Pearl Bodine, Jethro's mother, was advertising yodeling lessons and she was going to teach me how to yodel. When I walked onto the set for rehearsal, Max Jr. was sitting there and I asked him where I might find the director."

"Are you going to be on the show?" he asked.

"Yes, I am," Eddie replied.

"What's your name?"

"Eddie Dean."

"Eddie Dean!" Baer repeated enthusiastically. "When I was a little kid, my daddy took me out to see you on location at the Iverson Ranch when you were making your Western movies."

"I think I remember that," Eddie replied with a grin.

Eddie stated that he had fun being on *The Beverly Hillbillies* and that he spent his breaks on the set in between filming by reconnecting with Baer Jr.

After Eddie and Jimmie did their swan song at WAAW, they sent their wives and family to stay with their relatives until they got settled in Chicago: Dearest and kids stayed with her brother, Vern Donnelly, back in Yankton, while Ruth went back to Lawrence, Kansas.

Eddie and Jimmie went to Chicago and auditioned for Fleming Allen at

WLS and were hired on the spot. It was a sweet moment for Eddie since he was now back at the place that had turned him away six years earlier. Returning to Chicago to work at WLS was a great career move for the Dean Brothers, and it proved to be an important stepping stone for Eddie in bringing to pass the prediction his mother made about him when he was a little boy while on the road to stardom.

Above: Eddie and Jimmie Dean in a 1930 publicity photo for Sunshine Coffee. The brothers were the second manifestation of the "Sunshine Coffee Boys." They were the very popular celebrity spokesmen for the caffine beverage sponsored by WNAX radio in Yankton, South Dakota.

Above: Eddie and Jimmie Dean in 1930 at
radio station WNAX, Yankton, South Dakota.

Above: Eddie Dean broadcasting the news
over radio station WNAX, Yankton, SD, in 1930.

Below: The likeness of Abraham Lincoln on a pipe that Eddie carved of which
he showed Gutzon Borglum, the designer-sculptor of Mt. Rushmore.

Above: Eddie and Jimmie Dean, center, with unidentified accordianist and violinist, in Yankton, SD, ca. 1930.

Above: The Donnelly children, ca. 1915. Lorene "Dearest" Donnelly is the young girl standing in the front with her arms crossed. Standing behind her, left to right, is sister Dottie, brother Vernon, and sister Fern.

At right: A candid photo of Eddie and Dearest taken in an automated photo booth during a date in Yankton, SD, in 1930.

Above: Eddie, 24 and Dearest, 18, on their wedding day, September 11, 1931. This photo was taken of the happy couple outside Sacred Heart Catholic Church in Yankton, SD. Eddie and Dearest were married for over 67 years.

6

$\mathcal{WLS}$ and the
$\mathcal{N}$ational Barn Dance

Returning to Chicago during the last week of June 1934 was a homecoming of sorts for Eddie. Since forging a career in the entertainment arena, the "Windy City" had in some respects become his "home away from home." While Eddie's advent was marked without any celebratory fanfare, it was a sweet moment for him as he and his brother were now working together on the largest radio station west of New York City and were regulars on a hit program with a tremendous listener following that was heard nationally from coast to coast. Such an ideal situation meant greater professional exposure.

WLS was originally owned by the Sears-Roebuck and Company in 1924, but in four years time the large retail chain came to the realization that it was a better retailer than it was a broadcaster. So, in 1928, Sears sold WLS for $250,000 to ABC, the Agricultural Broadcast Company, a newly-formed holding corporation of which the *Prairie Farm Magazine* was the majority stockholder. The magazine went on to purchase the remaining shares of stock which enabled the publication to own the radio station outright.[1]

First published in 1841, the *Prairie Farmer Magazine* catered to the needs and interests of the American farmer. With *Prairie Farmer Magazine* ownership of WLS, service to the farmer remained the primary focus over the airwaves with up-to-the-minute weather information, agriculture and livestock reports, market updates, and other items of interest to farmers and ranchers throughout the rural Midwest. As such, WLS was proudly dubbed "The Farmers' Station."[2]

After the radio station's purchase, WLS' main studios were moved from Sears-Roebuck on Homan Avenue to the top floor of the four-story tall Prairie Farmer Headquarters on Chicago's West Side at 1230 West Washington Boulevard.

In addition to broadcasting farming interests, WLS also offered a wide variety of entertainment for its listeners. A pantheon of future well-known entertainers got their starts on WLS. The first was a comedy team of Charles Correll and Freeman Gosden. The duo appeared during the late 1920s before taking their "black face" minstrel show to Chicago's WGN as "Sam and Harry." A disagreement with the station brought them to nearby WMAQ where they became known as "Amos and Andy." Their act became so successful that it was eventually picked up by the NBC Radio Network.

Another comedy team debuted at WLS in 1927. "The Smith Family" featured the husband and wife team of Jim and Marian Jordan. Along with Correll and Gosden, the Jordan's also migrated to WMAQ and gained national notoriety as "Fibber McGee and Molly," which also aired over NBC.

Other early performers of future renown to have graced the WLS airwaves over the years include guitarist Les Paul, known as "Rhubarb Red"; Patti Page; and the Williams Brothers Quartet, featuring young Andy Williams.

Prairie Farmer owner and publisher Burridge D. Butler worked very hard to establish a "family atmosphere" at WLS among its listeners, staff, and performers. He set down a stringent station code of ethics for performers and staff in order to keep the station and its shows squeaky clean and family oriented.

Listeners could also read about their favorite WLS radio stars through the publication of *Stand By!*, a bi-weekly magazine which also contained a WLS programming guide. WLS would also release its version of a yearbook called the *WLS Family Album,* which featured photos and portraits of the station's performers as well as the station's personnel and their families. These yearbooks were published from 1930-1957. Eddie and Jimmie were profiled in the 1935 album.

The crowning jewel of all the entertainment programs broadcast over WLS was the *National Barn Dance.* The *National Barn Dance* was one of Country music's pioneering and longest running radio music jamborees. The show blended music, comedy, novelty acts, and homespun skits that lasted over five decades. Founded by broadcaster and Country music enthusiast George D. Hay, it first aired on WLS on Saturday, April 19, 1924, predating the *Grand Ole Opry* on WSM in Nashville by eighteen months.

The *Barn Dance* served two distinct audiences. It targeted the rural farm audiences as well as city listeners that had come from rural communities or those whom had been told about the "good old times."[3]

Starting in 1931, the show originated from Chicago's Eighth Street Theater located behind the Stevens Hotel on Wabash Avenue and Eighth Street. The show was picked up by the NBC Blue network in 1933, and became so popular that listeners showed up by the thousands to fill the 1200-seat theater twice every Saturday night (7:30 p. m. and 10 p. m.). Shows were sold out up to eight weeks in advance and patrons were willing to pay the ninety cents admission price to see some of their favorite Country artists in front of a radio microphone. Reaching a national audience, the radio program served as a marketing pioneer, making millions for network sponsors like Miles Laboratories, makers of Alka Seltzer.

The backdrop and set for the *Barn Dance* was constructed to look like the hayloft on a mid-Western farm complete with hay bales and occasional sounds of barnyard animals, courtesy of the show's entertainers.

Early stars of the *National Barn Dance* included Tommy Dandurand, Tom Owens, Chubby Parker, Pie Plant Pete, Walter Peterson, Rube Tronson, Cecil and Ethel Ward, and Bradley Kincaid, who was one of the first artists to popularize dozens of unpublished mountain and hillbilly tunes, among others.

At the time when Eddie and Jimmie became part of the *National Barn Dance* "family," a jovial cast of singers, musicians, and comedians were already established mainstays on the program including Pat "Uncle Ezra" Barrett, Lulu Belle and Scotty (the husband and wife singing team of Myrtle Cooper and Scotty Wiseman), the Hoosier Hot Shots (Paul "Hezzie" Trietsch, Ken Trietsch, Charles "Gabe" Ward, and Frank Kettering), Ford Rush, ventriloquist Max Terhune and "Elmer," Arkie, The Arkansas Woodchopper (Luther Ossenbrink), The Westerners (Louise Massey Mabie and her brothers "Dott" Curt Massey and Allen Massey, Larry Wellington, and Louise's husband, Milt Mabie), the WLS Rangers (Merton Minnich, Clyde Moffet, Osgood Westley, Lea Story, and Walter Tuite), the Hoosier Sod Busters (harmonica-playing duo of Reginald Cross and Howard Black), and Joe Kelly acting as Master of Ceremonies, who later hosted radio's *Quiz Kids* program.

Other star performers who were part of the *National Barn Dance* family at one time or another include Gene Autry, Rex Allen, "Ramblin'" Red Foley, the Prairie Ramblers (Tex Atchison, Salty Holmes, Chuck Hurt, Jack Taylor) featuring Patsy Montana (Ruby Blevens), George Gobel, Pat Buttram, and the singing novelty team of Homer (Henry Haines) and Jethro (Kenneth Burns).

The Dean Brothers were hired by WLS. In addition to performing in front of a live audience on the *National Barn Dance* on Saturday evenings, they worked throughout the week on the radio which broadcast from the Prairie Farmer Headquarters on Washington Boulevard. They went on the air every morning at 6:30 doing a thirty-minute show similar in format to what they had been doing on various radio stations in the past. Their show was sponsored by OshKosh B'Gosh overalls.

Since 1895, OshKosh began manufacturing hickory-striped denim bib overalls for farmers and railroad workers with the claim that the company made "The World's Best Overalls." Eddie's and Jimmie's show was such a hit with listeners that they sold OshKosh overalls faster than they were being manufactured.[4]

"We sold so much OshKosh overalls over the air that our contract was canceled after six weeks," Eddie recalled. "The company had to rebuild its factory in Oshkosh, Wisconsin, to keep up with the demand. That's how important radio was in those days."

After a few weeks working at WLS, Eddie asked permission from Burridge Butler, the owner of WLS, if he could go to Yankton to bring his family back with him to Chicago.

"Why did you leave them there?" the fatherly Butler asked.

"We didn't have the money to come here," Eddie said.

Eddie told Butler the whole story and he let Eddie take a few days off to bring Dearest and the children back to Chicago with him. Jimmie, in turn, sent for his wife, Ruth, from Lawrence, Kansas.

Eddie and family temporarily stayed in an apartment on the South Side of Chicago before locating a permanent residence in the 1500 block of North Leavitt Street on the North Side where Eddie could conveniently take the Washington Street Elevated Railway, commonly referred to by Chicagoans as "The Elevated" or simply, "The El," instead of driving his car to the radio station.

While at WLS and the *National Barn Dance,* Eddie became life-long personal friends with many of its entertainers. The following celebrities were some of Eddie's closest friends:

Known professionally as Lulu Belle and Scotty, the husband and wife team of Myrtle Eleanor Cooper and Scott Greene Wiseman, both natives of North Carolina, were one of the major Country Music acts during the 1930s and 1940s. They were affectionately dubbed "The Sweethearts of Country Music."

The duo is best known for their self-penned classic "Have I Told You Lately That I Love You?" that became one of the first Country songs to attract major attention in Pop circles and was recorded by many artists in both genres.

Cooper was the somewhat dominant half of the duo with a comic persona as a wisecracking country girl. In 1938, she was named "Favorite Female Radio Star" by the readers of *Radio Guide* magazine, an unusual recognition for a Country performer.

The couple recorded extensively and were regulars on the *National Barn Dance* into the 1950s. Upon their retirement to North Carolina from show business in 1958, Wiseman went into teaching and Cooper went into politics. From 1975 to 1978, she became a North Carolina state representative running on the Democratic ticket. In 1977, she made an impassioned plea for extending the death penalty to rapists, revealing that she had been the victim of a sexual assault while on a musical tour.

Wiseman died in 1981. Cooper was married to Ernest Stamey in 1983 until her death in February 1999.

Another of Eddie's friends, as well as a popular entertainer on WLS and the *National Barn Dance,* was Luther Ossenbrink, better known to his radio listeners as "Arkie, The Arkansas Woodchopper." Born in the Ozarks near Knob Noster, Missouri, to a family who owned a farm and general store, Ossenbrink did actually chop wood professionally in his younger days. He learned to play the guitar and fiddle (holding the instrument waist-high while bowing it as if he was "sawing" wood) to accompany his deep baritone singing voice.

Since coming to WLS in 1930, Ossenbrink hosted a daily radio show called "Arkie's Coffee Time." Ossenbrink enjoyed laughing and had a very robust and distinctive laugh. It's been said that on numerous occasions some of the WLS entertainers would plot to get him to laugh in the middle of a song, inventing the most outlandish stunts in order to make it happen. He never knew what to expect. Taking such fun with good graces, "Arkie" laughed and sang right through all the hijinks.

Eddie and Jimmie were coaxed to being part of the shenanigans to get "Arkie" to laugh during a song. Eddie explains:

"Normally, I wouldn't sabotage anyone's performance but it seemed that in 'Arkie's' case it helped his act and didn't hinder it any. I told 'Arkie' that I thought his guitar sounded a bit flat and that I would restring his guitar and tune it for him. He said he appreciated the gesture. While I was working on it, I had Jimmie take 'Arkie' off to the side to engage him in conversation away from what I was doing. What I did was restring his guitar so loosely that when he went to strum on the instrument, the strings would immediately fall off. I handed 'Arkie' his 'fixed' guitar just moments prior to him going on the air for his daily radio show. What happened next would infuriate anyone, but in 'Arkie's' case he rolled with the punches. As he started to sing his song while strumming his guitar, he quipped, 'Oh, my! No strings!' and let out a belly laugh and proceeded to sing all his songs *a coppella*. He did a fine job, too."

Ossenbrink also had a modest recording history in the early 1930s on the Champion, Columbia and Conqueror labels. He died in June 1981, at age seventy-five.

Eddie first became acquainted with Curt Massey as a featured member with his brother and sister (Allen and Louise) of the Western family band "The Westerners." This group, along with Larry Wellington on accordion, and Milt Mabie on bass who was also married to Louise Massey, came to WLS in 1933 and quickly won fan acclaim.

Born "Dott" Curtis Massey in Midland, Texas, Massey was a talented musician who learned to play piano, violin, trumpet, and cornet, as well as sing. He also had a distinguished career in radio broadcasting.

He was a regular from late 1945 through early 1946 on the *Nash-Kelvinator Musical Showroom* radio show hosted by the Andrews Sisters. Later during his career, he hosted his own radio show and co-hosted a fifteen-minute nationwide CBS musical program with singer Martha Tilton called *Alka-Seltzer Time*. In 1957, the pair recorded an album together on Tops Records entitled *We Sing the Old Songs*.

In the mid-1960s, Massey composed and sang the catchy theme song to the television comedy series, *Petticoat Junction*. Massey died in October 1991, at age 81.

Pre-dating Spike Jones and His City Slickers on wax by six years with their madcap version of music were the Hoosier Hot Shots. This four-man musical wrecking crew from Indiana developed their zany brand of musical comedy and developed a style that was uniquely their own. Their music contained elements of Dixieland, ragtime, a generous portion of novelty and laughs, and a searing rhythm to propel the numbers along.

The Hot Shots were Paul Trietsch, nicknamed "Hezzie," who played the whistle and "the Zither," describing it once as "an over-glorified washboard" consisting of a corrugated sheet metal washboard on a metal stand with various noise makers attached, including bells, and a multi-octave range of squeeze-type bicycle horns; and his brother Ken Trietsch, who played guitar and banjo while trading off solo vocal duties with master clarinetist Charles "Gabe" Ward; and Frank Kettering on string bass.

The group is noted for such classics as "Meet Me By the Ice House, Lizzie," "I Like Bananas Because They Have No Bones," "I've Got a Bimbo on Bamboo Island," "Red Hot Fannie," "Like a Monkey Likes Coconuts," and "From the Indies to the Andies in His Undies." Their recordings often included the signature spoken intro by Ken Trietsch to his brother Paul of "Are you ready, Hezzie?" It became one of the band's big tag lines, even entering the common vernacular.

The Hoosier Hot Shots joined the *National Barn Dance* in September 1933, staying for fifteen years.

In later years, Paul Trietsch was a neighbor along the lake to Eddie and Dearest in Westlake Village, California. Trietsch and Eddie were frequent golfing partners.

Frank Kettering was the first Hoosier Hot Shot to pass away in June 1973, followed by Paul Trietsch in April 1980. Ken Trietsch died in September 1987, with Gabe Ward passing in January 1992.

When Eddie decided to make his move to come to Hollywood in 1936, it was Gabe Ward and his wife, Marge, Hezzie Trietsch, and Curt Massey who helped finance Eddie's train ticket west as well as the shipping cost for his car on the same train.

"These were my dear friends who helped me tremendously," Eddie said. "I couldn't have done it without them."

Before coming to WLS and the *National Barn Dance* in 1933, Max Terhune was a veteran of vaudeville making a modest name for himself as a ventriloquist, whistler, animal imitator, and magician. A native of Indiana, Terhune was often referred to as the "Hoosier Mimic." After forming a close friendship with Gene Autry at WLS, it was Autry who introduced Terhune to Republic Pictures, where the comic actor went on to appear in nearly seventy films, mostly B-Westerns, between 1936 and 1956.

Terhune appeared in 21 episodes of a popular Republic Studios Western series called *The Three Mesquiteers* whose co-stars included Robert Livingston, Ray "Crash" Corrigan, and later, John Wayne, who replaced Livingston. Terhune played the comic sidekick, Lullaby Joslin, traveling the range with his dummy, Elmer, who shared his saddle. Elmer received film credit for his appearances.

Terhune (and Elmer) also co-starred in the *Ranger Busters* series of Westerns with Corrigan and John "Dusty" King. Terhune played the character of "Alibi" Terhune for these films. He later worked in some Johnny Mack Brown Westerns at Monogram Pictures. Terhune, Elmer and Eddie appeared together in the 1944 Ken Maynard film, *Harmony Trail,* their only film together.

Eddie's and Terhune's close friendship from their WLS days continued later on while in Hollywood. Both men would help each other out as they struggled to forge their respective careers in Tinseltown.

"I had recently arrived in Hollywood and I wasn't working as this time as I was struggling for money to feed Dearest and the kids," Eddie recalled. "It was rough. Nobody seems to care about you. I tolerated it and dear friends like Max helped me do it."

Eddie's creative and artistic abilities of working with wood aroused the interest of Terhune who asked Eddie to make another dummy to look exactly like him. Eddie tells the story:

"I got bass wood which was easier to carve and doesn't split. I then took Elmer a part to find out how he was made. I also made detailed drawings of Max's face. It took me about a month to finish the project and I was really proud of it. The dummy looked almost identical to Max. He worked up a character for this dummy I made and he gave me a sampling of his new 'act.' I howled with laughter.

"Max's wife, Maude, just hated this new dummy. She hated it because it looked too much like Max. She felt it was too eerie. She didn't want Max to have it."

Eddie said that when he went to see Max at his home a short time later, he saw the head of the Max-look-a-like dummy laying out in the front yard as the family dog was playing with it.

"It just broke my heart," Eddie said. "Max was upset too. I don't know exactly what happened but I suspect that Maude may have conveniently left the dummy out so that the dog could get a hold of it."

When Eddie left Terhune's house, the comic ventriloquist gave Eddie a folded piece of paper saying that he should call the person whose name was on the paper as it might lead to a job.

"I thanked Max and put the paper in my pocket," Eddie said. "When I arrived home to make that phone call, inside that piece of paper was a hundred dollar bill. Even though Max paid me for the work I did on the dummy, he knew I could use the extra money for the family. I took his kind gesture as a loan. This was in 1937, and it took me a long time to repay Max that hundred dollars."

Terhune died in early June 1973 in Cottonwood, Arizona. He was eighty-two.

Another WLS and *Barn Dance* regular with whom Eddie became good friends was comedian Pat Buttram. A native of Alabama and the youngest of six children born to a Methodist minister, Maxwell Emmett "Pat" Buttram is probably best remembered as Gene Autry's sidekick in more than forty of his movies and in all of his television shows and for playing the character of Mr. Eustace Haney in the1965-1971 television comedy *Green Acres*.

Buttram had a distinctive voice that he self-described as having ". . . never quite made it through puberty." Others have said his voice sounds like "a handful of gravel thrown in a Mix Master."

In the later years of his career, Buttram did voice work for several Disney animated features, was credited as one of the writers on the *Hee Haw* television show in its early years, and helped Ronald Reagan spice up his speeches with political quips.

Buttram died in 1994 at age seventy-eight of renal failure in Los Angeles.

Buttram joined the WLS family in early 1935 as a nineteen-year-old and was heard over the air during the early morning hours and at noon daily waxing his simple yet zany country philosophy on a variety of subject matter. His humor was witty and he appealed instantly with listeners.

Eddie said the first time he saw Buttram was when he was performing on the *National Barn Dance*.

"Joe Kelly, our announcer at WLS, asked me to listen to this new kid from Alabama they hired to be on the show. Before Jimmie and I went on with our act, I listened to Pat do his monologue from off stage. He had the audience in stitches. He was that good. He was a natural. He came off as a country bumpkin with some surprising savvy and with that recognizable crackly voice of his, you couldn't help but laugh. He and I were close friends. Years later, it was Pat who presented me with the Golden Boot Award."

The Golden Boot Award was the brainchild of Buttram to honor actors, actresses, and crew members that had made significant contributions to the genre of Western films and television. The award is sponsored and funded by the Motion Picture and Television Fund. Money raised at the award banquet is used to help finance services offered by the Fund to those in the entertainment industry.

The first Golden Boot Award was presented in 1983. Along with Eddie, other recipients that year included Roy Rogers and Dale Evans, Gene Autry, Rex Allen, Lash La Rue, Clayton Moore, Sunset Carson, Monte Hale, Bob Steele, Slim Pickens, Forrest Tucker, Lee Majors, Doug McClure, and Will Rogers, the latter given posthumously.

Probably Eddie's closest and dearest friend was fellow singing cowboy star Orvon Grover Autry, better known as Gene Autry. From 1934 to 1953, Autry popularized the musical Western and starred in ninety-three feature films with his horse, Champion. Eddie would later work in supporting roles in a handful of Autry's Western films and would, along with brother, Jimmie, become a member of the Gene Autry Trio providing musical backing for "America's Favorite Cowboy" on his recordings, personal appearances, and on his very popular weekly radio show *Melody Ranch*.

Autry, billed during his younger years as "The Singing and Yodeling Marvel," had made records for the American Record Corporation (ARC) and its affiliate labels (Conqueror, Silvertone, Perfect, Banner, Oriole and Romeo), along with the Gennet, Victor, and Columbia labels prior to coming on board WLS in 1931 and the *National Barn Dance* the following year.

Born in Tioga, Texas, in 1907, Autry was first discovered by cowboy humorist Will Rogers. By 1932, Autry scored his first hit recording with "That Silver-Haired Daddy of Mine," a tune he co-wrote with Jimmy Long. That recording, eventually selling 500,000 copies, launched Autry to recording prominence. The following year he gained national attention for his hit record "The Last Round Up."

During his long and illustrious career, Autry made 640 recordings, including more than 300 songs written or co-written by himself. His records sold more than 100 million copies and he garnered more than a dozen gold and platinum records. His Christmas and children's records of "Here Comes Santa Claus" (an Autry composition) and "Peter Cottontail" are among his platinum recordings. Autry's 1949 recording of "Rudolph, the Red-Nosed Reindeer," a Johnny Marks tune, remains the second all-time best-selling Christmas single (behind Bing Crosby's 1942 version of "White Christmas"), boasting in excess of 30 million in sales.[5]

In addition, Autry was an astute businessman who appeared to have had the "Midas Touch" which allowed him to amass a huge personal fortune. Some of his more noted business ventures include music publishing, production of a handful of popular Western shows for television, ownership of a radio and television station in the Los Angeles area, and ownership of the then California Angels baseball team (now the Los Angeles Angels of Anaheim). He died at home in Studio City, CA, on October 2, 1998. He was ninety-one.

It was while Eddie and Jimmie were working at WLS that Eddie said he first met Autry. During the few preceding years he was based in Chicago, Autry had developed a large and faithful following with mid-westerners. He had left WLS and the *National Barn Dance* to pursue a career in Western films a short time prior to the Dean Brothers arrival to the station. He had recently completed working in uncredited roles in a pair of Ken Maynard films and returned to Chicago to fulfill some prior contractual agreements doing stage shows at area theaters.

"Jimmie and I were rehearsing at the WLS studio at West Washington Boulevard when in walked Gene," Eddie recalls. "I had heard of him and seen his photo around the station. He was dressed sharply in a light gray tailor-made double-breasted Western suit, white Stetson, and brown cowboy boots. He was very popular in that part of the country. He came over to Jimmie and me and introduced himself. He was very nice.

"Gene was carrying a package that was about four inches thick. I asked him what was under his arm. He said it was a script to a movie and that he was going out to Hollywood to be featured in a film called *The Phantom Empire*."

Cowboy star Ken Maynard was originally tapped to be the lead in *The Phantom Empire*, a twelve-part serial for Mascot Pictures that combined the traditional "shoot-'em-up" Western with science fiction, but Maynard walked away to sign with another studio. The starring role was then given to Autry.

The Phantom Empire was released on February 23, 1935, and was considered a box office hit. It launched Autry's movie career as a singing Western star and gave birth to a new genre in Western films: the singing cowboy.

"It was Gene's efforts that helped pave the way to get guys like me in the business," Eddie said. "Gene was an unusual person. I always considered him a very good friend."

Eddie and Jimmie were enjoying a successful following at WLS and as regulars on the *National Barn Dance* when they caught the ear of Jack Kapp, the founder of Decca Records in the United States, who wanted the boys to be the very first to cut a session on his new record label. Decca Records began as a British record label established in 1929 by Edward Lewis. In late 1934, a United States branch of Decca Records was launched by Kapp, a former Brunswick Records General Manager, who went into partnership with Lewis. Kapp has been credited with turning Decca in to a major player in a depressed American record market by signing on to its roster popular artists such as crooner Bing Crosby and the decision to price Decca inexpensively at thirty-five cents. Other artists signed to Decca in its early years included Louis Armstrong, Jimmie Lunceford, The Andrews Sisters, Count Basie, Jane Froman, The Mills Brothers, Chick Webb, Bob Crosby, Guy Lombardo, Billie Holiday, Jimmy Dorsey, The Ink Spots, Ted Lewis, The Boswell Sisters, and Sister Rosetta Tharpe.[6]

Kapp was also instrumental in building the company's extensive hillbilly catalog, allowing Decca to corner the market on Country music for years. Ergo, enter Eddie and Jimmie Dean categorized as Decca's first Hillbilly artists, as well as holding the distinction of being Decca's very first artists to be waxed on the new American label.

In the early afternoon of Monday, September 10, 1934, Eddie and Jimmie entered a small make-shift recording studio near WLS to record a half-dozen Gospel sides. Those songs were "Tell Mother I'll Be There," "(There's) No Disappointment in Heaven," "There Shall Be Showers of Blessings," "Happy in Him," "There's No Friend Like Jesus," and "God Will Take Care of You." For some unexplainable reason, only four of the six selections were slated for commercial release here in the states. "There's No Friend Like Jesus" was targeted for release only in Great Britain, while the latter cut, "God Will Take Care of You," composed in 1904 by the husband and wife team of Civilla and W. Stillman Martin, was never issued.

All tunes were emblazoned in gold print against the record's navy blue-colored label as vocal duets with guitar accompaniment (courtesy of Eddie), while Jimmie retained the top billing spot for the duo's artistry credit: "Jimmie and Eddie Dean." Jimmie would sing tenor harmony while Eddie's rich baritone voice sang the lead and was spotlighted in solo passages. The Brothers were paid a flat fee of $20 per song without royalties yet sang these pieces with compelling harmonic honesty that not only tugged at the heart, but showcased their unique vocal styling. Despite such artistic quality, their recordings sold poorly.

Kapp, along with his younger brother, Dave, who worked as the recording engineer for Decca and who later founded Kapp Records in the early 1950s, recognized early on the talent they had with the Dean Brothers but failed to take the necessary action to invest the appropriate effort and resources to promote their artistry. But, hindsight is 20/20 vision and such miscalculations often breed regrets.

Seventeen years later when Eddie was recording for Capitol Records in Hollywood, Dave Kapp, who had an office in the Capitol Records building on Melrose Avenue, asked Eddie to come into his office. Kapp lamented to Eddie about not doing enough for he and Jimmie at the time.

"You probably don't know this, Eddie, but did you know you and your brother, Jimmie, made the first records we ever recorded?" Kapp asked.

"Yes. Whatever happened to them?" Eddie asked.

"We limited their releases and do you know why?"

"No, I don't," Eddie replied.

"We're Jewish boys and we didn't understand the attraction for Gospel music in the South. We didn't know anything about that. We were fools for not releasing those records because if we had known what we know now, and how popular Sacred music was in those days in that region, we'd have had some hit records."

This wouldn't be the only time Eddie would see his name on the Decca Record label. When Eddie made the move to California to get into motion pictures, he returned to record two handful of songs for the Kapp's on Decca in the fall of 1941 and in early 1942. (More on that later.)

Two months after making their recording debut on Decca, the Dean Brothers were invited to record for British-born record producer Art Satherley. Satherley went on to become one of the most respected and most revered Artist and Repertoire (A&R) men in the business, as well as one of the pivotal figures in the development of commercial Country music.[7] Among those he produced were such notables as Gene Autry, Tex Ritter, Roy Acuff, Bob Wills, Hank Penny, Carl Smith, Lefty Frizzell, Bill Monroe, and Marty Robbins, among others.

Known affectionately by those in the recording industry as "Uncle

Art," Satherley was born in Bristol, England, the son of a clergyman. At age twenty-four, he came to America in 1913 via Canada. He began his career working at a chair manufacturing company in Wisconsin. He later became Thomas Edison's assistant secretary, where he apprenticed in the facets of the newly established record business.

In addition to Country music, Satherley also was a fan of Blues Music and supervised recordings of such Blues icons as Ma Rainey, Bessie Smith, and Blind Lemon Jefferson.

According to Gene Autry biographer Holly George-Warren, Satherley, who claimed Autry as his greatest discovery, was a vain individual who would leave "prospecting recording artists with an 8 x10 photo of himself (and) his contact information printed on the back" while encouraging them to "think of him as their benefactor . . . and to call him Uncle Art."

Satherley was affiliated with American Record Corporation (ARC), a holding company that billed itself as the "World's Largest Manufacturer of Popular Priced Records." Labels under the ARC umbrella included Conqueror, Banner, Oriole, Romeo, Cameo, Regal, Melotone, and Perfect, which were primarily distributed through the Sears & Roebuck catalog.

Satherley's interest in Country music drew him to the Country music magnet in the Chicago area: The *National Barn Dance*. It was there that he recorded a number of *Barn Dance* regulars for ARC including The Hoosier Hot Shots, Lulu Belle and Scotty, and The Westerners, among others.

From November 2, 1934 to November 1, 1935, Satherley supervised twenty-three recordings of the Dean Brothers for American Record Corporation in Chicago in a small studio in the American Furniture Mart Building at 666 Lake Shore Drive on the North Side along Lake Michigan. Satherley asked Eddie to prepare some selections to record.

As had been with their experience with Decca Records, the Dean Brothers made some artistically fine recordings, but with ARC, the fruits of their efforts resulted in little fanfare.

Three selections of the twenty-three songs waxed were re-recorded at later dates: "The Soldier's Story" (recorded on November 2, 1934, and again on January 7, 1935, was not issued, while the January 24, 1935 recording was issued and distributed on the Conqueror, Banner, Oriole, Romeo, Melotone and Perfect labels). "Since My Mother's Dead and Gone"(originally recorded on November 13, 1934, was re-recorded two days later and distributed on the Conqueror and ARC labels). "End of the Bandit's Trail"(two recording attempts from November 15, 1934, and January 7, 1935, went unissued, while the recording of January 24, 1935, was accepted and distributed on the Conqueror, Banner, Oriole, Romeo, Melotone and Perfect labels).

Four cuts were never issued: "The Old Mill Wheel" (November 13, 1934), "Get Along Little Doggies" (October 29, 1935), "Barefoot Days" (October 29, 1935), and "Who's That Calling" (October 30, 1935).

Two songs from this recording period bear special mention. First, "The Soldier's Story" was written by Eddie when he was twelve years old. He said it was based on the Battle of Verdun, France, the longest and most devastating battle during the First World War on the Western Front. It was fought between the French and Germans from February to December 1916, resulting in a French victory at the cost of over 714,000 total casualties from both armies.

The pensive song is about two young lovers during a time when a great war ensues. The young man goes off to war and fights in the Battle of Verdun. He gets wounded and is crippled for the rest of his life. He fears returning to his love to ask her to be his wife as she might reject him. So he lives all alone with the hope he will meet her someday in heaven with "a love strong and true that will last."

"I grew up during World War I and I had heard so much about this battle that I wrote the song," Eddie said. "I saw our troops returning home from Europe after the war, some had limbs missing and some were confined to wheelchairs. I thought back to the notoriety of that battle and what must have been going through the mind of a soldier during that time. Uncle Art Satherley liked the song and wanted to record it. The song never mounted to anything much because, at the time, all of Uncle Art's concentration was on Gene Autry. Art told me one time, 'If I didn't have Gene, I'd put all my time in you, but I can't do that. I can't be dishonest to Gene.' I admired Uncle Art for his loyalty. We were good friends until he passed away (in 1986)."

Another interesting side note to "The Soldier's Story" is that Eddie wasn't given compositional credit for on the Conqueror Record label. On the record's flip side is "My Last Moving Day," a Gospel tune, that was the very first recording the Brothers did for ARC on November 2, 1934.

Another piece, "My Herdin' Song" (October 29, 1935, for Conqueror Records), was a collaboration between Eddie and Milt Mabie of "The Westerners." The composition would make its way onto the silver screen ten years later as one of three featured musical selections in *Song of Old Wyoming*, Eddie's first starring role. These ARC commercial recordings would be the last Eddie and Jimmie would make together as the Dean Brothers.

Satherley held the highest regard for Eddie personally and professionally. In an open letter dated January 30, 1972, the eighty-three-year-old record producer briefly wrote about his working relationship with Eddie and closed his missive with these gracious words: "He (Eddie) is what I would describe as a 'Country Gentleman' in every mannerism, whether at play or work. They (Eddie and his wife, Dearest, of whom he described as 'always very pleasant and gracious) are a real tribute to all that our America should stand for."

What Eddie stood for came directly from how he was raised by his parents. Both parents' respective values left their indelible mark on Eddie, but it was Eddie's mother, Eva Glosup, who was her son's biggest encourager. It was she who instilled in her youngest son to celebrate his uniqueness. It was she who believed in her son's impending greatness and told him so. As she was for all her children, Eva was their rock.

Just six weeks prior to the Dean Brothers making their final dozen recordings for Satherley, Eva suddenly took ill and died on September 22, 1935, from heart failure. She was fifty-seven years old. When Eddie heard of his mother's illness, he hurried by plane from Chicago to be at her bedside in time before her passing. It was a bitter pill for Eddie to swallow since he was close to his mother.

One can't help but wonder if Eddie's and Jimmie's final musical offerings on platter – "That Little Boy of Mine" and "We're Saying Goodbye" (both recorded on October 30, 1935) and "There's An Old Family Album in the Parlor" (November 1, 1935) – weren't done without Eva constantly in their minds. These pieces reflect a deep reverie for family.

While Eddie's and Jimmie's performances on radio, on stage, and on record may be considered impeccable, not everything went smoothly. Moments of stress and trauma did occasionally occur in their professional lives. One such stressful and traumatic incident involved Eddie as his guitar.

For Eddie, his guitar was an indispensable part of who is was as an entertainer. The Stella guitar that he bought at a hock shop in Dallas, Texas, in 1928 served him well until 1930, when he purchased a Nick Lucas Special that year for the hefty price of $125. Manufactured in conjunction with the Gibson Guitar Company, the Nick Lucas Special was considered to be the top-of-the-line guitar for its big, harp-like tone and for its crisp, sparkling treble and solid resonant bass. Designed by American crooner-pioneer jazz guitarist Nick Lucas, born Dominic Nicholas Anthony Lucanese, Lucas' career spanned seven decades until his death in 1982.

Best remembered as "The Crooning Troubadour" or "The Grandfather of the Jazz Guitar," Lucas introduced "Tip Toe Through the Tulips," an Al Dublin and Joe Burke composition, in the 1929 musical talkie *Gold Diggers of Broadway*. The song became an instant hit for Lucas, holding the #1 position on the pop charts for ten weeks. "Tip Toe Through the Tulips" was revitalized in 1968 and became a huge hit for the freakish-looking, ukulele-playing Tiny Tim (born Herbert Khaury), who sang with a distinctive high falsetto/vibrato voice.

A musical entertainer's worst nightmare is to have his prized instrument malfunction during a performance. The performer takes every conceivable precaution to insure nothing goes awry, but sometimes things just happen despite best efforts. What happened in Eddie's case was far worse than any nightmare; it was like driving a stake through his heart. While on stage performing on the *National Barn Dance*, Eddie's esteemed Nick Lucas Special slipped off the strap, hit an old fashioned chair, and broke into what seemed to be a hundred pieces.

"I was so upset I didn't know what to do," Eddie said in a November 1996 interview. "Luckily Jimmie was there with me to cover for me until I composed myself to pick up the other guitar we always had with us to resume our performance. Of course, seeing my shattered guitar laying on the stage floor broke my heart. It was the best guitar I had ever owned. I idolized Nick Lucas. He was a fine singer and a wonderful guitar player."

The following Monday, Eddie took the shattered pieces of his Nick Lucas Special to Lyon and Healy, one of larger music stores in Chicago, and asked if they could put his guitar back together. The news Eddie received wasn't good. He was told that the repairs would take about six months, the sound quality of the repaired guitar would more than likely be compromised, and that the repair cost would be as much as what Eddie originally paid for the instrument.

The music store associate suggested that Eddie take a look at a new guitar that was recently made called "The Dreadnaught," a D-28 model, manufactured by the Martin Guitar Company. Martin made it to compete with the Nick Lucas Special.

Eddie tried the Dreadnaught. Its beautiful tone so impressed him that he bought it right on the spot. In fact, Eddie said he had used that same guitar for sixty-one years from 1935 to 1996 to compose all of the music he used for his movies, recordings, and stage performances.

When Eddie first arrived in Chicago late in the previous decade, it had a well-documented reputation as a hedonistic, bootleg city filled with gangsters and gangland violence. Much of that dissipated with the repeal of the Volstead Act in 1933. However, Chicago still remained a tough town. Eddie recalled an incident in which a bigger man attempted to steal money from him but lived to regret it.

Dearest and Eddie would frequent a particular Polish restaurant located on the North Side a few blocks from where they lived. The place had good food. This one night Eddie was tired as he had worked a long day at the radio station so he stopped in the restaurant around 10 p. m. to grab a bite to eat before going home.

As Eddie entered the restaurant, Mr. Walkowski, the owner, was telling this big man who stood about 6' 2" to leave. He left but hung around outside. Eddie asked Mr. Walkowski what was wrong.

"He took the tip monies the customers left on the table for the waiters," he said.

Eddie ate a Polish sausage and was ready to go home. Upon exiting the restaurant, the same big man accosted Eddie and told him that he wasn't going anywhere. Eddie told him that he was tired and that he wanted to go home and asked if he would please move out of his way.

The stranger refused.

"I'll knock you across the sidewalk if you don't get out of my way," Eddie said warning his would-be attacker.

"I'd like to see you try it," the stranger said.

Eddie struck he man with a powerful right to his jaw that knocked him twelve feet across the pavement to the curb, rendering the would-be attacker unconscious.

Walkowski immediately came outside and told Eddie that he shouldn't hit a person so hard as he did.

"Is he alright?" Eddie asked.

"Just leave. We'll take care of everything," the restaurant owner said.

"I was just defending myself," Eddie said in defense.

"The police won't understand because there weren't any witnesses," Walkowski said. "Just go home."

Eddie then noticed that he had a bruised right hand from the punch, but managed to keep it from Dearest's awareness for four days.

The day following the incident Eddie went by the restaurant to inquire about the man he knocked out.

"We worked on him for about fifteen minutes," Walkowski said. "We finally got him up. He got into his car and left."

"This guy never came back to the restaurant," Eddie said.

Eddie and Jimmie were enjoying their time at WLS and as one of the stars on the *National Barn Dance*. The working conditions and pay were good, their fan base was growing, and their jobs provided stability to their respective domestic lives.

Life was going well until Burridge Butler, the owner of WLS, dropped a bombshell on all his employees just prior to Christmas 1935. Butler had worked passionately in helping to establish a "family atmosphere" at WLS between his entertainers, staff, and his radio listeners, but his passion now was taken to the extreme. Butler came out with a decree that all WLS employees had to sign a contact staying affiliated with WLS forever or leave. Deciding that Butler's demand was unreasonable, the Dean Brothers parted company with WLS after staying there over a year.

"What Mr. Butler was asking was ridiculous," Eddie said. "It would handcuff every entertainer by prohibiting them to pursue his or her career as they saw fit. He knew he had some wonderful people working for him and in his attempt to control them in case they got better offers from somewhere else, actually backfired. What he tried to do amounted to professional slavery."

Butler's intended actions proved to be the catalyst that broke up the Dean Brothers as an act. The parting of ways gave Jimmie a window of opportunity to branch out on his own, something he had been thinking about wanting to do for some time. He joined radio station WJJD in Chicago as a staff singer.

Eddie, on other hand, welcomed 1936 by being signed to do a radio drama series in Chicago on WBBM, a CBS affiliate, for General Mills. Eddie received a telephone call from Arthur "Tiny" Stowe, a 300-pound fellow Texan who had worked at WLS writing drama programs, tipping him off about an audition for the lead role in an upcoming soap opera series. Eddie worked with Stowe at WLS and had listened to him on KRLD radio in Dallas when he was younger.

The new soap opera was called *Modern Cinderella*, about a Texas cowboy who comes to the big city to make good in show business. The part would be perfect for Eddie as it reflected his own life experience.

After auditioning with over 165 hopefuls, Eddie was picked to play the part of "Larry Burton" on the sixty-minute network program that aired Monday through Friday from 10 a. m. to 11 a. m. CST.

Also on the show were leading lady Rosemary Dillon as "Hope Carter" and co-star Ben Gage. Gage would later marry actress/swimmer Esther Williams in 1945, and the couple would have three children together.

Eddie's role as Larry Burton provided him to be recognized as an individual star in his own right.

"Being on *Modern Cinderella* was a very pleasant job," Eddie recalled. "Dearest, the kids, and I lived on the North Side, and all I had to do was walk four blocks to catch the 'The El' and get off at the Wrigley Building at WBBM, walk into the Wrigley Building right into the studio. The daily ride to work was very comfortable for me as I could read the script on the way."

Eddie's character on the show also afforded him frequent opportunities to sing. The show sported a small orchestra, but most of the time Eddie's musical back up was done courtesy of guitarist Marvin Saxby. Saxby, who worked previously as a machinist and mechanic for the Ford Motor Company before becoming a professional musician, accompanied Dillon and Gage on their respective featured songs as well.

"Marvin was a wonderful guitarist," Eddie said.

Eddie and crew broadcast two *Modern Cinderella* programs per day: one for East Coast listeners and the other for West Coast listeners.

During this period, Eddie felt the need to engage himself in taking formal voice lessons in the hopes of expanding his musical horizons while improving his craft. He elected to study with Forrest Lamont, former star tenor with the Chicago Civic Opera company.

Lamont, a native of Canada, made his operatic debut in 1914 in Rome. He sang in various opera productions all over the world. For fifteen years, he was featured with the Chicago Civic Opera Company. After he retired from the concert stage, he became a voice teacher in Chicago. He died of pneumonia in December 1937, at age fifty-six.

When the network officials found out that Eddie was taking voice training lessons, they balked, fearing it would "hurt" his voice. They also pointed out that he couldn't make the kind of money singing opera as he could in Country music.

"I had thought about going into the classics more, but I just didn't *feel* the classics," Eddie said in a 1974 interview. "That's why I took lessons. And the Pop field, I didn't feel the Pop field either because some of the lyrics didn't do anything to me. They weren't earthy enough, weren't quite human enough. I realize that our business is basically a dream world anyway, but sometimes you can go a little bit too far away with the dream and get away from realism. So that's why I've stuck with . . . well, two reasons I've stuck with Country and Western is because first I love it, and secondly because I've been accepted by the fans, and to me, without them, I'd be nothing, believe me, *nothing*. The fans are the ones who make you what you are in show business. The fans are the ones who kept my longevity in the business."

Modern Cinderella started off with magical grace, receiving rave reviews from the media, but its "midnight" came around a fast thirteen weeks later, turning it in to a "pumpkin," as the show was suddenly canceled.

"I was disappointed about the show ending, to say the least," Eddie said. "It was a fun show and it gave me drama experience which eventually opened new avenues of opportunity for me."

Tiny Stowe, who produced *Modern Cinderella*, then made arrangements for Eddie to be part of a minstrel show that broadcast across the street on radio WGN, an ABC affiliate. On this show, Eddie did various dialects and gags while singing such old classics such as "Old Man River" and "Swing Low, Sweet Chariot." WGN billed Eddie as the "Gold Medal Baritone" for the *General Mills Minstrel Show* on the Mutual Broadcasting System.

However, after eighteen months, this show, too, was canceled. Then NBC brought Eddie and Jimmie back together again to sing duets for a thirteen-week pilot program in an attempt to sell them to a sponsor, but without success.

Eddie and Jimmie found themselves out of work because they had saturated themselves in Chicago. Eddie gave up trying to maintain a duet act.

"I didn't know what I was going to do at that point," he said.

One of the writers on the minstrel show suggested that he relocate to New York and get in to musical comedy as he seemed to have a natural flare for it.

Another person suggested that Eddie go to Hollywood to try to make good in motion pictures. That someone was singer Jimmy Atkins, the brother of Country guitar phenomenon Chet Atkins.

"Jimmy said to me that Gene Autry is out in Hollywood and is doing great and that I need to go out there," Eddie said. "He said that they need another singing cowboy out there and that I'd be perfect for it."

Both suggestions had merit. Remaining in a quandary about his future, Eddie decided to leave it all up to chance by a flip of a quarter. If the coin turned up heads, he would go to Hollywood. If tails, New York.

"I know making such a decision that way was crazy for a man with a wife and two beautiful children, but I really didn't know which direction I should take," Eddie confessed.

Eddie flipped the twenty-five-cent piece and it came up heads. Three days later, he was off to California to jump start his career and a new life with fear and uncertainties.

Above: Eddie and Jimmie Dean, The Dean Brothers, at radio WLS, Chicago, in 1934.

Above: A publicity photo of the Dean Brothers: Eddie and Jimmie, in 1934, soon after joining the *National Barn Dance* on radio WLS, Chicago. The brothers would also make some of the first recordings together on Decca Records during this period.

Above: The Dean Brothers: Eddie and Jimmie Dean in another 1934 publicity photo during their time on the *National Barn Dance* over radio WLS, Chicago.

Above: The Dean Brothers publicity photo
from the 1935 *WLS Family Album.*

Some of the stars of *The National Barn Dance* on WLS who became close friends with Eddie Dean were ventriloquist Max Terhume (right) shown here with Elmer, his dummy. Terhune went on to co-star in numerous B-Western films; and The Hoosier Hot Shots (above) whose comical music with a Dixieland-flavor predated Spike Jones. Pictured are Gabe Ward, clarinet; Frank Kettering, bass; Kenny Trietsch, guitar; and Paul "Hezzie" Trietsch, holding his "zither" (a glorified washboard with bells, horns and all sorts of other gadgets).

Above: Cast photo of members of *The National Barn Dance* from April 13, 1935. Eddie and Jimmie Dean are in the third row, third and fourth from the right. Other notables on the show include comic Pat Buttram, standing in the first row, far right; Max Terhune, standing fourth row, second from left; The Hoosier Hot Shots, third row fourth through seventh from the left; the WLS Rangers (wearing military-type outfits), first row, first through fifth from left; Malcolm Clair (a.k.a., "Spareribs"), black-face character, third row, middle; and "The Westerners," (l-r, Allen Massey, Larry Wellington, Louise Massey Mabie, Dott Massey, Milt Mabie), second row, right.

Above: Lulu Belle (Myrtle Eleanor Cooper) and Scotty Wiseman sang as a duo act as "Lulu Belle and Scotty" on the *National Barn Dance*. In real life they were husband and wife and became known as "The Sweethearts of Country Music."

Above: Arkie, The Arkansas Woodchopper (Luther Ossenbrink), left, was a very popular singer on the *National Barn Dance* from 1930 to 1959; while funnyman Pat Buttram, center, debuted on the *NBD* in 1935 and went to be Gene Autry's sidekick in films and television and became an icon as Mr. Haney on *Green Acres*. Singer and announcer Ford Rush, left, a stalwart in the early days of WLS, was also affiliated with the *National Barn Dance* and tried unsuccessfully to get Eddie Dean to be a regular on WLS when the young Texan first arrived in Chicago in 1928.

Above: The call letters for radio station WLS Chicago written in lightning bolt script.

Above: The Prairie Farmer Headquarters at 1230 West Washington Boulevard on the West Side of Chicago was also home to radio station WLS since 1928.

Above: The front cover to the 1935 *WLS Family Album,* an annual yearbook
for radio WLS listeners profiling the station's entertainers and
its personnel. The Dean Brothers were highlighted on page 44 in this book.

Above: Eddie Dean, left, enjoys a light-hearted moment with fellow cast members of the daily daytime radio soap opera, *Modern Cinderella*, broadcast over WBBM in Chicago. Pictured with Eddie are Rosemary Dillon, Ben Gage, center, and Arthur "Tiny" Stowe, right, the show's writer. For this particular program, Eddie went by the name of "Larry Burton." The program lasted thirteen weeks.

**Above: Eddie Dean as "Larry Burton" and Rosemary Dillon as "Hope Carter"
star as the principles in the daily daytime radio soap opera
Modern Cinderella over WBBM in Chicago.**

Above: A publicity photo of Eddie Dean in 1936 as "Larry Burton," the professional name he was known by in his role as the leading man in the daily radio soap opera *Modern Cinderella*, over WBBM in Chicago, and the *General Mills Minstrel Show.*

Above: The Dean Brothers on Conqueror Records from January 1935.

Below: The Dean Brothers on Decca Records from September 10, 1934.

7

Hurray for Hollywood, Part One

One of Eddie's biggest concerns at the immediate moment was how he was going to pay for his passage out to California. Money was tight for an aspiring entertainer with a wife and two small children. Thanks to friends such as Curt Massey, Hezzie Trietsch, and Gabe and Marge Ward, they pooled their financial resources together to help Eddie pay for his one way train ticket to Hollywood. They also agreed that Eddie shouldn't be without his own transportation out on the West coast, so they also helped to pay for his car to be transported on the same train.

Eddie and Dearest decided that Eddie should make the trip out to Hollywood alone to "test the waters," so to speak, and once he would get himself somewhat established, he would send for his family. In the meantime, Dearest and the children stayed behind in Yankton.

Jimmie, on the other hand, moved back to Kansas with Ruth. He wasn't seeing the immediate prospects of landing it big in the entertainment field, so he took a job working in an airplane factory in Abilene. His wife worked in the office of the same factory. However, Jimmie stayed connected in the entertainment arena doing some solo radio shows a few times a week on a local station in Wichita.

When Eddie arrived at the Union Train Station in downtown Los Angeles in the spring of 1937, the "City of Angels" was hosting a beautifully mild climate while the sweet, succulent scent of orange blossoms permeated the air.

While Eddie's arrival to "Tinseltown" went generally unnoticed, it did not escape the attention of Ben Paley, the head of the Columbia Broadcasting System in Los Angeles. Paley was a big fan of Eddie's and was familiar with what he had been doing in radio. Paley was initially under the impression that Eddie came out to California seeking radio work and attempted to redirect him toward New York, where all the big radio shows originated. When Eddie shared with the CBS executive that he was focusing on making a career in films, Paley tried diligently to sell Eddie to the movie industry, especially to Darryl F. Zanuck, the founder and head of Twentieth Century-Fox Studios and most arguably the most influential person in the movie industry.

Paley even arranged for Eddie to make a fifteen-minute transcription recording of a Western drama that featured a few songs sung by Eddie that was broadcast over CBS in Hollywood. Paley thought this unusual way of calling attention to Eddie's talents would pique Zanuck's curiosity while at the same time stroke film mogul's enormous ego.

The transcription recording was called "An Open Letter to Darryl Zanuck." Paley opened the broadcast by saying, "Mr. Zanuck, we have Eddie Dean here who is a Western character who can sing and act. He is a fresh new talent, and we feel he can be a great asset to the your studio in the making of Western films. We hope you will give him serious consideration."

Zanuck wasn't sold on the idea or the theatrics involved and nothing more was done. If Eddie wanted to get into movies, he would have to go through the conventional route as all aspiring actors had to do (joining the Screen Actors Guild and getting an agent to represent him to the studios) or leave it all to fate by being at the right place at the right time.

Although he was known professionally as Eddie Dean, Eddie believed he acquired greater recognition during his tenure on *Modern Cinderella* and the *General Mills Minstrel Show* as Larry Burton. Eddie figured that going by the name of Larry Burton would get his foot in the film industry door a lot easier and faster than going by Eddie Dean.

Eddie solicited the General Mills Corporation for permission to use the name of Larry Burton for himself but his request was denied. General Mills stipulated that Larry Burton was a trademark name and was therefore closely associated with General Mills products and services (i.e., sponsorship of radio programs such as *Modern Cinderella* and such monikers such as "The Gold Medal Baritone.")

Eddie, as Eddie Dean, decided to go the conventional route and sought professional representation from Columbia Management of California, whose managing director was W. Arthur Rush. Rush started his career by rising quickly through the ranks at RCA-Victor, becoming the recording company's West Coast manager before he was twenty-five. He then became an executive producer of many network radio shows before becoming a talent agent with Columbia Management, representing a pantheon of well-known performers.

In 1939, Rush formed his own management firm, Art Rush, Inc., where he continued to manage talent, and took on one of his most well-known clients: Roy Rogers, and a few years later, his wife, Dale Evans. Rush was the architect behind the polished and singular image of the much beloved cowboy husband and wife team, putting together what it meant to be Roy Rogers and Dale Evans. Rush's management of "The King of the Cowboys" and "The Queen of the West" drove their professional film, television, recording, and radio careers, their public appearances, and the production of scores of licensed merchandise, and later franchised Roy Rogers Restaurant chains. He continued to work with Rogers and Evans until his death.[1]

One of the first bookings Eddie was given through Art Rush and Columbia Management while waiting to make his break in films, was to appear on a Friday evening in October at an all-star Western music variety show dubbed "The Hollywood Barn Dance." Located in a theater on the west end of Hollywood Boulevard, this show was not to be confused with the popular radio program by the same name that was broadcast from 1943 to 1948 and hosted by Cottonseed Clark, and later Dusty King, or the 1947 movie.

"The Hollywood Barn Dance" theater show was hosted by popular Los

Angeles disc jockey Peter Potter (real name William Moore), who later on went on to win two Emmy Awards for creating the popular radio and television series, *Platter Parade* and *Jukebox Jury.*

Sharing the bill with Eddie on the show that evening were a number of popular Western music talents, as well as The Sons of the Pioneers, who with Bob Nolan and the group's founder, Leonard Slye (aka Roy Rogers), had already established themselves on records with their hit song, "Tumbling Tumbleweeds," and who had made some movie appearances together in a few Gene Autry films.

Eddie was slated to close the show. However, just prior to The Sons of the Pioneers going on, Bob Nolan asked Eddie if he wouldn't mind preceding the group on the show as a way to stall for time because Leonard Slye, the group's lead singer, had yet to arrive from a previous scheduled appointment. Eddie agreed to do it.

About that time, in walked the twenty-five-year-old Slye, enthusiastically excited and giddy as a school boy and clutching a paper in his hand. "Look what I got!" Slye said elatedly. "Look!"

What Slye was holding in his hand was a movie contract with Republic Pictures, one of the first major independent movie studios known for specializing in Westerns, movie serials, and B-films emphasizing mystery and action.

While all the members of the Pioneers were elated with Slye's good fortune, Eddie wondered in the back of his mind what would become of his chances with Republic, since Rush and fellow talent agent Cliff Carling had also booked Eddie with a movie audition with Republic Studios for the following day.

Republic was looking for a new singing cowboy because Gene Autry had gone on strike against the studio, demanding a salary increase. When Republic wouldn't budge with more money, Autry refused to do any more films for the independent studio until his demands were met. So Republic set up open auditions to find a new singing cowboy star.[2] Eddie was scheduled for a try out to be that new star.

The next morning, Eddie went to Republic Pictures in Studio City to do the audition for Herbert J. Yates, Republic founder and studio head. He sang about ten songs. After his final song, Yates slammed his fist on the desk and said to Eddie, "You have the greatest voice I ever heard! If we didn't sign this kid yesterday, you would have gotten the job."

To say that Eddie felt dejected and even devastated upon hearing such news would be an understatement.

"All of a sudden I felt a big curtain draw down on me," Eddie recalled. "That curtain was Len Slye. I knew I had missed one of the biggest chances a man could ever have to do a series of Westerns from a studio which made the majority of Western movies."

Slye's first starring role for Republic Pictures, *Under Western Stars*, was released in April 1938. The fledgling actor made the picture under his new name, Roy Rogers, a name that would become the most recognizable of all the singing cowboys.

Although Eddie was initially discouraged over how the Republic Pictures audition turned out, he looked at it as a temporary setback. He nevertheless kept his perspective and kept moving forward. He vowed that some way, somehow, he would find work in films. Scrounging around Hollywood for work in motion pictures can be a pretty frustrating and lonely place, and Eddie did what he could to provide for Dearest and the kids.

In mid-October 1938, Eddie ran into another aspiring actor, who suggested to him that he return to Republic Pictures to try to get a job there. Eddie was focusing on getting lead parts instead of trying to start out finding steady work in supporting roles.

"Go see the Casting Director," the actor told Eddie, "and if he asks you if you can ride a horse, tell him you can ride anything you've got."

Eddie went to see the Casting Director at Republic and told him that he wanted to talk to him about getting a job in pictures and that he was a cowboy from Texas.

"Can you ride a horse?" the Casting Director asked.

"I sure can," Eddie replied enthusiastically. "I can ride anything you got."

The Casting Director then handed Eddie a script and said, "Take this script into the hall and learn a line and come back and do a character for me."

Eddie took the script, read two pages, and learned the lines of two characters. He returned ten minutes later stating what he was able to do.

"I was used to reading a script from my time in radio in Chicago," Eddie explained. "We read the lines of the script together as a cast."

Impressed, the Casting Director called for his secretary saying, "Prepare Mr. Dean a Letter of Introduction for membership in the Screen Actors Guild."

Eddie was told to report back to the studio the following morning at 5 a. m. to begin work on a new Western film.

Elated, Eddie immediately raced over to the Screen Actors Guild office at the west end of Hollywood Boulevard just moments before they closed, presented the clerk with his Letter of Introduction, and was given his union card.

The next morning, Eddie arrived at the Republic Pictures Studio in Studio City, where all the supporting actors working in the new Western movie were to be bused to the set at Iverson Ranch in the northwest corner of Chatsworth in the Simi Hills, about twenty-five miles away.

The new movie to be filmed was *Western Jamboree*, starring Gene Autry. Four pictures earlier, Republic Pictures caved in to Autry's salary demands, recognizing that the cowboy balladeer was too hot of a property to let go. This was to be his fifth and final movie for 1938.

Directed by Ralph Staub, *Western Jamboree* co-starred Smiley Burnette as Autry's sidekick, Frog Millhouse, and Jean Rouverol (Autry's leading lady), as Betty Haskell. Based on a story by Patricia Harper, the film is about a singing cowboy who goes up against a gang of outlaws who are looking to steal the valuable helium gas beneath the cowboy's ranch.

This would be Autry's twenty-fifth starring Western role since doing *Phantom Empire* in 1935. *Western Jamboree* was filmed October 18–27, 1938. The film had an operating budget of $55,462 (equal to approximately $904,500 today).[3]

After all the supporting actors were appropriately fitted in wardrobe, they boarded the bus for the forty-five-minute ride to Iverson Ranch. Sitting across the aisle from Eddie on the bus was a big guy telling stories that had everyone laughing. One of the other actors sitting near Eddie told him that the 6-foot, 5-inch man was from West Texas.

"I finally said to the man across from me, 'What part of Texas are you from anyway?'" Eddie said.

He looked over at Eddie and said, "Move over. They call me 'Pee Wee.' My name is Glenn Strange. I'm not from West Texas. I'm from New Mexico."

From that moment on, Strange became one of Eddie's best buddies. Strange had a long career in films playing in countless Westerns either as a sheriff or a henchman. He played the Frankenstein Monster three times for Universal Pictures in the 1940s and later played a long-standing role on television's *Gunsmoke*, as Sam Noonan, the bartender. He also collaborated with Eddie on a number of songs.

Eddie's unaccredited role as an extra in the Autry film was that of Thompson, a ranch hand. His first ever on-screen motion picture appearance came within the first five minutes of the movie. He can be seen mounted on his horse keeping watch over a herd of cattle at night. He saw a light in the nearby distance and went to investigate. Two men with sonar equipment were working surreptitiously trying to locate helium deposits on the ranch. When Eddie came upon them, he was overpowered by the pair and knocked semi-unconscious. After he fired shots as the two were getting away, Autry and Burnett came riding by to investigate. When Eddie told them what happened, they gave chase.

Later during filming, Eddie was with a group of other cowhands that were directed to run up to some horses that were at the hitching rail, mount up, and ride quickly away. Eddie did as he was directed but did so with a personal flare that caught the eye of the director.

"Before we shot the scene, the director told us extras to pick a horse to get on," Eddie said. "I picked out mine. I was twenty yards away from where the horses were hitched and when the director yelled, 'Action.' I made a running dive for my horse, getting my left foot in the stirrup and body in the saddle all in one motion. I was one of the first guys to break out riding."

After the scene was filmed, Staub was impressed with what Eddie had done, called him over, and asked if he wanted to make an extra $36. Eddie told him he was ready and asked what he needed to do.

Staub said that in this particular scene Eddie would do a "running fall" off his horse after engaging Autry and Burnett in a brief dialog along the trail. After Autry and Burnett had past him a ways, Eddie would ride down the hill carrying the mail and would then be shot dead by one of the henchmen hiding behind some rocks, thus doing the "running fall" off his horse.

"I did the fall off the running horse, got up, dusted myself off, and they printed it," Eddie recalled.

"The director yelled, 'Hey, guys! We have a new stunt man here!' I said, 'Wait a minute I did that to prove to you that I could do it. I've done these things ever since I was a kid. I don't want to be a stunt man. I want to be an actor.'"

As it turned out, both the running mount and running fall scenes were deleted from the final edited production.

During the lunch break on the set, Eddie saw Autry sitting underneath the shade of a large tree and Burnett was sitting next to him leaned up against the same tree. Eddie went up to Autry to say hello. It was a few years since they first met at WLS in Chicago, but Autry remembered him.

"After engaging in some small talk, Gene said to me, 'Eddie, I want to ask you something. Do you think this kid Leonard Slye, is going to hurt me in the business?'"

"Well, Gene, I don't think he'll hurt you, but he'll give you some good competition," Eddie replied. "You know, a funny thing, Gene, I wish I was in your spot. You need competition. You haven't had any competition. Competition is what America has been built on. Gene Autry is not going to be anything for very long if you don't have competition. With competition you'll be bigger than you ever were and you'll make more money than you ever made because of Roy Rogers."

"Eddie, I think you are right," Autry said slowly nodding his head reflectively. "Competition is good. Yeah, competition is good."

By the time *Western Jamboree* was being made, Roy Rogers had two Republic films under his belt (the second, *Billy the Kid Returns*) At that point in time, Autry had nothing to worry about from Rogers. A *Motion Picture*

Herald survey placed Autry as the top Western star of 1938.

Western Jamboree was released during the Christmas holiday season on December 2, 1938, providing Eddie with his first appearance on the silver screen. He was on his way to becoming an actor.

Between 1939 and 1941, Eddie appeared in four Gene Autry flicks: *Rovin' Tumbleweeds* (1939), in an unaccredited role as a cowhand singer; *Sunset in Wyoming* (1941), as a cowhand (unaccredited); *Down Mexico Way* (1941), as a guest at a barbeque (unaccredited), and *Sierra Sue* (1941), as Jerry Willis, a pilot.

On a break during the filming of *Sierra Sue* on location near Bishop, CA, Burnett casually asked Eddie, "Are you getting any breaks at all in the film industry?"

"No, not so good," Eddie replied.

"Go over and touch Gene," instructed Burnett. "It will bring you good luck. You'll be working the rest of your life."

Autry was playing poker with some of the film crew in a tent nearby.

Eddie went to Autry and said, "Gene, Smiley told me if I were to touch you, it would bring me luck. I need a lot of work."

"Go ahead and touch me then, Eddie," Autry said lightheartedly while dealing a round of five-card stud.

Eddie said he did just that and he claimed he hadn't been out of work since.

"Gene had a great charisma and was very likeable, but he never looked very comfortable acting," Eddie said.

Eddie's second movie role as an extra occurred two months later when filming began in December 1938, on the fifteen-chapter Republic serial of *The Lone Ranger Rides Again*, starring Robert Livingstone as the Lone Ranger and Chief Thundercloud as the Ranger's faithful companion, Tonto. It was a sequel to Republic's earlier 1937 serial *The Lone Ranger*, which had been highly successful.

In this second Lone Ranger serial, Eddie is in an unaccredited role as Cooper, a settler, who appears in Chapters 1-3, 6-7, and 12. This "shoot-'em-up" cliffhanger was released in February 1939. Production costs went

$20,000 over budget for a total of almost $214,000, making it the most expensive 1939 Republic serial.[4]

Eddie would take on unaccredited roles in two other serials from Universal Pictures during the next four years, *Gang Busters* and *Don Winslow of the Coast Guard.*

Based on the popular radio crime drama by the same name, *Gang Busters* stars Kent Taylor as Detective Lieutenant Bill Bannister, Robert Armstrong as Detective Tim Nolan, Irene Hervey as news photographer Vicki Logan, and Ralph Morgan as the evil Professor Mortis.

In this thirteen-chapter serial released in March 1942, a city is terrorized by a gang of known criminals who are officially listed as dead in police records. Eddie briefly portrays Blair, a police lab technician, in a scene in Chapter One.

The follow year, in April 1943, *Don Winslow of the Coast Guard* was released starring Don Terry as Commander Don Winslow, Walter Sande as Lieutenant "Red" Pennington, and Nestor Paiva as the "The Scorpion," a fascist sympathizer who plots to lay the ground work for another Japanese attack on the Pacific Coast of the United States. This was the follow up to *Don Winslow of the Navy*, made a year earlier.

In *Coast Guard*, Eddie plays Clark, Commander Winslow's aide, in Chapters 2, 3, 9, 12, and 13.

Thanks to Art Rush, Eddie's third movie extra role was in the Hopalong Cassidy Western *Renegade Trail.* This began a long and close relationship with William Boyd, who starred as Hopalong Cassidy. Co-starring with Boyd in *Renegade Trail* were Russell Hayden as "Lucky" Jenkins, George "Gabby" Hayes as "Windy" Halliday, the town marshal, Charlotte Winters as Mary Joyce, and Roy Barcroft as "Stiff-Hat" Bailey, the villain. *Renegade Trail* was the twenty-fourth of the sixty-sixth Hoppy Westerns that were made.

Filmed in early 1939 at Lone Pine, CA, and released in July 1939, Eddie plays "Red," a singing cowhand, who joins in the vocal fun with the King's Men quartet. The King's Men were the first singing quartet to appear in a Hopalong Cassidy Western, later singing in sixteen Hoppy films. The King's

Men quartet was comprised of Ken Darby, arranger and bass, Rad Robinson, baritone, Jon Dodson, lead tenor, and Bud Linn, top tenor. The film features two songs, "Lazy Rolls the Rio Grande" and "Hi Thar, Stranger!" both written by Foster Carling and Phil Ohlman.

The King's Men quartet was the basis of the Ken Darby Singers, featured on many Decca recordings including Bing Crosby's original 1942 recording of "White Christmas." The group was also featured as regulars on *The Jack Benny Show* on radio. Darby, who later worked in close association with Disney Studios on *The Wizard of Oz*, went on to win three Academy Awards (*The King and I, Porgy and Bess,* and *Camelot*) as Associate Musical Supervisor with Alfred Newman and Andre Previn.

"The King's Men were a wonderful quartet," Eddie recalled. "The one song that was written and given to me to sing was "Hi Thar, Stranger!" I sang the song in the movie welcoming people to Hoppy's camp. I think they cut the song out of the film. It didn't work out for me singing in those Hoppy movies. Bill (Boyd) and I got along great, but he didn't want anything to take away from his action films."

In *Renegade Trail*, town marshal "Windy" Halliday sends for his old Bar-20 Ranch friends, Hopalong Cassidy and "Lucky" Jenkins, to help fight a gang of outlaws led by "Stiff-Hat" Bailey. Hoppy becomes interested in Mary Joyce, whose ranch is the main target of the Bailey gang. Things get complicated by the fact that Mary's husband, Rusty Joslin, an escaped convict, is involved with the outlaws.

This was the final Hopalong Cassidy entry to feature "Gabby" Hayes, who left the series over a contract dispute. Hayes was eventually replaced with veteran slapstick comic Andy Clyde, as "California," who pals around with Hoppy and Lucky.

To help promote the release of *Renegade Trail*, a special Hopalong Cassidy show was booked in San Diego. It was a variety show with music by Eddie and the King's Men, as well as live action cowboy drama with shoot outs, fist fights, trick horse riding, and roping featuring Hoppy and the majority of the film's cast. Eddie was asked to drive Hayes to the event to do the show.

During the 120-mile drive from Los Angeles to San Diego, Eddie said he personally got to know Hayes a little better outside of his theatrical character.

"That was the closest I got to getting to know him outside of his Gabby Hayes persona," Eddie said. "He was a wonderful guy, kind of serious at times, and a really sharp dresser."

For the next year, Eddie worked as an extra in six additional Hopalong Cassidy films: *Range War* (1939), in an unaccredited role as Pete, a henchman; *Law of the Pampas* (1939), a credited role as Curly Naples, a henchman; *Santa Fe Marshal* (1940), as the town marshal (unaccredited); *The Showdown* (1940), as the marshal (unaccredited); *Hidden Gold* (1940), a credited role as Logan, the Express Agent; and *Stagecoach War* (1940), as Tom, a henchman (unaccredited).

During this time, Eddie also developed a close personal and professional friendship to Harry "Pop" Sherman, the producer of all the Hopalong Cassidy films. Born in 1884, Sherman went into producing during the silent era, and then in 1935 formed Harry Sherman Productions, planning to produce low-budget Westerns. His claim to fame was the introduction of the Hopalong Cassidy character (based on the books by Charles E. Mulford), which made his films so exceptionally popular that he became one of the few B-film independents distributed by major studios, including both Paramount and United Artists. He was very popular among his workers, who nicknamed him "Pop."

After making fifty-four films, Sherman turned over the production of the Hopalong Cassidy series to Boyd, so that he could concentrate on moving into the A-picture market. Sherman was one of the many independent producers aggressively expanding in the immediate post-war era, only to find the boom market suddenly and unexpectedly decline. The independent veteran was plagued by financial problems brought on by the film recession in the late 1940s. Sherman was forced to drop out of the Society of Independent Motion Picture Producers (SIMPP), but a few years later renewed his membership with the Society as he tried to jump-start his career.

Sherman was so taken with Eddie's singing abilities that the veteran producer held three different meetings with the heads of Paramount Pictures to try to get them interested in doing a series of Westerns with Eddie. It was to no avail. They kept turning the idea down.

"Pop Sherman was a wonderful man and an influential and talented producer," Eddie said. "I appreciated all that he tried to do for me. He had three daughters and he paid me the highest compliment a man could ever receive. He said that if he could ever have a son, Eddie Dean would be his son. When a man like Pop Sherman says something like that about you, that's really saying something!"

In 1940, Eddie appeared in a pair of Tex Ritter films from Monogram Pictures, which began a close, life-long friendship between the two cowboy singers. The first flick was *The Golden Trail*, released in July, in which Eddie plays Bart, a henchmen. In the second film, *Rolling Home to Texas*, released on December 30, Eddie plays himself but as a town sheriff that helps Ritter capture a gang of outlaws that smuggle prisoners out of the local penitentiary to commit crimes. They are later gunned down by the same outlaws in order to collect the lucrative rewards.

Eddie was given co-star billing in *Rolling Home to Texas,* as well as a featured solo spot singing the romantic ballad, "Desert Moonlight," backed by Cal Shrum and his Rhythm Rangers. Playing guitar for the six-member Rhythm Rangers was Hal Blair, with whom Eddie would form a tight, symbiotic musical relationship and close friendship, collaborating a canon of numerous songs together over the years.

Allowing Eddie to sing in his movie was not only very gracious and benevolent of Ritter, but audacious, as well. After all, Ritter was *the* star of the film as well as *the* singing star noted for his deep, husky vocal interpretations. No such veteran star relishes the possibility of being over-shadowed by any up-and-coming singer/actor, especially when they appear together in the same film. Ritter didn't possess an over-inflated ego and didn't feel threatened by Eddie's musical contributions.

"How many guys that you know would let another man sing in his pictures?" Eddie asked rhetorically. "Only Tex Ritter."

For the next four years, Eddie continued to appear in a variety of unaccredited roles in B-Western flicks including those starring Don "Red" Barry, Bill "Cowboy Rambler" Boyd, George Houston, Victor Jory, Johnny Mack Brown, John Wayne, and various manifestations of "The Three Mesquiteers," a series of movies in which each film featured a trio of stars such as Bob Steel, Tom Tyler, Robert Livingston, Raymond Hatton, Rufe Davis, Duncan Reynaldo, and the Mesquiteers series imitators from Monogram Pictures, "The Range Busters," featuring Ray "Crash" Corrigan, John "Dusty" King, and Eddie's close friend, Max Terhune.

In 1943, Eddie appeared unaccredited in the Roy Rogers movie, *King of the Cowboys*. In the opening scenes as Tex, a lawman, Eddie is overpowered by thugs and rescued by Rogers. Rejoining Rogers as his film sidekick was Smiley Burnett, due to Gene Autry being inducted into the Army a year earlier.

"I liked and respected Roy Rogers," Eddie said. "He wasn't a phony."

Finally, Eddie was beginning to get some breaks with more visible exposure in his final two non-starring roles. The first was the 1944 Western, *Harmony Trail*, starring Ken Maynard. Originally titled *White Stallion*, the film also co-starred Gene Alsace, Max Terhune, and Terhune's dummy, Elmer Sneezeweed, Glenn Strange, perennial bad guy Charles King, Robert McKenzie, and the screen debut of twenty-two-year-old leading lady Ruth Roman.

In a modified remake of John Wayne's *Paradise Canyon* (1935), Marshall Rocky Camron (Alsace) is given the task of solving a $100,000 bank robbery. Camron enlists the aid of his friends, Ken Maynard, Eddie Dean, and Max Terhune. "Doc" Martin (McKenzie) and his daughter, Ann Martin (Roman), are fleeing a nearby town in a hurry, as some of the local citizens are somewhat incensed regarding the imitation elixir sold them by Martin.

An ambush attempt is made on Maynard's life as the bank robbers, aware of the coming of a marshal, mistake Maynard for Camron because of the identical white stallions ridden by both. Maynard, Eddie and Terhune, posing as performers with Martin's traveling medicine show, hunt for the bandits.

Released on December 1, 1944, *Harmony Trail* was filmed at Corriganville, Ray "Crash" Corrigan's movie ranch in Simi Valley, CA. Eddie was prominently showcased in the motion picture singing "Down Harmony Trail,"

"Boogie Woogie Cowboy," a lyrical collaboration between he, Hal Blair, accordionist Jack Statham and guitarist Gus Snow, and "On the Banks of the Sunny San Juan," a romantic ballad written by Eddie and Glenn Strange.

Eddie's final non-starring role in films occurred the following year in *Wildfire* starring Bob Steel. Filmed in "gorgeous color," as it was billed, Eddie plays Sheriff Johnny Deal. Other co-stars in the movie are Sterling Holloway, John Miljan, Virginia Maples, and Sarah Padden. Eddie's vocal talents are spotlighted on an abbreviated a cappella version of "By the Sleepy Rio Grande" and his tour de force piece, "On the Banks of Sunny San Juan."

Pete Fanning (Miljan) and his men are rustling horses from the local ranchers and blaming it on a wild horse they named "Wildfire." "Happy" Haye (Steele) and his sidekick "Alkali" Jones (Holloway) ride up on two local ranchers after they shoot Wildfire in the leg and are about to finish him off. Happy stops them and nurses the horse back to health. They ride into town to sell their horses but Fanning tells one of his men to say that the two pintos are his and that he bought them from an Indian that's been dead for six months so no one can say differently. Happy shows Sheriff Johnny Deal (Eddie) his Bill of Sale and they back off, still bent on stealing Happy's horses and more local horses. Happy gets the sheriff to deputize him and they go after Fanning and his gang.

Released in mid-July 1945, *Wildfire* was directed by Robert Emmett Tansey, who would later direct Eddie's initial starring roles in his own series of Westerns. Eddie was paid $500 for his role in *Wildfire*.[7]

Although Eddie was appearing mainly as an extra in films and was mostly paid minimum scale wages as outlined by the actors' union, these early years in Hollywood were tough for him to support Dearest and their two school-age children. Until the next B-Western film came along, Eddie would earn a living singing at theaters, rodeos, or any venues that would appreciate his music.

From September through December 1941, Eddie was hired to do singing commercials on *The Lone Ranger* radio program starring Brace Beemer. He was paid $55 per show.[8]

Things began to open up more for Eddie as World War II approached with opportunities to record on commercial records and transcriptions, being a member of a talented vocal trio for America's Number One Cowboy, gaining a following as a featured vocalist on a hit radio show, and of course, getting to star in his own series of action packed Westerns.

8

Hurray for Hollywood, Part Two

By 1941, Eddie, Dearest, and the children were ready to settle into a new home of their own. They had been renting a house at 902 Rose Street in Burbank.[1] Eddie was now making enough money to buy a relatively-inexpensive single family home with a modest mortgage payment. A recent water pipe breakage causing a flood inside the rented home was the actual catalyst for Eddie and family to move. Dearest didn't want to participate in any further clean up gaffs. It was time to move. Such a house was recently built and for sale at 124 North Naomi Street in Burbank.

The three-bedroom two-bathroom 1,569-square-foot home located off West Olive and Alameda avenues just a few blocks from Disney Studios sold for $12,000. That was quite a hefty sum back then. The Dean Family lived at that address for over twenty-eight years. It was a spacious home for them at the time, and over the years did not "depreciate" in its suitability due to Eddie's "stardom" status.

Seventy-two years later, that same home had an estimated value at $615,000, but in 2005 the home sold for $740,000.[2] Eddie and Dearest wanted to provide their children with a stable and relatively "normal" family environment while growing up. Both Donna and Edgar attended parochial schools throughout their formal education period as per Eddie's and Dearest's commitment to each other concerning their children's education.

Both children initially attended Saint Charles Borromeo Catholic School in nearby North Hollywood and then Saint Robert Bellarmine and Saint Finbar, both in Burbank.

For her high school education, Donna matriculated to the all-girls Our Lady of Corvallis High School in Studio City (operated between 1941 and 1987). Edgar attended the all-boys Notre Dame High School in Sherman Oaks. Notre Dame became a co-ed campus in 1982.

It had taken Eddie only a few short years since initially relocating to Los Angeles for him to quickly become a recognizable talent within the area Country music community. However, by the spring of 1940, the Los Angeles Country music community was buzzing over the news that Roy Acuff was coming to Hollywood to appear in *Grand Ole Opry*, a musical B-film based on the famed Country music hall in Nashville, Tennessee. Two years earlier, Acuff joined the Grand Ole Opry and became one of its hottest and most popular acts with his "Smokey Mountain Boys."

Known as the "King of Country Music," Acuff is often credited with moving the genre from a "hoedown" format to the star singer-based format that helped to make it internationally successful. Acuff's 1936 rendering of the popular Gospel tune, "The Great Speckled Bird," and his own "Wabash Cannonball," brought him such notoriety.

"Roy Acuff sang like my dad used to sing, but Roy sang more with a nasal tone," Eddie said.

To honor Acuff's advent to "Tinseltown," Max Terhune rolled out the red carpet by hosting a welcome party for Acuff at his home. All of the *Who's Who* of the Hollywood Country music scene were in attendance, including Eddie and Roy Rogers, who both performed.

Eddie recalled taking a drinking break with Acuff that evening. "Roy said to me, 'I'm so tired. Do you happen to have any whiskey?' I said, 'Yes, I have a quart bottle with me in the trunk of my car. I carry it for snake bites.' He and I sat down and drank half of it and then we went back in the house to the party."

During his sojourn to Hollywood, Acuff met with American songwriter Fred Rose, who was based in Hollywood writing songs for RKO Pictures B-Western film star Ray Whitley, the composer of "Back in the Saddle Again," Gene Autry's theme song. Rose had also collaborated with Autry on a number hit songs.

Acuff and Rose immediately hit it off together and the pair talked about joining forces to form a music publishing company. Impressed with Eddie's ability to write a song, Rose invited Eddie to be a part of his and Acuff's intended business venture. Eddie refused Rose's offer at the time citing family concerns, but looking back in hindsight, he said passed up a gold mine financial opportunity.

Eddie explains: "Fred Rose called me one day and said he was writing some songs and asked if I would come over to his home in the Hollywood Hills and sing them in order to help him out. I did. After working over the pieces of music, Fred said, 'I'm going back to Nashville with Roy Acuff to form our music publishing company. We need a third partner and we'd love to have you join us.

"I figured Fred said that to a lot of people even though I never heard him say it to anyone. I told him that I was just starting to get myself situated in Hollywood with singing and in films. I didn't want to move my family again as I had my kids in school out here. Fred called me a few times about it and I turned him down. I told him I'd love to go, but I wanted to have my kids educated in one place."

In 1942, Rose returned to Nashville and teamed up with Acuff to create Acuff-Rose Music, the first Nashville-based music publishing company. It was almost immediately successful due in large part to Rose's ASCAP (American Society of Composers, Arrangers, and Publishers) connections and gifted ability as a talent scout. Acuff-Rose quickly became the most important publishing company in Country music.[3] In 1946, the company signed Hank Williams, and four years later published their first major hit with Patti Page's rendition of "Tennessee Waltz."

"Fred and I remained friends," Eddie said. "Later on, I played a lot of rodeos and we played one out at the fairgrounds near Nashville and Fred came out to see the show."

Rose died Nashville in December 1954. He was fifty-six. Along with

Hank Williams and Jimmie Rodgers, Rose was one of the three charter members of the Country Music Hall of Fame when it opened in 1961.

Acuff, who became the first living inductee into the Country Music Hall of Fame in 1962, died in Nashville in November 1992 of congestive heart failure. He was eighty-nine years old.

During this period, more opportunities came knocking for Eddie to branch out musically. While promoting his movie, *Rancho Grande,* in Oklahoma City, Oklahoma, during the spring of 1940, Gene Autry asked the Jimmy Wakely Trio, regulars at Oklahoma City's WKY, to back him for some live performances. Wakely, a native of Arkansas, and fellow trio members Johnny Bond and Dick Reinhart, so impressed Autry that he invited them to California to work for him. By September, they were hired as Autry's new back up group for his Sunday evening radio program, *Melody Ranch,* sponsored by Wrigley chewing gum.

Melody Ranch aired for an unprecedented sixteen years from 1940 until 1956. The program featured songs, comedy, and action-filled drama. Autry's musical director was Carl Cotner.

In late 1941, Wakely left Autry because of movie commitments and a new recording contract with Decca Records. Bond also left, briefly leaving Reinhart as the lone man standing. Needing to fill two slots in his *Melody Ranch* Trio, Autry looked to Eddie.

"Gene called me at two in the morning asking me for my help," Eddie recalled. "He said, 'Eddie, I'm in trouble. I need some help. Wakely just quit on me tonight and I want you to get a trio together for me.' I said, 'Well, Gene, I don't know. I've been working as a single. I don't want to get mixed up in a trio again. I'm trying to build myself up as a single act, and I've sort of had it with the other fellow's wives and things like that.' The bottom line was Gene talked me into it.

"He asked me if I would get my brother, Jimmie, to come out to California to join me. Jimmie was living in Wichita, Kansas, working at an airplane plant. I told Gene yes. I don't know why I did, but I did. I called Jimmie and he came out the next day."

After the first few weeks together, Reinhart left the trio and tall and lanky

Johnny Bond, a native of Oklahoma, returned to round out the group. He would become a main-stay on *Melody Ranch*, later becoming Autry's radio sidekick for the drama sequences in addition to providing musical offerings.

Eddie sang the lead in the trio and played different characters on the radio show's fifteen-minute drama offering each week. The trio also accompanied Autry on the road doing live performances at theaters, rodeos, as well as on recordings.

Eddie earned $34.94 for four days of work singing in Autry's rodeos with the trio. The following week, he was paid $67.88 for eight days of work singing at another venue.[4]

Dearest was also part of the Flying "A" Ranch Rodeo working as the organization's secretary.

While Eddie seemed to be doing well as a member of the Gene Autry *Melody Ranch* Trio, Jack Kapp of Decca Records contacted Eddie to wax some solo vocal numbers for his record label. Kapp always liked Eddie's vocal styling as it had been six years since Eddie, along with brother Jimmie, graced the label back in Chicago. Unfortunately, Eddie's Decca solo recordings also went nowhere fast.

For this record date of September 4, 1941, Eddie was teamed up with Gus Snow on guitar, Martin Kob on bass, and Jack Statham on accordion in a Los Angeles studio to record "A Little Grey Home in the West," "It's Harvest Time in Peaceful Valley," "Where the Silvery Colorado Wents Its Way," and the inaugural version of "On the Banks of the Sunny San Juan" that Eddie and Glenn Strange wrote together.

Five months later on February 25, 1942, with America freshly engaged in World War II, Eddie waxed his final half-dozen cuts with Decca with "I'm Back in the Saddle Again," Gene Autry's theme song, "Sleepy Time in Carolie," "How Can You Say You Love Me," "I'm Comin' Home, Darlin'," "The Land Where the Roses Never Fade," and "Don't Forget That Jesus Loves You," a Gospel piece. For this session, Eddie was backed by Herb Kratoska on guitar, Paul Sells on piano/accordion, Budd Hatch on bass, and Frank Marvin on steel guitar. Frank Marvin was the brother of Johnny Marvin, Gene Autry's long-time business associate and musical collaborator.

"I'm Comin' Home, Darlin'" was one of many team efforts between Eddie and Carl Hoefle, whom Eddie knew from his radio days Chicago. Hoefle led a popular vocal trio back in the "Windy City" called "Tom, Dick, and Harry." After Hoefle came to California, Eddie and he reunited to compose songs together.

When Eddie signed on to do his own series of Westerns beginning in 1945, Hoefle came on board as musical director in *Song of Old Wyoming, Romance of the West,* and *The Caravan Trail,* Eddie's first three films respectively. He also collaborated with Eddie as a songwriter on "Wild Prairie Rose," that was showcased in *Song of Old Wyoming* and "Ridin' to the Top of the Mountain," along with Del Porter, who gained distinction recording with Spade Cooley and as clarinetist and lead singer for the musically outrageous Spike Jones and His City Slickers. The piece was featured in *Colorado Serenade* (1946).

The partnership of Hoefle and Porter helped to enlarge the Spike Jones "musical depreciation" canon with such zany pieces as "Pass the Biscuits, Mirandy" (1942) and "You Wanna Buy a Bunny?" (1949). Hoefle went on to work on the musical score for *Flight to Nowhere* (1946), a low-budget espionage picture starring Jack Holt and Evelyn Ankers, and *Scared to Death* (1947), the only color movie that veteran horror actor Bela Lugosi ever made.

On February 24, 1942, Eddie, Jimmie, and Johnny Bond were on hand in Hollywood joining Carl Cotner and crew to help Autry cut back-to-back hits on Okeh Records, an inexpensive subsidiary of Columbia Records, with "Deep in the Heart of Texas," "I'm Thinkin' Tonight of My Blue Eyes," and "Tweedle-O-Twill," a quirky Autry-Fred Rose ditty.

On June 10, 1942, less than two months before the musicians union strike would take effect, Autry, with his trio and Cotner's orchestra, waxed on the Okeh label in Hollywood the popular "(I've Got Spurs That) Jingle, Jangle, Jingle." The Frank Loesser and Joseph Lilley composition was written for *The Forest Rangers,* which starred Fred MacMurray, Paulette Goddard, and Susan Hayward. On the flip side of that recording was the Autry-Fred Rose piece, "I'm A Cow Poke Pokin' Along."

Other versions of "(I've Got Spurs That) Jingle, Jangle, Jingle" were later recorded by Tex Ritter, Glenn Miller, The Merry Macs, and Burl Ives, with the most successful commercial recording done by Autry's Columbia label mate, bandleader Kay Kyser, whose rendition reached Number One on the *Billboard* charts in July 1942.

Autry also acknowledged Eddie's compositional artistry from time-to-time by featuring some of his songs on *Melody Ranch* and on record, including "I'm Comin' Home, Darlin'" (recorded August 11, 1941), "I'll Be Back," a collaborative piece between Eddie, Rex Preis and Bill Bryan (recorded November 29, 1944, after Columbia Records settled its two-year dispute with the musicians' union).

This new manifestation of the *Melody Ranch* Trio with the Dean Brothers and Johnny Bond provided a creative and versatile aggregation for Autry. Eddie's rich baritone vocal styling provided the perfect complement to the other singing voices involved. Johnny Bond also contributed to the mix with his lively but offbeat novelty pieces.

However, Autry felt a bit intimidated by Eddie's abilities and was afraid that somehow Eddie would eventually overshadow him in the singing arena; and rightly so. Eddie had the better, more versatile singing voice. Autry told Eddie a number of times that if he had come out to Hollywood three years before, he wouldn't have had a chance at stardom. In an attempt to put his fears at ease, Autry coaxed Eddie to reposition himself from in front of the microphone so as not to be too aurally recognizable to the listening audience.

"Gene came up to me very quietly pulling me to the side and asked me to change positions in the trio," Eddie recalled. "As the lead singer of the trio, I always stood in the middle right in front of the microphone. Gene told me that people were starting to recognize my voice. He asked me if I would mind putting one of the other two guys in the middle. So, I did. Why he didn't want people to recognize my voice, I'll never know. I guess it goes back to the situation I had with Wayne King in Chicago. He didn't want someone else in the band to overshadow him. If I had a show, I'd want the best people in the world involved in it. Gene was the kind of guy that if he asked you to do something, you'd do it for him."

After the Japanese attack on Pearl Harbor, Hawaii, which brought the United States in World War II, Autry was determined to join the armed forces. Although Autry was in his mid-thirties, he had taken flying lessons, earned a private pilot's license, and his goal was to become a flight officer. On July 26, 1942, during a broadcast of *Melody Ranch* from Chicago, Autry was inducted into the Army Air Force as a technical sergeant.

Eddie, Jimmie, and Johnny were on hand at that special *Melody Ranch* broadcast. To honor their boss just moments prior to his taking the Oath of Allegiance, the trio sang a lively Dick Reinhart piece called "I'll Trade My Horse and Saddle (For a Pair of Wings)." Autry was correct. During the singing of this song, Eddie's lead vocal styling can be recognized amidst the group setting.

Autry was first sent to Santa Ana Air Force Base for basic training, then to Luke Field in Phoenix, Arizona, for additional training. He was granted permission by the Pentagon to broadcast *Melody Ranch* every Sunday evening with his radio cast, no matter where he was. It would prove to be a good morale booster for American radio listeners to hear "America's Favorite Cowboy" regularly on radio while he was doing something "irregular" for his country. Since Autry was now the property of Uncle Sam, his radio show was renamed to broadcast under the title of *The Sergeant Gene Autry Show*.

"We'd travel to Luke Field every Sunday to do Gene's radio show," Eddie said about the radio cast. "We'd rehearse with Gene for a bit just prior to air time and then we did the show. Gene would have advance copies of the script and music so he would be prepared."

By mid-1943, Autry was transferred for more flight training to Love Field in Dallas. The difficult traveling distance from Los Angeles to do weekly radio shows were a burden for Eddie. In addition, he was more than ready to shed group vocal work and move forward to further pursue his career as single. So, he gave Autry his notice.

Through his association with Pete Canova, Eddie auditioned and was hired to be a part of a new musical comedy show hosted by Pete's sister Judy Canova. *The Judy Canova Show* ran for twelve years on Tuesday evenings, first on CBS and then on NBC. Eddie only worked on the show during its first season, playing on fifty episodes from July 6, 1943 to June 27, 1944. The show was sponsored by Colgate tooth powder.

Canova, known as "America's Wacky, Wistful, Wonderful Scatterbrain," sang, yodeled, and played guitar and was typed as a wide-eyed, love-starved Ozark bumpkin with her hair in braids that was at times topped with a straw hat. As part of the show's on-going story line, she divided her time between home in the Ozarks and the fictional "Rancho Canova" in Southern California. Canova's theme song was the tune "Scatterbrain."

In addition to Eddie, who played himself and was always given a featured vocal selection on the thirty-minute show, Canova was accompanied by a talented cast that included voice master Mel Blanc as Sylvester and Pedro, Ruth Perrott as Aunt Aggie, Ruby Dandridge as Geranium, Joseph Kearns as Benchley Botsford (Kearns, a seasoned veteran of radio, would later be known as "Mr. Wilson" on the *Dennis the Menace* television show in the early 1960s), announcer Ken Niles, and Charles Dant and his Orchestra.

"Pete wanted to have a contrast of a cowboy with Judy's hillbilly persona," Eddie said about the makeup of the show. "We had a good, unified, overall show with Mel Blanc doing his thing with all his different characters, the good music that the Charles Dant Orchestra provided, Judy's clown singing and yodeling, and my cowboy-type singing. The producers of the show were pleased."

Some of the featured songs Eddie sang on the show were "Ridin' Down the Canyon," "The New San Antonio Rose," "I'm Gonna Lasso a Rainbow For You," "Goodbye, Little Darlin'," "I'm Comin' Home, Darlin'," "The Song of the Trail," "I'll Take You Home Again, Kathleen," and "There's a Star Spangled Banner Waving Somewhere."

"I had a lot of fun working on the show with Judy," Eddie said. "She was a wonderful gal who was very supportive of the war effort and of the troops. She was more than generous in allowing me to be showcased singing a song each week. Jack Benny used to do that for Dennis Day on his radio show. I guess you say I was the sort of the Dennis Day of *The Judy Canova Show*."

In 1983, Canova died from cancer at age sixty-nine.

When Eddie joined *The Judy Canova Show*, it brought an end to the *Melody Ranch* Trio. As a result, brother Jimmie was again out of a job. A short time later, Country singer Foy Willing called Eddie because he was looking for a lead singer for his trio, Riders of the Purple Sage, and wanted to know if Eddie would be interested in the job. Eddie wasn't, but he suggested to Willing that he get Jimmie.

"Dearest didn't want me to get tied up in a trio again." Eddie said. "I got tired of having to split money because I could make as much on my own as with a group. She also got tired of me taking care of someone else. Foy asked me if Jimmie was a good singer. And I said, 'For a trio? You won't find a better one. He'll blend in perfectly.' So Foy hired him. When my brother Jimmie was with the Riders of the Purple Sage, it was one of the greatest Western groups that I ever heard. One of the smoothest, too."

In 1942, Willing co-founded the group with Iowa musician Al Sloey. The initial band included fiddler Johnny Paul, accordionist Ken Coopern, and a fifteen-year-old gal singer from Oklahoma named Clara Ann Fowler, who would later gain renown after World War II as hit maker Patti Page.

During the group's various manifestations during their ten-year career, their smooth, tight harmonies helped them to create a number of hit recordings, such as "Texas Blues" (1944), "Detour" (1946), "Have I Told You Lately That I Love You" (1946), "Anytime" (1948), and "Brush Those Tears From Your Eyes" (1949), among others, as well as Willing's sentimental composition, "No One to Turn to." In addition, they appeared in Western films starring Roy Rogers, Jimmy Wakely, and Monte Hale, and were regulars on *The Hollywood Barn Dance* through 1945 before hosting their own radio drama-music program *All-Star Western Theater* from 1946-1947, sponsored by Weber's Bread. A guest Western star appeared on the show to participate in the drama sequence and then sang a song or two backed by Willing and the Riders of the Purple Sage. Eddie appeared twice on *All-Star Western Theatre* just as his own series of Western films were taking off.[5]

Willing and Sloey made up the core of the group with Sloey singing a smooth tenor and Willing a rich baritone. Dick Reinhart joined the group briefly after leaving the Autry Trio and sang lead.

In 1944, Jimmie Dean replaced Reinhart and stayed with Foy Willing and the Riders of the Purple Sage for a over a year. Charlie Morgan, who went on to become the lead singer with Andy Parker and the Plainsmen, became a "Sager" during this period, expanding the group to a robust quartet sound.

Prior to becoming a "Sager," Jimmie was one of "The Red River Valley Boys," a backup group led by Johnny Bond that appeared in *Arizona Trail*, a Tex Ritter film from 1943. Rounding out the group were Wesley Tuttle and Paul Sells.

After his time as a "Sager," Jimmie formed a Western trio in late 1945 with Wesley Tuttle and Merle Travis, calling themselves "The Trail Riders." This short-lived ensemble was created as a replacement group for Foy Willing and the Riders of the Purple Sage for their CBS radio show while the "Sagers" were on a month's vacation. "The Trail Riders" also made a handful of transcription recordings for C. P. MacGregor Transcriptions of Los Angeles.

"I was working at CBS and Foy brought in Wesley and Merle to sing with Jimmie Dean," recalled Marilyn Tuttle, who became the wife of Western artist Wesley Tuttle. The Tuttle's were bedrocks in the Western music scene in California, performing together from the late 1940s and throughout the 1950s as original regulars on *Town Hall Party*, a weekly Western music radio and television show originating from Compton, CA, of the greater Los Angeles area. In addition to that radio-television program, the Tuttle's recorded Western and Gospel music together in their own right and performed live shows with many top Western stars, including Eddie and Tex Ritter.

"It wasn't the first time I had seen Wesley but it was the beginning of a wonderful romance between us," Tuttle said. "When Foy returned he let Jimmie Dean go. Foy used to tell me, 'Jimmie Dean sounds like an old man.' That sounded harsh, but Jimmie didn't have the voice that his brother (Eddie) had."

This was probably Jimmie Dean's final work as a Western group singer. After this group split up, Jimmie tried his hand at raising chinchillas at his home at 11851 Archwood in North Hollywood, and he eventually went back to work in the airline industry, landing a job at the Lockheed plant in

Burbank. He worked his way up to a fairly high level management position and remained in that industry until he became ill and died.

Over the years, Jimmie's alcohol drinking worsened and he developed cirrhosis of the liver. Toward the end of his life, he remained hospitalized for two-and-a-half years. During Jimmie's hospitalization, Dearest worked tirelessly behind the scenes to get all of her brother-in-law's affairs in order.

"Nobody will ever know, I think, or any of our family will realize how wonderful (Dearest) was to my brother, Jimmie, to help take care of him," Eddie confessed.[6] "She got all his books and papers together to figure out what insurance he had through Lockheed. He owed taxes on his home and he was about to lose it, so she got everything squared away with that. Lockheed was really wonderful concerning coming through on the insurance and everything. Dearest kept all the books down to the very penny, so that anyone could come in and look at these books and know *exactly* how everything was handled. For her to do that, day after day, every day, for two-and-a-half years while he was ill was something else, for which I'm very grateful, naturally."

Jimmie Dean lost the fight with cirrhosis of the liver and succumbed to death on February 7, 1970. He was sixty-six. He was survived by his wife, Ruth, and their adopted son, Kent.

Of all his siblings, Eddie was the closest to Jimmie not only because of their close proximity in birth order but because of the musical gifts they shared, as well working together professionally. Jimmie's death left a void in Eddie's heart for a long time.

While Eddie was appearing as an unaccredited extra in films, he was also creating a name for himself in the music arena. That would be the forte of where his talents lay. Between 1942 and 1945, he cut sixty-six transcription recordings for Standard Transcription Company. At that time, commercial recordings were pressed onto 12-inch 78 rpm discs for private use only, while transcription recordings were 16-inch, recorded at 33-1/3 rpm, and played over the radio.

Eddie's transcription recordings covered a variety of songs ranging from his own compositions of "My Old Herding Song," "On the Banks of the

Sunny San Juan," "Boogie Woogie Cowboy," "I've Got a Cowboy Song For Sale," "Prairie Moonbeams," "When I Move to That New Range," and "I'm Comin' Home, Darlin'" to Western standards as "Palomino Pal of Mine," and "Ridin' Down That Utah Trail," and crossovers pieces, such as Ernest Tubbs' "Walking the Floor Over You" and "I Wonder Why You Said Goodbye."

Eddie had a little more success on platters when he signed on with Bel-Tone Records, an independent label that had been active in Los Angeles for sixteen months in 1945 and 1946. Bel-Tone opened for business in late July 1945. Much of Bel-Tone's Country recordings took place in the first month after the company opened its doors even though it didn't have a recording studio to call its own. The label had to contract out with established commercial studios in Los Angeles to record their artists.[7]

The man responsible for most of Bel-Tone's Country sessions was singer, musician, radio personality, and record producer Cliffie Stone, who was pivotal in the development of a thriving California Country music scene. Also on the label's artists' roster was Dale Evans.

During that summer of 1945, Eddie waxed eight sides, all backed by Cliffie Stonehead (aka, Cliffie Stone) and his Orchestra. Eddie's music was categorized by the company on its red label with silver printing as "Folk Singer – Instrumental." Those sides were "Careless Darlin'," "This Lonely World," "Born to Be Blue," "The Low Road's Good Enough For Me," a collaborative effort between Eddie and Pete Canova, "Cry, Cry, Cry," "For Better Or Worse," "Fifteen Hundred and One Miles of Heaven," and "Dream Rose."

Bel-Tone put some money behind Eddie's releases because of his status as a new cowboy star.[8] A pair of his recorded songs were currently featured in two of his films: "Careless Darlin'," an Ernest Tubb, Lou Wayne, and Bob Shelton offering, was in *Tumbleweed Trail* (1946), and "Fifteen Hundred and One Miles of Heaven," Eddie's and Dearest's own composition, was in *Stars Over Texas* (1946).

By June 1946, Stone moved on to Capitol Records, and soon after, Bel-Tone began its financial descent, filing for bankruptcy in late November 1946, owing $40,000.[9]

To revitalize its Country music market, Gold Seal Records purchased the Bel-Tone masters in November 1947.[10] Gold Seal was one of the more obscure independent labels headquartered in postwar Chicago. The company was in business for almost two years and employed an unconventional release numbering system that was difficult to follow. The Gold Seal label was more well known for the release of some significant Jazz recordings.

As did Bel-Tone, Gold Seal also helped to promote Eddie's 1945 recording of "Cry, Cry, Cry," an Eddie Dean-Hal Blair opus, that found a spot in *West to Glory* (1947), Eddie's eleventh cowboy motion picture. By the time the record was re-released, Eddie had already signed on with Majestic Records the previous year.

Just after World War II ended in 1945, Eddie reconnected with Les Paul, his friend from his days in Chicago. The guitar genius relocated to Los Angeles after being discharged from the Army while serving in the Armed Forces Network. Paul came over to Eddie's home in Burbank one evening to discuss the possibility of working together as a musical team as Paul greatly admired Eddie's singing style as well as his creative compositional abilities.

Born Lester William Polsfuss from Waukesha, Wisconsin, he took his stage name of Les Paul. He also used the nickname of "Rhubarb Red," a moniker which Paul proudly described as his "hillbilly alter ego."

Paul gained renown for his creative and imaginative guitar prowess, his multi-track recording innovations, his design of fastidiously and expertly crafted guitars, and of course, for his numerous hit recordings throughout the 1950s with his wife Mary Ford. Eddie was also responsible for bringing Les Paul and Mary Ford together as a musical entity.[11]

"While Les felt that he and I would be a good team, he wanted a female singer," Eddie explained. "He described the kind of female he was looking for. I thought about it and knew of the right girl for him. Her name was Iris Colleen Summers, a twenty-one-year-old from Los Angeles. She was singing in an all-girl Western trio called 'The Sunshine Girls' who sang back up to Jimmy Wakely and his trio and who were regulars on *The Hollywood Barn Dance* program. She was also a very popular vocalist on KXLA's *Dinner Bell Round Up Time*.

"I called Colleen and told her to go see Les Paul at his home in Holly-wood as he had a job waiting for her there. She went to see Les. Les called me back a few hours later and asked, 'How did you know this is the gal I wanted to record with?' I told him, 'You described her to me and I know her.' Colleen changed her name to Mary Ford and she and Les made a lot of hit recordings together."

In 1949, the couple married.

"Every time Les would see me he'd call me 'Mr. Cupid' for bringing he and Mary together," Eddie said.

Between 1950 and 1957, Paul and Ford put out twenty-eight hits for Capitol Records including "How High the Moon," "Vaya Con Dios," "Mockingbird Hill," "Bye Bye Blues," "The World Is Waiting for the Sunrise," and "Tiger Rag." These songs featured the novel sound of Ford harmonizing with herself. In 1953, the couple also hosted *The Les Paul and Mary Ford Show,* their own television program which ran for three years.

They divorced in 1963. Ford died in 1977 from complications from diabetes at age fifty-three.

In 1997, Paul made an appearance at the Gene Autry Museum in Los Angeles. Eddie wanted to attend but was too ill at the time to do so. The two friends had not seen each other for a long time.

"If I had gone to the museum to see Les, there would be only one thing I'd ask him that had been bugging the heck out of me for years," Eddie said. "I would ask him, 'Where is my Les Paul guitar?'"

On August 13, 2009, Paul passed away from complications with pneumonia at age ninety-four.

While Eddie's musical momentum would continue to receive accolades in the years to come and would prove to be his most creative and enduring forté, his film career took a lucky turn. He finally would get to star in his own series of color Western flicks for young post-World War II movie goers.

Movie poster of the 1938 Gene Autry film, *Western Jamboree,* in which Eddie made his very first on-screen appearance in an uncredited role.

Eddie Dean as "Red," a cowhand, looks on as William Boyd as Hopalong Cassidy attends to a man that has been shot in *Renegade Trail* (1939). This was the first of seven Hopalong Cassidy flicks that Eddie appeared in. He had a singing part in *Renegade Trail* with The King's Men Quartet.

Eddie Dean (in back facing front) as Pete, a henchman, listens to what William Boyd as Hopalong Casssidy (dressed in black) has to tell Padro De Cordoba, far right, and fellow bad guy Ray Bennett in the Hoppy film, *Range War* (1939). Behind Boyd at far left is Britt Wood as Hoppy's sidekick, Speedy MacGinnis.

William Boyd as Hopalong Cassidy, dressed in black, gets the drop on bad guys Ray Bennett as Stokey and Eddie Dean, far right, as Pete, in *Range War* (1939). At Boyd's right is Britt Wood as Speedy MacGinnis, one of Hoppy's sidekicks.

Eddie playing one of the bad guys.

Cast and crew photo for the Hopalong Cassidy film *Range War* (1939). Eddie Dean is pictured at front left under the film camera. Seated in the middle with hat off is William Boyd as Hoppy, seated to his right is producer Harry "Pop" Sheran, seated at Boyd's left is Russell Hayden. Monte Montana is standing in the fourth row, middle, wearing dark shirt with hat off.

Eddie and Dearest with Dearest's sister and brother-in-law, Lawrence and
Fern Wirth, posing with Tex Ritter on the movie set in June 1940.
The Wirth's were on their honeymoon.

Tex Ritter overpowers Eddie Dean as Bart, the henchman, in the Tex
Ritter film *The Golden Trail* (1940).

Eddie as Bart, the henchman, seems to have the drop on Tex Ritter from the Tex Ritter film *The Golden Trail* (1940).

Movie poster for the Tex Ritter film, *Rollin' Home to Texas* (1940).
Eddie is given billing credit in the film and on the poster. He plays
himself as the sheriff who helps Tex catch the bad guys. Eddie is also
given a singing spot in the movie. *Rollin' Home to Texas* was the second
of two Tex Ritter films in which Eddie appeared.

Above: Tex Ritter joins in some musical merrymaking with Cal Shrum and his Rhythm Rangers from the 1940 film, *Rollin' Home to Texas*. Shrum is behind Ritter's right shoulder, while Hal Blair, standing to Ritter's right wearing the black hat, is playing the mandolin. Eddie and Blair met during the filming and would form a long-standing musical partnership.

Below: Eddie fighting for control of the gun with bad guy Dan White from the Ken Maynard film, *Harmony Trail* (1944). Eddie was featured singing three songs in that movie.

Eddie Dean posing for a publicity photo in the early 1940s.

Another Eddie Dean cowboy still from the early 1940s.

Eddie Dean a-pickin'-and-a-grinin' in
another publicity still from the early 1940s.

Eddie (standing second from right) in a non-starring role in a scene from the 1942 PRC film, *Rolling Down the Great Divide*. Also pictured standing is Rex Lease, Charles King, and Glenn Strange, while Lee "Lone Ranger" Powell and Charles "Slim" Whitaker try to get the drop on them. The film was part of "The Frontier Marshal" series.

Eddie walking behind Gene
Autry in early 1942 during a
candid moment while on
the streets of Chicago.

Eddie (second from left), with brother Jimmie (on Eddie's left) and
Dick Reinhart (on Eddie's right) along with Horace Murphy with
Technical Sergeant Gene Autry during a broadcast of *The Sergeant
Gene Autry Show* on radio.

Eddie, at left, along with Johnny Bond, middle, and Jimmie Dean, far right, as members of the Gene Autry Trio having a light moment with Technical Sergeant Gene Autry prior to a radio broadcast from Luke Field in Phoenix, Arizona. Standing in the center playing the fiddle is Autry's long-time musical director, Carl Cotner.

The Gene Autry Trio in 1942. (L-R)
Jimmie Dean, Johnny Bond, Eddie Dean.

Poppa James Glosup, center, visits with Jimmie, left, and Eddie, right, in Los Angeles in 1943 while his two sons were members of the Gene Autry *Melody Ranch* Trio.

Judy Canova, pictured here, known as "America's Wacky, Wistful, Wonderful Scatterbrain," hosted her own radio show for twelve years beginning in 1943. Eddie was a cast member and featured vocalist on *The Judy Canova Show* during the program's first year.

Eddie shares a light-hearted moment with cast members Ruby Dandridge and Ken Niles during a break on *The Judy Canova Show* in late 1943. Eddie was the show's featured vocalist while Dandridge played Geranium, Canova's sassy and vivacious domestic, and Niles was the show's announcer.

Eddie was the catalyst in bringing hit makers Les Paul and Mary Ford
together professionally and personally. Paul would always
refer to Eddie as "Mr. Cupid."

Above: Jimmie Dean (left) with Wesley Tuttle, Paul Sells and Johnny Bond as "The Red River Valley Boys" from a scene from *Arizona Trail*, a Tex Ritter film from 1943.

Below: Jimmie Dean (center) with Wesley Tuttle and Merle Travis as "The Trail Riders."

Publicity photo of Jimmie Dean in cowboy duds while holding his guitar.

Above: Jimmie Dean, center, as a member of Foy Willing and the
Riders of the Purple Sage, with Foy Willing, left, and Al Sloey, right,
at the 443rd Army Air Force Unit, Ontario Army Air Field, Ontario, CA, circa 1944.

Below: Eddie on the Bel-Tone Records label from 1945.

9

Silver Screen Cowboy, Take One

Movie studio publicity would have liked fans to believe that Eddie Dean got signed on to do his own Western film series because moviegoers vigorously clamored to see more of his rugged good looks, to hear more of his magnificent singing voice, or to watch his "natural" acting abilities in starring roles. It's the type of romanticized fodder that made Hollywood the "Land of Make Believe."

In truth, Eddie became a cowboy star because he possessed exclusive rights to a color film process called Cinecolor. That is the only reason he got his break at Western star-status. Nothing more, nothing less. Period.

The story is not a glamorous testament to him, but sometimes one has to make the breaks that are given to him, and Eddie responded to such an opportunity by running with it for all it was worth. He waited patiently too long for that moment. It was about *carpé diem* – seizing the day – and seize it he did.

Cinecolor was an early subtractive color-model, two-color film process invented in 1932 by English-born cinematographer William T. Crespinel (1890–1987).

Unlike the Technicolor two-color processes that photographed both color elements on the same piece of black and white negative, Cinecolor used two films in "bi-pack," meaning the photographer would load a standard camera with two films, one orthochromatic and dyed red, and another panchromatic strip behind it. Color light would expose the cyan (greenish-blue) record on the ortho stock, which also acted as a filter, exposing only red light to the panchromatic film stock.[1]

In the laboratory, the negatives were processed on duplitized film and each emulsion was sensitized and/or filtered to record its appropriate portion of the color spectrum, red or cyan. While Cinecolor could produce vibrant reds, oranges, blues, browns and flesh tones, its renderings of other colors such as bright greens (rendered dark green) and purples (rendered a sort of dark magenta) were muted.

Although limited in tone by comparison, Cinecolor's chief advantages over Technicolor were that color rushes were available within 24 hours and the process cost only 25 percent more than black-and-white photography (the price grew cheaper as larger amounts of Cinecolor film stock were bought), and could be used in modified black-and-white cameras.[2]

Before 1945, Cinecolor was used almost exclusively for short films. From 1932 to 1935, Cinecolor was used in at least twenty-two cartoons including Max Fleischer cartoons featuring Betty Boop, two *Merry Melodies* from Warner Bros., and a pair of MGM's *Happy Harmonies* cartoons.

Low-budget companies such as Monogram, Producers Releasing Corporation, and Screen Guild Productions were Cinecolor's chief employers. Most features made in Cinecolor were Westerns, because the primary colors in those films were blues, browns and reds. While the color recording capability of Cinecolor was not accurate, it was, nonetheless, realistic looking.

While Eddie was in his final few months as a regular on *The Judy Canova Show*, Crespinel brought Cinecolor to Eddie's attention. Crespinel owned and operated a small processing/editing studio across the street where Eddie lived in Burbank. He knew of Eddie and liked his singing. Crespinel had only done commercials and shorts in Cinecolor and was unsuccessful at getting major studios interested in his process, so he pitched Eddie the following proposition: He'd give Eddie an exclusive on Cinecolor for a year if Eddie would sell a series of Westerns in color to the studios.

Eddie went to Monogram, but they turned him down, as did Paramount and Republic.

"People knew me at Republic and they weren't interested," Eddie said.

At the suggestion of Pete Canova, Eddie approached Producers Releasing Corporation, and they accepted the series. Producers Releasing Corporation was one of the low-end Hollywood film studios on "Poverty Row" from the late 1930s to the mid-1940s.

"Poverty Row" was a slang term used in Hollywood from the late silent period through the mid-1950s to refer to a variety of small and mostly short-lived B-movie studios. While many of them were on or near today's Gower Street in Hollywood, the term did not necessarily refer to any specific physical location but was instead a kind of figurative catch-all for low-budget films produced by these lesser tier studios.[3]

In comparison with the Big Five major studios of Metro-Goldwyn-Mayer (MGM), Paramount Pictures, Twentieth Century-Fox, Warner Bros., and RKO Pictures, and the Little Three majors of United Artists, Columbia Pictures, and Universal Studios, the Top Four Poverty Row studios ranked as follows: Grand National (which operated from 1936 to 1939), Republic Pictures, Monogram Pictures, and Producers Releasing Corporation (PRC).

A few of the films made through Producers Releasing Corporation or PRC, as it was commonly known, had gained a respectable reputation over the years, but the majority of its output was routine. The company was substantial enough to not only produce but distribute its own product and some imports from the United Kingdom, and operated its own studio facility, the complex used by the defunct Grand National Films, Inc.[4]

Most of the movies PRC made were Westerns, action melodramas, and horror movies, and each took about a week or so to shoot. Typical PRC efforts included *The Devil Bat* with Bela Lugosi and jungle and Western thrillers with Larry "Buster" Crabbe.

PRC was purchased by Pathé Industries, though the only noticeable change was of the name of the company's production arm to PRC Pictures,

Inc. The company otherwise continued to flourish within its own element until after World War II, due in large part to Eddie making his series of singing cowboy Westerns in Cinecolor, the first Western *series* to be filmed in color.

The distribution arm of the company was absorbed in the formation of Eagle-Lion Films, Inc. in 1946, and the production arm (and, therewith, the entire company) followed shortly thereafter in 1947.

During its existence, PRC released 179 feature films and never spent over $100,000 per film.[5]

Just about the time Eddie pitched the idea of Cinecolor to PRC, he happened to bump into producer and director Robert Emmett Tansey during a break from rehearsals on *The Judy Canova Show*. Tansey was exiting the same studio building on Vine Street in Hollywood from a business appointment.

"You're just the guy I'm looking for!" Eddie said to Tansey.

"I am? What do you want? What have you got?" the producer replied.

"Well, I want to do a series of Western pictures," Eddie said.

"Aw, come on, Eddie you know I've been trying to sell you out here for the past five years," Tansey said. "They just won't buy you."

"They're going to buy me now!"

"Why is that?" Tansey queried.

"I've got a color process, that's why," Eddie said.

"You have?" Tansey asked, almost disbelieving what he had just heard. "Let's talk about this some more."

"Tansey and I met the next day and worked out the details," Eddie said. "I actually hired him as my producer!"

Robert Emmett Tansey had a long history in motion pictures, first as an actor in silent films during the 1920s and then as director and producer of Western films at Lone Star, Republic, Grand National, and Monogram. The forty-eight-year-old Brooklyn-born movie maker had worked twice with Eddie as director, first in Ken Maynard's *Harmony Trail* and then in Bob Steele's *Wildfire*.

For some unexplainable reason, Tansey utilized a variety of names during a sound film career that lasted about twenty-five years. He was credited on film as Robert Emmett Tansey, Robert Tansey, Bob Tansey, Robert Emmett, Al Lane, and Bobby Lane.[6]

Tansey was president of Action Pictures, Inc., a small independent film company. He signed on to PRC, producing and directing nine of Eddie's Westerns before passing away in June 1951, at age fifty-three.

"Tansey was a fabulous director," Eddie said. "He had a fabulous mind."

Tansey brought Frances Kavanaugh on board for all the original screen play duties. Known affectionately as "The Cowgirl of the Typewriter," Kavanaugh, a native Texan, grew up around ranching. She was one of the few women who wrote screenplays for B-Westerns in the 1940s and early 1950s.

In 1940, she moved to Los Angeles with her parents. She attended a drama workshop when, for fun, she began writing two-person dialogue sketches for her fellow acting students. Her sketches intrigued Tansey, a workshop visitor, who offered her a job with his production company on the Monogram lot.

Kavanaugh began by polishing dialogue on scripts in an office that adjoined Tansey's office. Not liking how many of the scripts were originally written, she rewrote them, much to Tansey's approval, who hired her to be his script writer.

Between 1941 and 1951, Kavanaugh wrote more than thirty Western scripts for cowboy stars other than Eddie including Tom Keene, Bob Steele, Jimmy Wakely, Ken Maynard, and Duncan Renaldo.

(1) *Song of Old Wyoming* (1945)

Everything was in place by August 1945, when filming began at Corriganville in Simi Valley, CA, on *Song of Old Wyoming*, Eddie's first picture for PRC. Eddie's contract stipulated that he was to do eight pictures a year for three years. With a budget of $36,000, the movie was completed within a tight ten-day production schedule.

"All was done at a pretty hectic pace," Eddie recalled. "It was all about the budget, the budget. Things moved so quickly that sometimes I didn't receive any advance notice of knowing my lines. The color process and everything to shoot it took ten days instead of six days. PRC as well as other film companies didn't want to spend that much on a Western picture, but in the end the movie was profitable."

Color Westerns weren't anything new. There were a number of color films that were made during these years, most notably, *Wildfire*, in which Eddie co-starred. What made Eddie's color movies so unique was that his was the first *series* of B-Westerns filmed in color.

As director of color supervision, Crispenel was also a regular face on the set whenever the cameras rolled as he had final approval whenever his process was used in a movie.

Co-starring with Eddie on this break-through film were Emmett Lynn as Eddie's sidekick, "Uncle Ezra," Sarah Padden as "Kate 'Ma' Conway," Al La Rue as the "Cheyenne Kid," Jennifer Holt, daughter of actor Jack Holt and sister of cowboy star Tim Holt, as "Vicky," Ian Keith as "Lee Landow," Robert Barron as "Jesse Dixon," Gene Alsace as henchman "Ringo," and Horace Murphy portraying editor "Timothy Meeks."

Kate "Ma" Conway, owner of a cattle ranch and publisher of the *Laramie Bulletin*, wages an up-hill battle to have Wyoming join the Union. She refuses to be intimidated by corrupt politician Lee Landow and crooked banker Jesse Dixon who have teamed up to fight her.

Eddie is the Conway Ranch foreman who is reluctant to use his guns because of an incident in which a man was killed. Eddie and ranch hand Uncle Ezra lead the Conway cattle drive to market but is blocked by Dixon henchmen, led by Ringo. A fight ensues and Eddie is saved by the quick trigger hand of the Cheyenne Kid, a notorious outlaw. Vicky, whom Ma has raised as her daughter, admires Cheyenne's courage to the chagrin of Eddie, who is in love with her.

Cheyenne, on his way to a job in Laramie, turns down Ma Conway's offer for work but when he gets to Laramie he finds he has been hired by Landow and Dixon to ruin Ma's cattle business. In order to carry out the plan, he accepts Ma's ranch-job offer. Accidents quickly begin and Eddie suspects Cheyenne but Ma refuses to listen to his warnings, as she has become fond of the young outlaw.

Eddie subsequently learns that Cheyenne is really Ma's long-lost son, missing from twenty-five years past in an attack by renegade white men, but Ma does not know this. Cheyenne begins to regret his deeds and turns against the gang leaders and helps Eddie to save the day.

While Kavanaugh's script gave birth to a new leading singing cowboy star in Eddie, the film also introduced movie goers to a new face riding the Western trails. At Tansey's suggestion, Kavanaugh wrote a bullwhip into the script for the Cheyenne character played by La Rue, who physically resembled A-List actor Humphrey Bogart.

La Rue looked so much like Bogart that Sarah Padden asked if the two were related. La Rue said he didn't think so. After a long pause studying the young actor's face, she asked, "Did your mother ever meet Humphrey Bogart?"[7]

The Cheyenne character caught on with the young Saturday matinee audiences and after a spate of fan mail, the unknown supporting player soon began starring in his own Westerns as the whip-wielding, black-outfitted "Lash" La Rue. La Rue had such exceptional skill with the bullwhip that he taught Harrison Ford how how to use a bullwhip in the Indiana Jones movies.

"Eddie had a very beautiful voice," Kavanaugh was quoted as saying. "He was very good in (the movies that he made). We all really enjoyed Eddie because, we thought of all the singing cowboys, he had the greatest voice. He was a very good actor for the roles he played. Some writers have said he wasn't known for being a great actor, but that isn't true. He played his part. I can't understand reviewers who don't understand the underlying motive. They weren't suppose to be Westerns like Gary Cooper did, they were entirely different pictures . . . in the context of the times and for whom they were made. He was a devoted family man. He lived the part he played. He was kind, sweet, gentle, and stood up for what was right."[8]

Before passing away in February 2009 at age ninety-three, Kavanaugh wrote eight screenplays for Eddie's pictures. Remaining films include *Ro-*

mance of the West, The Caravan Trail, Colorado Serenade, Wild West, Driftin' River, Tumbleweed Trail, and *Stars Over Texas.*

Eddie's saddle pal in *Song of Old Wyoming* was Iowa-native Emmett Lynn, an old grubby prospector-type who also supplied the comic relief in a number of Republic Westerns through the forties and early fifties. He made several television appearances from 1949 until his death, especially in Westerns. He was featured in nine episodes of *The Lone Ranger* during the final decade of his life. He also appeared with the Three Stooges in *The Yokes on Me* (1944). His last two films were *A Man Called Peter* (1955) and *The Ten Commandments* (1956). He appeared in over 140 films between 1940 and 1956 before dying of a heart attack two years later.[9]

Lynn was Eddie's sidekick in his first three films. Lynn wanted to leave the series earlier due to a personality dispute with Tansey, but stayed on as a favor to Eddie.

"I told Emmett that he wasn't walking out on the studio, that he was walking out on me," Eddie recalled. "He said, 'Eddie, I'll stay for you until until you find somebody else.'"

Like Gene Autry, Eddie was a prolific composer. Eddie was able to incorporate his own songs in about 80 percent of his films. It was more cost-effective for the studio to do so. Not only did it cost the studio less money to shoot a scene doing a close up of Eddie singing a song than it would be to do a chase scene or a fight scene, it also had to do with the cost of musical material used in the films.

"I didn't charge the studio that much on most of the songs I wrote, so it was to my interest not to break the budget of the picture!" Eddie said. "I didn't overcharge for a lot of the songs so we could keep things going, to keep things in balance."

Using other people's material in a picture could be a pricey proposition, as was the case when the writers of "Along The Navajo Trail" (Dick Charles, Larry Markes, and Edgar DeLange) came to Eddie to pitch him the song to do in one of his pictures.

"They wanted like $2,400 for the song, and the studio just couldn't see spending, taking out of the budget, that kind of money for a song," Eddie said. "The writers said if we didn't buy it, they'd give it to Roy Rogers. Republic Pictures wanted it, but these writers wanted me to do the song. Well, the studio didn't buy it, so Roy got the break on the song."

In *Song of Old Wyoming*, Eddie sings the title track of "Hills of Old Wyoming," a Ralph Ranger and Leo Robin offering. Eddie then follows up with "My Herding Song," a piece he worked out with Milt Mabie, from "The Westerners," during both their days at WLS and *The National Barn Dance*. Finally, Eddie sings the romantic "Wild Prairie Rose," a piece he and Carl Hoefle composed.

It was customary that all the movie singing cowboys in their films shared star billing with their horses. Their horses were an intricate part of their hero persona, and in many instances heroes in their own right. You couldn't have one without the other, or so it seemed. In the opening credits of a Roy Rogers movie, for example, it was always "Roy Rogers and Trigger (The Smartest Horse in the Movies)" before co-stars such as Dale Evans and Gabby Hayes were even mentioned. It was the same with "Gene Autry and Champion (World's Wonder Horse)," or "Tex Ritter and "White Flash," or "Rex Allen (The Arizona Cowboy) and Koko (The Miracle Horse of the Movies)."

But Eddie was a different breed of singing cowboy. While he rode handsome looking steeds, the horses he rode (there were four) did not detract from himself as the main character in his films. Eddie commented in a later interview that he kept changing mounts so he would never be upstaged by his horse.

Eddie's first mount, a paint named "War Paint," trained by famous rodeo performer, Johnny Agee, went uncredited in his first three films. Agee was Tom Mix's former horse trainer, known to be the best in the business.

After *Song of Old Wyoming* was released on October 12, 1945, the film was well-received by moviegoers and PRC had a hot new prospect even though Eddie was thirty-eight years old when he started his series. He was about a dozen years older than when his contemporaries started. Rogers was twenty-five years old when he signed on with Republic. Autry was twenty-eight. Ritter was thirty-one.

In 1946, Eddie fulfilled his contractual duty to make eight pictures. As soon a film was "in-the-can," he went on the road to promote his latest film.

"I had brokers back East to book our shows in theaters and such to promote my films," Eddie said. "That's where I made most of money. I was only making about $2,500 per film. Even though my films were in color, I had to really work to get this series going. I told the studio that I would go on the road, and I got Del Wagner, a former film distributor, to book me. He'd never booked anybody like me before, but he had contacts with all the theaters throughout the country.

"We'd do three shows per venue guaranteed and I'd sometimes do as high as seven shows. If I had to do extra shows I got 50 percent of the house. It was stipulated in my contract with PRC that I be given three weeks' notice of the starting day of my next picture. I had that done because I'd be on the road and I'd have dates booked and if the studio suddenly called me back to do a picture, I'd have to cancel out. This would be unfair to the theaters, so the studio agreed to that."

(2) *Romance of the West* (1946)

Eddie's second film, *Romance of the West*, also filmed in Cinecolor, showed moviegoers something new and different in a hero: a cowboy who cried. That display of emotion was not suppose to be part of the Western hero's persona, but Eddie made his character believable, more human-like.

Filmed at both Corriganville in Simi Valley and next door at Iverson Ranch in Chatsworth, Eddie's co-stars were Emmett Lynn as "Ezra," Joan Barton as "Melodie," Forrest Taylor as "Father Sullivan," Robert McKenzie as "Lem Matthews," Jerry Jerome as "Duke Morris," Stanley Price as "Jim Lockwood," Chief Thundercloud (Victor Daniels) as "Chief Eagle Feather," Don Reynolds as "Little Brown Jug," Lottie Harrison as "Miss Twitchell," and Gene Alsace as "Chico" (unaccredited). Jay Silverheels, who would go on to greater fame a few years later as Tonto, the Lone Ranger's faithful Indian companion, appears in this film in an unaccredited role as "Young Bear."

The Indians, led by Chief Eagle Feather, live peacefully in Antelope Valley and Eddie is the new Indian Agent. Everything seems fine until the town selectmen do not want the valley occupied by the Indians because it contains silver. So they hired outlaw Indians organized by a henchman named Chico to start trouble hoping that the U. S. Calvary will forcibly remove the Indians from the valley so they can claim it. But Father Sullivan and Eddie believe the Indians are being wronged even though they cannot convince anyone else.

The villain mercenaries kill an Indian family leaving an orphaned Indian boy whom Ezra, Eddie's bearded old sidekick, named "Little Brown Jug" and whom Eddie adopts with the help of Father Sullivan.

Little Brown Jug is shot dead during gun fighting when the mercenaries try to overtake "The Compound," the place where Father Sullivan ministers to the Indians. Learning that Little Brown Jug is dead, Eddie is sorrowful and cries. In his grief, he gains renewed inner strength to lead Ezra and friends to overcome the bad guys.

When *Romance of the West* was released on March 20, 1946, it proved to be another box office success.

In this film, Eddie sings three romantic ballads that were not his own but showcased his beautiful baritone voice outside of a Country Western genre: "Indian Trail" by J. S. Zamenick, "Ridin' the Trail to Dreamland," by Sam Franklin, and a Bob Nolan, Bernard Barnes, and Carl Winge composition, "Love Song of the Waterfall."

When Eddie toured with his live shows to help promote his pictures, "Love Song of the Waterfall" was one of his most requested numbers.

"I knew it was a great song because people always asked me to sing it," Eddie said.

A few years later when Eddie was signed on to Capitol Records, he wanted to record "Love Song of the Waterfall" as part of a theme album of songs from his pictures. Ken Nelson, Capitol's A&R man, refused to do it because Eddie was categorized as a Country Western singer, and the song did not fit the perimeters of a Country Western song. Eddie proved over the years that he could sing songs such as "Love Song of the Waterfall" just as well or even better than any pop singer. So what did they do with the song? They gave it to Jimmy Wakely to record!

"I don't blame Jimmy at all because he's a good friend of mine," Eddie said. "He recognized that it was a good song, so I highly respect him! It's just that the Capitol people at the time had me boxed in a certain category and there wasn't a whole lot I could do about it."

Forrest Taylor, who played "Father Sullivan" in *Romance of West*, had an extensive career in films, often vacillating between playing roles of good guys such as a priest, a judge, an Army cavalry officer, and "brains heavy" roles. He appeared in four of Eddie's early films playing a priest, an honest judge, a military officer, and a crooked judge.

Born in 1883, in Bloomington, IL, Taylor was a stage veteran by the time he started appearing in silent films in 1915. After military service in World War I, Taylor returned to films. During the 1930s, he gained notoriety as a supporting player in B-Westerns and several cliffhanger serials.[10]

Taylor retired in 1963. Two years later, he died of natural causes in Garden Grove, CA, at the age of eighty-one.

(3) *The Caravan Trail* (1946)

Shortly after the release of *Romance of the West*, Eddie's third Cinecolor production was in the works with *The Caravan Trail*. Filmed at Iverson Ranch in Chatsworth, CA, Al La Rue rejoins Eddie in this action packed adventure as "Cherokee." Other support cast members include Emmett Lynn as "Ezra," Jean Carlin as "Paula Bristol," Robert Malcolm as "Jim Bristol," Charles King as "Reno," Robert Barron as "Joe King," Forrest Taylor as "Judge Silas Black," Bob Duncan as "Poker Face," Jack O'Shea as one of the "killers," and Terry Frost as "Bart Barton."

Eddie and Ezra lead a caravan of settlers to new homestead land. When they arrive at their destination, the homesteaders discover that the land is controlled by Joe King, who also controls the town. King is willing to rent out the land to the new settlers while demanding 50 percent of the profits on whatever the homesteaders make. Eddie and Ezra also thwart a robbery attempt for food on the homesteaders by Cherokee and his two pals. When Eddie arrives in town he finds that his good friend the marshal has been murdered. Eddie is appointed marshal by King's crony judge thinking that Eddie will be a token lawman acting on the whim of King. When Eddie catches Cherokee and his pals robbing the bank, he gives them a chance to go straight by making them his deputies. Still outnumbered against King and his henchmen, things get worse when one of the new deputies becomes a double-crosser. Using their wits, Eddie, Ezra, Cherokee and Reno team up together to defeat the bad guys.

The Caravan Trail's color supervision was under the direction of Arthur Phelps. No explanation was given as to why Crispenel wasn't overseeing color supervision for this film. Eddie sings the soothing and flowing "Wagon Wheels" by Billy Hill and Peter DeRose, "Crazy Cowboy Song," a novelty collaboration between Eddie and Johnny Bond, and "You're Too Pretty To Be Lonesome," a lovely ballad that was a team effort between Eddie, Lewis Hersher, and Lew Porter.

Seeing how successful Eddie's first three films fared, Monogram Pictures approached Eddie and PRC to buy his Western series and the Cinecolor process.

"I wasn't going to let them have it," Eddie said. "While Monogram was better financed than PRC, I refused. Monogram originally turned my offer down. Why would I let them have it now when they didn't have faith in me in the first place?"[11]

Charlie King is probably the most-recognized villains in B-Westerns. Born in 1895 in Texas, King played henchman roles early in career, but later graduated to be the boss of outlaw gangs.

King made about three hundred fifty sound films between 1935-1949, two hundred sixty-four Westerns and thirty-eight serials.[12] King only appeared in two of Eddie's films, as "Reno," the bumbling outlaw turned deputy in *The Caravan Trail,* and in an unaccredited role as "Muscles," a ranch hand in *Colorado Serenade.* Both roles were comic in nature and did not reflect the "nastiness" that was reflective of King's persona as the lead bad guy in other films. Eddie stated that King was his favorite villain.[13]

King had an ongoing battle with alcoholism and died from cirrhosis of the liver.[14]

(4) *Colorado Serenade* (1946)

Eddie's fourth Cinecolor flick for PRC was *Colorado Serenade*, another Frances Kavanaugh original screenplay, which introduced moviegoers to three new faces. The first was Roscoe Ates, Eddie's new comic sidekick, who played the stuttering "Soapy Jones," Emmett Lynn's replacement.

The second new face(s) was Eddie's back up vocal group, The Sunshine Boys. The last new face was the handsome veteran stunt man David Sharpe, who made his first major co-starring "acting" appearance in color.

Born in 1895, in the rural hamlet of Grange, Mississippi, Roscoe Ates was a distinguished military veteran in both World War I and II. He was a stutter until he was eighteen. He was able to overcome this debilitation by talking in front of a mirror. He attended the Music Conservatory in Warren, Ohio, and became an accomplished violinist. In between wars, he gave up a violin career to tour the vaudeville circuit using his violin and occasional stuttering as part of his comedy "schtick."

By the time Ates teamed up with Eddie, he had a number of movie credits under his belt, mostly various B-Westerns, and had a somewhat brief but memorable moment in the 1939 epic film, *Gone with the Wind*, where he plays a convalescing Confederate soldier. While scratching his back on a tent pole, he utters the line, "These *animules* is driving me crazy!"

While Ates' stuttering was meant to accent humor in a particular scene, many educational groups, such as the National Parents-Teachers Association (PTA), objected to his prolific use of the practice and asked him to stop.[15]

"I only stuttered occasionally in pictures after that," Ates was quoted as saying in an interview.[16]

Ates was so popular that he remained Eddie's sidekick for the balance of Eddie's fifteen films. With the advent of television, Ates rejoined Eddie in 1950 on the short-lived thirty-minute live television series, *The Marshall of Gunsight Pass*.

Ates worked throughout the 1950s on various television programs, mostly Westerns, before succumbing to lung cancer in 1962 at age sixty-seven.[17]

The Sunshine Boys were the first singing group to be in Eddie's films at PRC. The group started in 1938 as "The Red River Rangers" in Charleston, West Virginia, by bassist Milton "Ace" Richman (born August 14, 1916, death unknown), and the Smith Brothers – guitarist A. L. "Smitty" Smith and fiddler J. O. "Tennessee" Smith.[18]

They were offered $15 per week to come to Macon, Georgia and sing on a radio station. They were asked to be part of radio station WSB's *Barn Dance* program in Atlanta in the early 1940s, where they met Ed Wallace (born February 2, 1924) who played piano and accordion, and who attended Georgia Tech University. Radio station management wanted the "Rangers" to also do Gospel quartet music (which they didn't know anything about). So, Richman asked Wallace to help them do the Gospel quartet style, which he did between classes at George Tech.

When performing Country Western music, the group was known as "The Red River Rangers." When the station went to Gospel time they put down their instruments and were "The Sunshine Boys." They also did a stint as "The Light Crust Doughboys" at WSB, as they were filling three roles.[19]

During the war years, the group would appear at War Bond rallies around Atlanta with whichever celebrity was in town at the time. After Wallace graduated from Georgia Tech with an engineering degree, he took his physical to join the Army. One officer recognized him in line and asked Wallace if he was still doing shows at WSB and War Bond rallies. Wallace said he was. The officer told Wallace that he was doing more good in that role than if he were drafted. So, Wallace rejoined the group.

In an undated interview, Ed Wallace recounts how The Sunshine Boys got the nod to be in Eddie's pictures: "Eddie was a nice guy. In early June 1946, he did a Cliffie Stone radio show with "Tennessee" Ernie Ford, and I just happened to have the radio on. Eddie mentioned that he was going to begin a new picture in a week-and-a-half and he needed a group to sing in it. Merle Travis was on the show at the time and said his group could do it.

"Eddie said, 'No, I need a group with a sound like the Sons of the Pioneers.' I called him up and put our group out there. He invited us to his house to give us a listen. While we were there, Tennessee Smith picked up his fiddled and started playing. 'Do y'all play instruments?' he asked. When we said we did, he said, 'Let's hear some Western stuff.'

"When we finished, he said, 'That's exactly what I'm looking for.' He introduced us to Robert Tansey, the producer, and we worked the rest of 1946 with Eddie, making five pictures. Eddie was a great singer, but he was too smooth to really hit it big. Ken Curtis was like that, too. He just didn't look the part of a hard-riding cowboy. It's just one of those things."[20]

The Sunshine Boys also appeared in four other of Eddie's productions: *Driftin' River*, *Tumbleweed Trail*, *Stars Over Texas*, and *Wild Country*.

After departing from making films with Eddie, The Sunshine Boys also appeared in other B-Westerns. By the mid-1950s, they were working with a young Elvis Presley. Because of their smooth,flawless style, they recorded a number of Gospel pieces and became more synonymous with that genre.

David Sharpe was called the "Crown Prince of Daredevils" and ranks alongside Yakima Canutt as one of Hollywood's all-time greatest stuntmen. He appeared in more than 5,000 films over six decades, although most were unaccredited.[21]

Born in 1910, Sharpe won the U.S. National Tumbling Championship in 1925 and 1926. He began his film career as a child actor in the 1920s. Eventually he became the "Ramrod" (stunt co-coordinator) for Republic Pictures from 1939 until mid-1942, when Sharpe joined the Army Air Corps.

Colorado Serenade was Sharpe's first major co-starring role in a color adult B-Western, and what damage he and Eddie caused in the bunkhouse scene when they took to fisticuffs! It looked like a cyclone hit the set! Sharpe was also showcased doing some unbelievable high-action stunt work toward the end of picture in a major brawl scene in the saloon, joining Eddie against Duke Dillon's men.

Sharpe was inducted into the Stuntman's Hall of Fame in 1980 before succumbing Lou Gehrig's disease later that same year.

There was actually a fourth "character" whose presence in the film is an enigma. It's Eddie's horse. Eddie is riding a palomino and the horse is unidentified in the film credits. There was some speculation that the steed may have been "Falcon," previously ridden by Buster Crabbe in his PRC Billy the Kid/Billy Carson series. No one seems to know who this mystery horse was.

"No one back then didn't expect for this stuff to be analyzed as much as a lot of other people are doing 66-plus years later," said Boyd Magers. "They were turning these movies out for the Saturday matinee crowd and they didn't think that a seven or ten-year-old kid was going to notice that or even care."[22]

Helping Eddie to bring *Colorado Serenade* to life were Roscoe Ates as "Soapy Jones," David Sharpe as "Nevada," Mary Kenyon as "Sherry Lynn," Forrest Taylor as "Judge Roy Hilton," Dennis Moore as "Duke Dillon," Abigail Adams as "Lola," Duke Dillon's girl, Warner Richmond as "Dad Dillon," Lee Bennett as "Parson Trimble" (in real life Bennett was the son of William T. Crispinel), Robert McKenzie as "Colonel Blake, Town Manager," Bob Duncan, as "Ringo," a Dillon henchman, Charles King, as "Muscles," a cowhand in an unaccredited role, and The Sunshine Boys (Eddie Wallace, M.H. "Ace" Richmond, A. L. "Smitty" Smith, and J. O. "Tennessee" Smith) in unaccredited roles.

Eddie and Soapy foil an attempted stagecoach holdup designed to murder Circuit Judge Hilton, bound for Rawhide to restore law and order. The Judge and the other passenger, Parson Trimble, decide to put up at the ranch owned by Sherry Lynn, Eddie's sweetheart, and her mother Ma Lynn. They are waylaid again, but the outlaws are driven off, and Nevada, an undercover man for the Judge, allows one of captured men to escape so he can follow him to the gang hideout. The Judge also deputizes Eddie. Nevada gets in with the gang as an undercover agent for Judge Hilton, led by Duke and Dad Dillon, and is given the assignment to kill the Judge, whose first act in Rawhide was to close Duke's saloon and fire the city manager, Colonel Blake, a hireling of the Dillon's. Eddie, Nevada, and Soapy find evidence at the Dillon mine that they have been stealing government gold shipments. Colonel Blake is preparing to skip town and reveals to Sherry and saloon girl Lola, Duke's girlfriend, that Duke is really the son of Judge Hilton, kidnapped in infancy by Dad Dillon as an act of revenge.

The Dillon's and Eddie and his men are in a gunfight outside of the Palace Saloon when Judge Hilton, having learned that Duke is his son, goes out on to the street to look for him. Duke, not believing the story, is looking to kill the judge. Dad Dillon shoots Judge Hilton, not mortally wounding him. Duke and Dad shoot it out in which Duke is killed. Dad Dillon is killed by Eddie in gun play. Judge Hilton, sorrowful that he never got to have a relationship with his real son, is gratified knowing that Duke did the right thing by coming on the side of law before dying.

Selections that were sung by Eddie in *Colorado Serenade* were a schmaltzy version of "Home on the Range," and two romantic pieces that The Sunshine Boys provided color and shading on in "Ridin' to the Top of the Mountain," a collaborative effort between Eddie, Lew Hersher, and Lew Porter, and "Western Lullaby," a joint venture by Eddie and Pete Canova. Eddie, Roscoe Ates, Charlie King and an uncredited ranch hand join in together on the jovial "Ridin' Down to Rawhide," by Sam Armstrong.

Signing on as Eddie's musical director for his films beginning with *Colorado Serenade* was Karl Hajos, a two-time Academy Award nominee. Born in Austria-Hungry in 1889, Hajos was educated at the University of Budapest and the Academy of Music in Budapest before immigrating to the United States in 1924. He worked on stage musicals in New York before entering movies three years later. He was with Paramount Pictures for a number of years before turning to freelancing.

Hajos also worked as musical director on popular films including the 1935 Universal Pictures horror classic, *The Werewolf of London*, starring Henry Hull and Warner Oland, as well as Monogram's *Charlie Chan in the Secret Service* (1944), starring Sidney Toler.

Hajos was nominated for an Academy Award in the category for Best Music, Scoring of a Dramatic or Comedy Picture for *Summer Storm* (1944), starring Linda Darnell and George Sanders. The following year, he was nominated in the same category for his second Oscar for the comedy, *The Man Who Walked Alone*, starring Dave O'Brien and Kay Aldridge.[23]

Other Eddie Dean films that Hajos was associated with include *Wild West, Down Missouri Way, Driftin' River*, and *Stars Over Texas*.

Hajos died on February 1, 1950, in Los Angeles. He was sixty-one.

Bad guy Dennis Moore played the lead "heavy" in three of Eddie's films (*Colorado Serenade, Driftin' River*, and *The Tioga Kid*). Born Dennis Meadows in Ft. Worth, TX, in 1908, he went by the last name of Moore when he got into acting during the 1930s. His film career resume lists his experience as playing roles of the hero, second lead, sidekick, and villain. From 1932 to 1958, Moore was a stable fixture in Westerns.

There was a disturbing dark side to Moore's personality that was referenced in *See You Up There, Baby*, a book written by Linda Lee Wakely, daughter of singing cowboy star Jimmy Wakely.[24] Moore was selected, along with Lee "Lasses" White, to play sidekick roles in a Wakely series at Monogram. Moore's ego was such that he apparently felt it demeaning to play second lead to a singing cowboy.

On the night of August 29, 1945, during a drinking session with Foy Willing and some other lesser known Hollywood cowboys in one of Hollywood's watering holes, Moore was bemoaning his fate, when he drunkenly announced he was going out to Wakely's ranch to "kill that singing cowboy (S.O.B.)."

After midnight, Moore arrived at Wakely's home (7600 Lankershim Blvd.), called Wakely outside, and armed with a knife, stabbed Wakely in the head. The police arrived, took Moore into custody, but in court, Wakely refused to press charges, according to an article in the September 1, 1945, *Los Angeles Times*.

According to the book, the judge's words were, "My God, Mr. Wakely, this man tried to kill you and it could happen again. He should be put away."

Wakely still refused to press charges, and the judge ruled, "If Mr. Wakely won't have you jailed, then you will have to leave town for sixty days. If you come back to Los Angeles during that time, I will have you jailed."

John James replaced Moore as the third member of the star trio.

Moore played "El Azote" ("The Whip"), the whip-welding adversary to "Lash" La Rue in *King of the Bull Whip* (1950). The two are pitted against each together for a climatic whip fight at the end of the flick.

Throughout the 1950s, Moore found work in numerous television Westerns. Moore and his wife moved to Big Bear Lake and operated a gift shop for four years until he died of acute circulatory failure, rheumatic heart disease, and rheumatic fever on March 1, 1964.

Colorado Serenade was hailed by critics as one of the better Westerns filmed in Cinecolor.

(5) *Wild West* (1946)

Eddie's fifth picture was *Wild West*, and his fourth production of 1946. Produced and directed by Robert Emmett Tansey with color direction by William T. Crispinel (unaccredited), and original screenplay by Frances Kavanaugh, this was considered by many to be one of Eddie's better Western dramas.

The production once again co-starred Al La Rue this time as "Stormy Day" for his third and final appearance as a supporting character in Eddie's films before signing on to do his own series of PRC Westerns as "Lash" La Rue, the bullwhip-wielding cowboy hero who always dressed in black.

"Al La Rue made such an impression with moviegoers in the three Eddie Dean films he appeared in that at one point he was receiving more fan mail than Eddie was," said Boyd Magers. "It was just a matter of time before La Rue would star in his own series of Western films."[25]

Wild West also introduced fans to Flash, Eddie's new horse, which shared star billing with Eddie in the opening film credits. Flash was a black gelding marked with a white splotch on its nose and another white mark between its eyes, which Eddie saddled in eight of his PRC productions. Flash was bridled and harnessed in attractive yet classy silver sun-dial-type gear that accented its sleek, ebony body.

Rounding out the cast members in *Wild West* are Sarah Padden as "Carrie Bannister," Robert "Buzzy" Henry as "Skinny Bannister," Louise Currie as "Florabelle Bannister," Jean Carlin as "Mollie Bannister," Lee Bennett, as " Bill Butler," the telegraph engineer, Terry Frost as "Drake Dawson," Warner Richmond as "Judge Templeton," Lee Roberts as "Captain Rogers," Chief Yowlachie as "Chief Black Fox," Bob Duncan as "Rocky," a henchman, George Chesebro as "Commissioner" (unaccredited), and I. Stanford Jolley as a rustler (unaccredited).

Wild West is about a gang of thugs interfering with the building of the telegraph. Town boss Drake Dawson (Terry Frost) and a crooked lay judge (Warner Richmond) fear the coming of the telegraph will bring an end to their lawless activities in the town of Preston. Dawson's gang stirs up trouble among the local Indians, who are persuaded that the telegraph may mean the end of the buffalo. Dawson's henchmen are wantonly killing buffalo belonging to the Indians in order to bring about an uprising against the telegraph company.

Enter rangers Eddie, Soapy Jones, and Stormy Day (Al La Rue), who are persuaded back in harness to secure the prompt continuation of the building project. The trio of lawmen loosely resemble in scope their movie predecessors of "The Three Mesquiteers" or "The Range Busters." They work with Bill Butler, the telegraph engineer (Lee Bennett), to see that the job gets done.

Carrie Bannister (Sarah Padden), the widow of a slain ranger captain, persuades her friend Chief Black Fox (Chief Yowlachie) to help secure the telegraph rather than oppose its construction.

On their way to gather more information on the outlaws, Soapy and Skinny (Robert "Buzzy" Henry), Mrs. Bannister's young son, are ambushed by Dawson's men. Discovering an abandoned gun near a wounded Skinny, Soapy recognizes the weapon as belonging to the murdered Captain Bannister. When Eddie learns that Dawson himself is carrying a matching gun, Bannister's murderer has finally been found. The rangers arrive just in time to round up the gang and with peace finally restored, a recovered Skinny is made an honorary ranger.

There is also a subplot to this film between Eddie and La Rue vying for the romantic favors of Carrie Bannister's two daughters: Florabelle Bannister (Louise Currie), who clearly prefers Eddie, while La Rue settles for Mollie Bannister (Jean Carlin), her tomboy sister.

Eddie's musical offerings for *Wild West* included "Ride on a Tide of a Song," the romantic "I Can Tell By the Stars," and the pensive "Journey's End," all penned by Dorcas Cochran and Charles Rosoff; and the humorous "Elmer, the Knock-Kneed Cowboy," a collaborative effort between Eddie and Ruth and Louis Herscher.

Wild West would also be Eddie's final movie to be filmed in Cinecolor. PRC was always strapped for financial backing as Cinecolor pictures usually cost twice as much to make as opposed to a black and white picture. Originally, Eddie was signed by PRC to do three Cinecolor films on a "trial basis." When Eddie asked why he would only be signed to three color films, he said the response he received from studio executives was that he sings too smoothly and they considered him too high class for the people in the South where there were going to release his films. If he did well in those three pictures, fine. If he didn't, they would get someone else even though Eddie would still retain the rights to use the color process.

"I wasn't worried about, "Eddie said. "I was raised in the Bible Belt, so that's why I agreed to their terms. My first picture made so much money within the first six weeks of release that they called me in and signed me up for three years!"

Eddie made good on his first three color films and then some, adding a fourth and fifth for good measure. But what proved to be Eddie's "Waterloo" in regards to the continuation of the Cinecolor process for his Western pictures had to do with weather conditions.

The cost of production for *Wild West* ran afoul of rainy weather that forced players and technicians to stay with camera and equipment for twenty-one days, more than double the shooting time to make a movie. The final cost of production rocketed to nearly $80,000, which put PRC in a financial predicament.[26] It was then decided by studio execs to film the remaining Eddie Dean series in black and white.

Non-use of Cinecolor was a major disappoint for both Eddie and Robert Emmett Tansey, who "desperately" wanted to maintain color for Eddie's films.[27] PRC's new black and white policy for the remainder of Eddie's films was officially announced in the August 6, 1946, edition of *Daily Variety*, a film trade publication.

Two years later, *Wild West* was edited, shortened, and released in a black and white version called *Prairie Outlaws*. This truncated version has the dubious distinction of being the number eighteenth picture out of nineteen that was released in Eddie's PRC series of Westerns. *Prairie Outlaws* was released in 1948, presumably in order to cash in on the appearance of "Lash" La Rue, who by then had his own starring series. This version contains new footage of Eddie and Ates at the start of the film, the removal of two songs ("Ride on the Tide of a Song" and "Journey's End" were retained) and the romantic scenes with the sisters edited out.

Louise Currie, who played "Florabelle Bannister," Eddie's love interest in *West West*, was quoted in an interview as saying her association with Eddie was a pleasant, happy one.[28]

"(Eddie) was a very, very nice individual, and he had talent," Currie said in the article. "He could sing very well. *Wild West* was the only color feature I made and it was an enjoyable experience."

Down Missouri Way (1946)

Eddie's next PRC production took a pronounced detour from his Western films by driving head-on into a musical comedy entitled *Down Missouri Way*. Roscoe Ates is once again teamed up with Eddie in this low-budget piece. Eddie plays second lead in the film as "Mortimer," caretaker at an agricultural college for Shirley, the mule, and for Martha O'Driscoll who plays "Dr. Jane Colwell," who has been training Shirley as part of her scientific research. Eddie's character can best be described as one of an "enlightened but savvy country bumpkin" who has Shirley's and O'Driscoll's best interests at heart.

The beautiful Martha O'Driscoll was a veteran of about fifty films during her acting career including *Lil' Abner* (1940), *House of Dracula* (1945) with John Carradine playing Count Dracula, and *Carnegie Hall* (1947), her final film before retiring. She died in 1998 at age seventy-six.

Produced by Josef Berne, *Down Missouri Way* also stars John Carradine as "Thorndyke 'Thorny' P. Dunning, the movie's director, William Wright as "Mike Burton," the movie's producer, Roscoe Ates as "Pappy," Renee Godfrey as "Gloria Baxter," Mabel Todd as "Cindy," Eddie Craven as "Sam," Chester Clute as "Professor Shaw," Will Wright as "Professor Morris," Paul Scardon as "Professor Lewis," Earle Hodkins as a "Hillbilly scene actor," The Tailor Maids (Joline Westbrook, Marian Bartel, and Marilyn Myers), and The Notables, an all male singing group.

Dr. Jane Colwell, an associate professor at an agricultural college, thinks that a trained mule she has been working with needs a rest and takes it to her farm in Missouri's Ozark Mountains. Shirley's indubitable talents, however, are discovered by a movie company, whose producer, Mike Burton, sets out to win the affection of both Dr. Colwell and her obstinate animal, a feat accomplished much to the consternation of the company's star, Gloria Baxter.

An expected romantic confusion ensues, and three professors from the Midlands College Department of Agriculture descend on the movie location to put a halt to Shirley's promising screen career. But Mike Burton and his flamboyant director do their best to placate both the prominent faculty and their beast, and soon everyone is enjoying a typical Missouri hayride. After many complications, the mule is featured in the film, and Mike Burton wins the heart of Jane.

Eddie performs "There's a Rose That Grows in the Ozarks" and joins Mable Todd on the raucous "Monkey Business." Renee Godfrey and the Tailor Maids take care of "Big Town Gal" while leading lady Martha O'Driscoll warbles "I Never Knew That I Could Sing" and "I'm So in Love with You." The entire company, including John Carradine, goes on an old fashion hayride and sings the finale opus, "There's Nothing Like an Old Missouri Hayride."

Appearing in *Down Missouri Way* as one of the Tailor Maids was Marilyn Myers, who later became Marilyn Tuttle, the wife of Western artist Wesley Tuttle.

"Eddie was a really nice man, a wonderful singer and a great friend," Tuttle said in a telephone interview from her home in San Fernando, CA. "I've always enjoyed hearing him sing. I loved his stuff. Wesley and I did shows together with Eddie and traveled with he and his wife Dearest. They were wonderful people."

Although Tuttle couldn't recall anything specific about Eddie that took place during the week-long filming of *Down Missouri Way*, she did say that he was "always friendly, always nice, and that he was a good man. Wesley and I enjoyed him immensely."

However, Tuttle did recall a negative impressionable incident during the filming of the movie that involved actor John Carradine.

"The cast members had to sit on a hay wagon during the finale," Tuttle said. "Prior to the actual filming all Carradine did was tell dirty jokes. He was very crude and rather obnoxious. I don't know what else I could say about him."

These days Tuttle sits as a member of the Advisory Board of the Western Music Association, an organization that since 1988, encourages and supports the preservation, performance and composition of historic traditional and contemporary music and poetry of the West. Eddie was honored in the Western Music Association Hall of Fame in 1990, while Wesley Tuttle was so honored in 1997.

Down Missouri Way, with the attention focused on Shirley, the mule, may very well have been the catalyst that helped to launch Francis, the Talking Mule, series of films four years later starring Donald O'Connor and the distinctive off-camera voice of Chill Wills as Francis.

Released on August 15, 1946, *Down Missouri Way* caused little stir at the box office. However, the film did show Eddie's acting capabilities in a different light. He demonstrated versatility at his craft from being typecast as a rather dour-looking cowboy actor to someone who can do light comedy roles with integrity and authenticity while showcasing his ever-ingratiating smile.

While *Down Missouri Way* may have been a pleasant diversion for Eddie, he was eager to get back where he was most comfortable and where his fans expected to see him: riding tall in the saddle fighting the bad guys by resuming his series of Western flicks.

A press book page of *Song of Old Wyoming* from 1945,
Eddie Dean's first starring role in a series of westerns
that was contracted to be filmed in Cinecolor.

A small poster advertising Eddie Dean's first starring role, *Song of Old Wyoming*.

A lobby card advertising *Song of Old Wyoming*, Eddie Dean's first film in a starring role. Also pictured are (l-r) Sarah Padden, Emmett Lynn, Eddie, Jennifer Holt, and Al La Rue.

Above: A letterpress printer's movie block depicting Eddie Dean and
Jennifer Holt in *Song of Old Wyoming*.

Below: Veteran comic actor Emmett Lynn was Eddie's
sidekick Ezra, in his first three Cinecolor films.

A young-looking 38-year-old Eddie Dean in 1945
starring in his own series of westerns.

Eddie Dean with his first of four movie steeds,
War Paint, from 1945. Eddie rode War Paint in his first
three Cinecolor productions.

Eddie Dean and his mount, War Paint, study the script for the next scene in Eddie's
starring film debut in Producers Releasing Corporation's *Song of Old Wyoming.*

A publicity photo of Eddie Dean in early 1945
being advertised as PRC's newest western star.

A lobby card from Eddie Dean's third PRC film, *Caravan Trail*. Pictured with Eddie who is riding on War Paint is Jean Carlin.

Another lobby card showing Eddie Dean and Emmett Lynn getting the drop on Al La Rue (second from left) and Charlie King (second from right) in *Caravan Trail*.

Above: Eddie Dean and Emmett Lynn leading settlers
to their new homesteads in *Caravan Trail*.

Below: Veteran comic actor Roscoe Ates (left) appeared as
Eddie Dean's sidekick Soapy Jones in 15 of his films while veteran stuntman
David Sharpe (right) appeared in thousand of films and co-starred with
Eddie in the Cinecolor production of *Colorado Serenade*.

The front cover of the pressbook announcing *Colorado Serenade*,
PRC's newest Eddie Dean film release in Cinecolor.

Above: Eddie Dean (middle) points the way for Al La Rue (left) and
Roscoe Ates (right) in *Wild West*, the last of Eddie's movies to be filmed in
Cinecolor. *Wild West* was the third and last appearance of La Rue in Eddie's films
and movie goers were introduced to Eddie's new horse, Flash, pictured above.

Below: Frances Kavanaugh (left) wrote nine original screen plays for Eddie Dean's films
while Robert Emmett Tansey (right) produced and directed them.

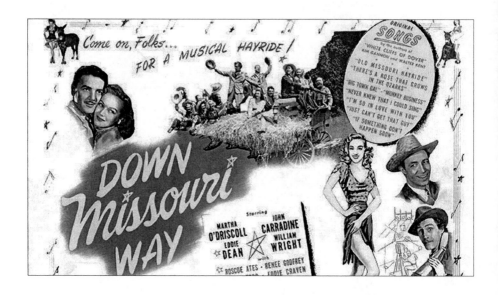

Above: A poster advertising the PRC musical comedy *Down Missouri Way*. Eddie Dean plays Mortimer, caretaker to Shirley, the mule, who stars in her own film.

Below: Eddie Dean in a publicity shot for his role as Mortimer in PRC's musical comedy *Down Missouri Way*.

Producer-director Josef Berne gives last minute directions to Martha O'Driscoll before filming the finale to *Down Missouri Way*. Other cast members pictured on the hay wagon are Renee Godfrey, seated to O'Driscoll's right, John Carradine, standing at left wearing hat, William Wright, to Carradine's left, Eddie Dean holding the reigns, Mabel Todd and Roscoe Ates seated next to him. The Tailor Maids and the Notables are seated at the other end of the wagon.

10

Silver Screen Cowboy, Take Two

In the aftermath of PRC's decision to scrap the Cinecolor process on the remainder of Eddie's series of Western motion pictures, the first flick that he filmed in living black and white was *Driftin' River*. Production began on July 12, 1946, with filming at Corriganville in Simi Valley, and the Monogram Ranch and the Walker Ranch on Placerita Canyon Road in Newhall, CA.

(6) *Driftin' River* (1946)

Driftin' River was produced and directed by Robert Emmett Tansey, with Jerry Thomas working at Tansey's right hand as associate producer, and Frances Kavanaugh once again writing an original screen play.

Joining Eddie in this "shoot 'em up" adventure is Roscoe Ates as "Soapy Jones," Shirley Patterson as "Jenny Morgan," Lee Bennett as "Tucson Brown," William Fawcett as "Tennessee," Dennis Moore as "Joe Moreno," Robert Callahan as "Clem Kensington," Lee Roberts as "Trigger," Forrest Taylor as "Major Hammond," Don Murphy as "Captain Rogers," Lottie Harrison as "Senora," Wylie Grant as "Whistling Sam Wade" (uncredited), and The Sunshine Boys (Eddie Wallace, M.H. "Ace" Richmond, A. L. "Smitty" Smith, and J.O. "Tennessee" Smith), as singing ranch hands.

Eddie and his partner Soapy Jones, under government orders, proceed to the J.C. Morgan's ranch to buy cavalry remounts for the Army. At the ranch, they find out that J.C. Morgan is a female (Shirley Patterson). The nearby town of Dow City is under the control of a lawless trio headed by Trigger (Lee Roberts), Clem Kensington (Robert Callahan), and Joe Moreno (Dennis Moore). A member of the gang is Tucson Brown (Lee Bennett), one of J. C.'s trusted hands. When Eddie decides to buy the horses, Tucson steals the herd to prevent the sale. Soldiers, sent to investigate, are brutally murdered in an ambush organized by Tucson.

The aroused townspeople elect Tennessee (William Fawcett), J.C.'s foreman, as sheriff. Moreno and his gang mistaken Eddie for "Whistling Sam" Wade, a notorious outlaw hired by Moreno, and Eddie joins the outlaw gang in an attempt to get the goods on them, but is in trouble when his true identity becomes known. When the real "Whistling Sam" Wade murders Tennessee, Eddie and Soapy, along with the reformed Tucson, swing into action to clean up the town and put the bad guys away for good. The climax of the film is when Eddie and crew stampede the stolen horses they've confiscated from Moreno through town that as a diversion which ends in a major gunfight.

During a solemn moment during the film, Eddie branches out showing the spiritual side of his persona by saying a few words of eulogy over the grave on Tennessee at his funeral.

> "Oh Heavenly Father, our beloved Tennessee has gone to join the great roundup in Heaven. He left us here on earth his will. Not the kind of will that most men leave of gold and riches, but a will full of truth and beauty, something money cannot buy. He left us the rolling hills of the West which he loved so dearly, the glorious sunrise, the magnificent sunset of each new day. He left a memory of a courageous spirit undaunted by trails and hardships. He left us his love to enjoy and to share with our fellow man. We humbly ask for understanding and appreciation for all these things. Amen."

In this film, it can be truly said that Eddie was a man who wore many hats. In fact, he switches color cowboy hats a few times during *Driftin' River's* fifty-nine-minute run. In the opening scenes, Eddie is wearing a black cowboy headdress. During the middle of the picture, he is seen wearing a white cowboy hat. In the concluding moments, he reverts back to wearing a black hat.

Eddie sings the beautifully grace-filled and gently rolling film's title song composed by Lewis Porter and Robert Tansey, and "Way Back in Oklahoma," a collaboration between Eddie and Johnny Bond that's a fun-filled ditty about a teller of tall tales. Ates chimes in on a half-chorus while the Sunshine Boys supply the engaging music and vocal refrain.

Eddie's leading lady in *Driftin' River* was the beautiful twenty-four-year-old Canadian-born Shirley Patterson. This would be Patterson's first of four leading lady roles she would play in Eddie's Westerns.

Patterson began her acting career after graduating from the Mar-Ken School in Sherman Oaks, CA, in 1941, signing a contract with Columbia Pictures. Her career spanned forty films, a small quantity of television appearances, and a serial.[1] Batman aficionados will recognize Patterson as Linda Page, Bruce Wayne's love interest, in the 1943 fifteen-chapter *Batman* serial from Columbia Pictures.

In addition to *Driftin' River,* Patterson performed her leading lady roles with Eddie in *Tumbleweed Trail* (1946), *Stars Over Texas* (1947), and *Black Hills* (1947).

In later years, Patterson also joined Eddie as guests at Western film conventions. She succumbed to a losing fight with cancer in 1995, in Fort Lauderdale, Florida. She was seventy-two.

Driftin' River tried to do for Lee Bennett what *Song of Old Wyoming* had done for Al La Rue. Bennett had the handsome looks of a leading man but lacked La Rue's charisma. He was given another shot at a strong co-starring role in *Stars Over Texas,* but he never caught on with fans. As a result, he never rose above being a supporting player.

Eddie's last Western, *The Tioga Kid,* is actually a remake of *Driftin' River* as PRC's and Eagle Lion's way of cutting production costs. The film has slight plot changes and contains a large percentage of previous footage from *Driftin' River*.[2]

Bennett reprises his early scenes as Tucson from *Driftin' River,* but this time remains with the villains and is shot by the good guys in the same street fight. As a bit of trivia, portions of *Driftin' River* footage was used in "Lash" La Rue's PRC film, *Border Feud,* from 1947.

Bennett died in 1954 at age forty-three.

William Fawcett began his film career late in life at age fifty-two, playing a variety of old timers from cooks to judges, clerks, doctors, and ranch hands. He was born William Fawcett Thompson in Minnesota in 1894, the son of a Methodist clergyman who came from Australia, and his mother from Wales. His Fawcett middle name was in honor of the doctor who delivered him when he was born.

It was anticipated that Fawcett was to follow his father into the ministry. That wasn't the case. When Fawcett returned from military service with the ambulance corps during World War I, he elected to become an actor.

Fawcett worked repertory theater and stock companies into his 20s and 30s. He became a teacher of English and dramatic literature at the University of Nebraska. He earned his Master's and Ph.D. degrees and became professor of theater arts at Michigan State University.[3]

In 1946, Fawcett headed for Hollywood and started working in Eddie's films for PRC. He appeared in seven of Eddie's films mostly portraying crooked judges and dishonest clerk roles.

Fawcett worked in about 400 movie and TV productions, including over 60 Western movies, 19 serials, and over 200 TV episodes, mostly Westerns.[4] Fawcett is probably most remembered for his role as Pete Wilkey, the ranch foreman, on NBC TVs *Fury* (1955-1960), with Peter Graves and Bobby Diamond.

Fawcett died on January 25, 1974, of circulation problems, at age 79 in Sherman Oaks, CA.

Filming *Driftin' River* ended around July 20, 1946, and went over budget for an approximate negative of cost of $32,000.[5]

(7) *Tumbleweed Trail* (1946)

Tumbleweed Trail, Eddie's seventh film, was produced and directed by Robert Emmett Tansey, with yet another original screen play from the pen of Frances Kavanaugh. It was based loosely of a remake of *Riding the Sunset Trail* (1941), a Monogram Pictures production which starred Tom Keene, that was also produced and directed by Tansey.[6] Jerry Thomas worked as associate producer of this film while musical direction came once again under the baton of Karl Hajos.

In this film, Eddie is riding Flash and packing a pair of six-guns around his waist while wearing a black cowboy hat. Also appearing as Eddie's leading lady for her second straight film was Shirley Patterson playing the part of "Robin Ryan." Assisting Eddie in the development of the plot of *Tumbleweed Trail* which was filmed at the Andy Jauregui Ranch in Newhall CA, was Roscoe Ates as "Soapy Jones," Johnny McGovern as "Freckles Ryan," Bob Duncan as "Brad Barton," Ted Adams as "Lawyer Small," Jack O'Shea as "Gringo," and imported gunman, Kermit Maynard as "Bill Ryan," William Fawcett as "Judge Town," and The Sunshine Boys (Eddie Wallace, M. H. Richman, A.L. Smith, J. O. Smith), as "singing cowhands." The film was released to theaters on October 1, 1946.

Eddie is assigned to thwart the efforts of Brad Barton, a crook, to take over the property of his half-brother Bill Ryan. In order to secure the ranch, which is believed to hold large silver deposits, the scheming relative contracts to have Ryan killed. He then presents a forged will to the court naming himself as the sole heir. Shocked by the tide of events, Ryan's two rightful heirs, his grown daughter Robin and young son "Freckles," are determined to remain on their father's property. Eddie and his sidekick, Soapy Jones, arrive on the scene in time to enter the fight on the side of Robin and "Freckles."

Eddie sings three songs in this film beginning with the hauntingly beautiful yet pensive title track, "Tumbleweed Trail," co-written with Glenn Strange. Eddie then sings "Lonesome Cowboy," a novelty ditty he composed with Johnny Bond. Ates and Johnny McGovern saddle up to join Eddie on the final verse as these three "lonesome" cowboys ride along the trail "searchin' for a cow." Later, Eddie croons "Careless Darlin'" to Shirley Patterson under a full moon in order to win her sympathy. Backed by The Sunshine Boys, the tune is an Ernest Tubb, Lou Wayne and Bob Shelton original.

Bad guy Bob Duncan, who played Brad Barton in *Tumbleweed Trail,* worked in over thirty movies from 1944 to 1957, mostly Westerns. His credits include appearances in five of Eddie's films with major "heavy" roles in *Tumbleweed Trail, Range Beyond the Blue* (1947), and *The Westward Trail* (1948).

Not much is really known about Duncan, but it appears that over the years since his movie career faded out, he had his own demons with which to contend. He resided in North Hollywood, a suburb of Los Angeles. On the morning of March 13, 1967, Duncan put in a call to the North Hollywood Police Department and told them he was about to commit suicide. When officers arrived at the sixty-two-year-old's home a short time later, they found him on his couch, dead from a self-inflicted gunshot wound fired from a .22 rifle.[7] Such a sad epitaph to one of the B-Western films' bad guys that fans loved to hate.

(8) *Stars Over Texas* (1946)

Stars Over Texas was Eddie's eighth PRC Western drama and his third production filmed in black and white. Not making movies in color didn't seem to hurt Eddie's popularity one bit with moviegoers. They were eating up Eddie's pictures as fast as he could make them. Released on November 18, 1946, this was Eddie's final film made in that year.

Robert Emmett Tansey was once again at the helm directing and producing this film for which Frances Kavanaugh wrote the original screenplay. Jerry Thomas was apprenticing as associate producer waiting in the wings for his turn to assume his role as producer. Karl Hajos once again oversaw the musical direction for this fifty-nine-minute piece.

Filmed at Corriganville in Simi Valley, CA, Eddie and his horse Flash are once again joined by Roscoe Ates as "Soapy Jones," Shirley Patterson as "Terry Lawrence," and Lee Bennett playing dual roles as "Bert Ford," the Lawrence ranch foreman, and "Waco Harper." Other support cast members include Lee Roberts as "Hank Lawrence" of the Bar L Ranch, Kermit Maynard as "Knuckles," a henchman, Jack O'Shea as "Ringo Evans" owner of the Cross E Ranch, Hal Smith as "Peddler Tucker," Matty Roubert as "Bugsy," a henchman, Carl Mathews as "Two-Horn," a henchman, William Fawcett as "Judge Diamond Smith," and The Sunshine Boys (Eddie Wallace, M. H. Richman, A. L. Smith, J. O. Smith), as "singing cowhands."

When Eddie, wearing a black cowboy hat, Soapy, and the Sunshine Boys deliver cattle to the Lawrence Ranch (the Bar L), they run into trouble with Ringo Evans and his gang. Ringo's men are rustling Bar L cattle and attempting to kill Bert Ford, the Bar L foreman. Riding into town, rancher Hank Lawrence and Ford are fired at from a distance by three of Ringo's men. Out-riding the gunmen, the two men suspect that they were rustlers.

Seeing the resemblance between Ford and his pal Waco Harper, who is handy with his guns, Eddie has Waco impersonate Ford so they can get to the bottom of the cattle rustling. They then find proof that Ringo is behind the rustling by having altered the Bar L brand in order for it to blend in with the Cross E brand.

The plot builds to a heated climax as Eddie and company find themselves greatly outnumbered in town when Ringo and his gang attacks. Peddler Tucker saves the day in a surprise move by lighting up the shoot out with fireworks, thus enabling Eddie and friends to round up Ringo and his gang.

In *Stars Over Texas*, Eddie sings a trio of songs that he helped to compose. The film's opening selection is the title piece that is saturated with pride, sentiment and reverie. Hal Blair assisted Eddie with its creation. Eddie sings "Fifteen Hundred and One Miles of Heaven," a lively salute to Texas that acknowledges the total distance of "The Lone Star" State from north-to-south and from east-to-west. Eddie gets assistance from Roscoe Ates and The Sunshine Boys who supply the music and who join in on the chorus. Finally, Eddie croons to Shirley Patterson the romantic ballad, "Sands of the Rio Grande," co-written with Eddie's good friend Glenn Strange.

Composer Pete Gates, with whom Eddie had collaborated on a number of scores for his films, had an unaccredited role as a musician in *Stars Over Texas*.[8]

Hal Smith, who played "Peddler Tucker," went on to become a character actor and voice actor. Smith was probably best known as "Otis Campbell," the town drunk on television's *The Andy Griffith Show* during the 1960s. Smith also previously worked with Eddie by appearing in *Down Missouri Way.*

Smith also did voice characters for cartoons including Walt Disney's Goofy, the Owl in the three original Winnie the Pooh featurettes, as well as for other major studios and production companies such as Hanna-Barbera and Warner Bros.

In 1962, Smith was the bungling but melodramatic King Theseus of Rhodes in the feature film, *The Three Stooges Meet Hercules.* Smith manipulates Moe, Larry, and Curly Joe, with Schuyler, their muscle-bounded pal, in getting rid of a two-headed Cyclops and other problematic creatures that plague his island kingdom of Rhodes in exchange for their freedom.

Smith died in 1994 at age seventy-seven.

As the year 1946 wound down, Eddie was voted tenth of the "Top Ten Money Making Western Stars" for that year by the Exhibitors of the United States and Canada in the poll conducted by *Motion Picture Herald* and *Fame.*

The *Motion Picture Herald* poll, under the auspices of the Quigley Publishing Company, listed those Western stars that were voted ahead of Eddie in order respectively as Roy Rogers, "Wild Bill" Elliot, Gene Autry, Gabby Hayes, Smiley Burnette, Charles Starrett ("The Durango Kid"), Johnny Mack Brown, Sunset Carson, and Fuzzy Knight.

Eddie was elated, humbled, and greatly appreciative of the results of that poll. He said he never had a big star complex, which is probably why he rated #10 instead of higher. However, the polls were significant as the bar had now been raised and brought Eddie major Western star status.

"When I work, I just try to do the best I can," he stressed.

The new year looked even more promising, as he was more than willing to meet and exceed such a challenge of maintaining his status, not only for himself but to his fans.

Eddie Dean with his horse Flash.

Eddie Dean and Flash in 1947.

Eddie Dean on top of Flash ready to to chase the bad guys.

The cover of the pressbook heralding Eddie Dean's newest PRC picture *Driftin' River*. Notice the mention that Eddie has a new horse named Flash even though Flash first appeared in *Wild West*. Flash is even given equal credit as Eddie.

Above: A lobby card showing Roscoe Ates, Lee Bennett,
Eddie Dean, Shirley Patterson, and William Fawcett in
Driftin' River (1946 PRC).

Below: A lobby card showing Eddie Dean and sidekick
Roscoe Ates rounding up outlaw leader Dennis Moore and
his gang in *Driftin' River* (1946 PRC).

Pressbook covers for *Tumbleweed Trail,*
Eddie Dean's seventh Western for PRC (1946).

Pressbook cover for *Stars Over Texas,* the eighth
Eddie Dean Western for PRC (1946).

Eddie Dean (wearing black hat), stops Leo Bennett from firing his six gun
in a scene from *Stars Over Texas* (PRC 1946). Seated at the table looking
on are Leo Roberts and Roscoe Ates as Eddie's sidekick "Soapy Jones."

11

Silver Screen Cowboy, Take Three

Having made the Western movie fan polls, Eddie continued to be a major box office draw. The year 1947 would be another banner year for him professionally, producing some of the best action-packed Westerns on the silver screen.

(9) *Wild Country* (1947)

In *Wild Country*, Eddie's ninth picture for PRC, he was under the creative supervision of a new producer and director. Jerry Thomas worked as associate producer in the shadow of Robert Emmett Tansey on the last handful of Eddie's films. Here Thomas debuted as producer on his first film after Tansey's departure from PRC. This fifty-seven-minute production was released on January 17, 1947.

Ray Taylor got the nod to direct the remainder of Eddie's PRC productions after Tansey's departure. Taylor was a veteran filmmaker who liked to keep the action moving in his productions.

Born in Minnesota in 1888, Taylor was an actor and theatrical stage manager prior to World War I. After leaving the Army, he joined Fox Films and became an assistant to John Ford. He moved to Universal in the 1920s, where he mostly directed short subjects before moving up to serials and B-action thrillers during the silent era.[1]

Taylor made the transition to sound, and by the middle of the 1930s, he was one the film capital's top hands at making chapter plays, fast-moving programmers, mostly crime thrillers and action films. Among his best works were *Return of Chandu* (1934) starring Bela Lugosi, *Dick Tracy* (1937) starring Ralph Byrd, and *Flash Gordon Conquers the Universe* (1940) starring Buster Crabbe.

Taylor and Eddie weren't strangers as Taylor previously directed the serial *Don Winslow of the Coast Guard* in 1943, of which Eddie played a supportive role. In the late 1940s, with the decline of the serial form, Taylor finished out his career directing low-budget Westerns, such as those made by Eddie and Lash La Rue.[2] Taylor died in 1952.

Arthur E. Orloff appears on the film's list of credits for his second original screenplay, the only time he worked on one of Eddie's films. After this, his resume expanded to include working on other B-Western films with Lash La Rue, Rex Allen, and Monte Hale before branching out writing for various television programs, such as two *Perry Mason* 1963 episodes.[3]

Orloff, a native of Brooklyn, New York, died in September 1994, in Beverly Hills, CA. He was eighty-five. His daughter is the noted publicist/journalist Katherine Orloff.

Unlike the consistency of Frances Kavanaugh's creative screenplays for Eddie's first eight pictures, all the series' remaining screenplays showcased different writers' talents. Musical supervision for *Wild Country* is once again under the direction of Karl Hojas.

Assisting Eddie and his horse Flash in bringing *Wild Country* to life on the silver screen include his pal, Roscoe Ates as "Soapy Jones," leading lady Peggy Wynn as "Martha Devery," Douglas Fowley as "Clark Varney," I. Stanford Jolley as "Rip Caxton," Lee Roberts as "Sheriff Josh Huckings," Forrest Mathews as, "Sam," a henchman, William Fawcett as "Judge Joe Spindle," Henry Hall as "Marshal Harlan G. Thayer," Charles Jordan, as "Brown," a convict, Richard Cramer as "Prison Guard No. 1," Gus Tante as "Dilling," and The Sunshine Boys (Eddie Wallace, M. H. "Ace" Richmond, A. L. "Smitty" Smith, and J. O. "Tennessee" Smith), as singing ranch hands.

Rip Caxton (I. Stanford Jolley) escapes from a convict road gang and seeks out revenge on Sheriff Bill Devery (Steve Clark), the man responsible for his conviction. United States Marshal Harlan G. Thayer (Henry Hall) sends Marshal Eddie and his pal Soapy Jones (Roscoe Ates) after Caxton. The trail leads to Silver Springs, where Caxton has brutally murdered Devery while in jail on trumped charges. Caxton joins forces with local bad man Clark Varney (Douglas Fowley), and they appointed Josh Huckings (Lee Roberts) as the new sheriff.

The gang plans to kill Devery's daughter, Martha (Peggy Wynn), and take over the Devery Ranch to use as a base for their cattle rustling operation. Learning that Caxton wears a polka dot hatband as a trademark, Eddie has Soapy were a similar one, figuring that Caxton will come out in to the open to investigate a rival. The townspeople mistake Soapy as the wanted outlaw and jail him. On a visit to the Devery Ranch, Eddie meets Martha and her hired hands (The Sunshine Boys) and devises a plan to capture Caxton and the gang. Caxton, planning to use Soapy as a lure to trap Eddie, frees him. Eddie escapes the trap by beating the truth out of the crooked sheriff.

Meanwhile, Soapy and Martha are held hostage in a line shack by Caxton and Varney's men. Eddie and The Sunshine Boys come to rescue Soapy and Martha in a major shoot out with Caxton and the Varney gang.

Probably the most dramatic scene in the film is when the shootout continues in town with Eddie and the sheriff having their own private gun battle, or so it seems. Eddie counts the bullets that the sheriff has fired against him. After the sixth bullet has been fired, Eddie, unarmed, bold and audacious, rushes the sheriff and takes to fisticuffs. As predictable, the bad guys are defeated as Eddie and company save the day.

Eddie sings the gently flowing title song, "Wild Country," which he composed with Hal Blair, along with a pair of tunes written by Pete Gates: "Saddle With a Golden Horn," and "Ain't No Gal Got a Brand On Me," a novelty opus espousing confirmed cowboy bachelorhood, with musical support provided by The Sunshine Boys.

Isaac Stanford "Stan" Jolley, a native of New Jersey, earned his paychecks as a veteran villain in scores of B-Westerns and serials beginning on the late 1930s and throughout the 1940s. It's been calculated that Jolley worked in approximately 250 films in his career ranging from the Charlie Chan series to *White Christmas*.[4] He's been in 167 Westerns working with everyone in the business from Tex Ritter to the Range Busters and everyone in between, and in two dozen serials. He was the voice of the skeletal bad guy in the Republic serial, *The Crimson Ghost* (1946).

Jolley's performance as Rip Claxton in *Wild Country* was one of his more memorable appearances on screen. He gave a textbook example of Western villainy at its best. He was ruthless, calculating with a total disregard for the law, and a cold-blooded killer without scruples. He worked in another one of Eddie's films: *Check Your Guns* (PRC, 1948), as Brad Taggert, the town boss and bad guy.

As B-flicks phased out, Jolley found supporting work in television with appearances on *Gunsmoke, Wagon Train, Wild Bill Hickok,* and *Perry Mason,* among others.

Jolley died on December 6, 1978, in Los Angeles. He was seventy-eight.

(10) *Range Beyond the Blue* (1947)

Range Beyond the Blue was Eddie's tenth production for PRC. Produced by Jerry Thomas and directed by Ray Taylor, the original screen play for *Range Beyond the Blue* came from the creative pen of Patricia Harper.

By the time Harper was given the assignment to write for this picture, she already had written fifteen Western screenplays, most of which were original material. Ironically, Harper got her first start at writing original stories in Gene Autry's *Western Jamboree,* the same film in which Eddie got his initial start as an actor. Other screenplay credits for Harper include *Death Rides the Plains* with Robert Livingston as The Lone Rider, *Western Cyclone* starring Buster Crabbe, and *Secret Agent X-9,* a thirteen-Chapter serial about Nazis espionage in America starring Lloyd Bridges and Keye Luke. Harper later wrote a pair of screen plays for Lash La Rue.[5]

Orchestration duties for *Range Beyond the Blue* was provided by Walter

Greene and Karl Hajos (unaccredited). Greene was a prolific film and (later on) television composer who worked on numerous productions for over thirty years. In 1946, the Missouri native earned an Academy Award nomination for his score to the 1945 film *Why Girls Leave Home*.

Greene worked on four Eddie Dean films. In addition to *Range Beyond the Blue*, he worked on *Black Hills, Shadow Valley*, and *The Tioga Kid* (uncredited). He also provided musical scores on a number of Lash La Rue films.

When Greene made the transition to television, he provided musical scores for seventy-three episodes of *The Gene Autry Show* from 1951-1955, thirty-five episodes of the *Range Rider* series starring Jock Mahoney from 1951-1953, and the *Tarzan* series during the 1960s.

Greene composed for a variety of genres. He is probably known most for scoring numerous *Pink Panther*, *The Inspector*, and *Misterjaw* animated shorts in the 1960s and 1970s. Greene died in Victorville, CA, in 1983, two days prior to Christmas Day. He was seventy-two.[6]

Eddie and Flash roar into action in this fifty-five-minute flick with the help of Roscoe Ates as "Soapy Jones" and Helen Mowrey as "Margie Rodgers." Other support cast include Bob Duncan as "Lash Taggert," Ted Adams as "Uncle Henry Rodgers," Bill Hammond as "Kyle," a henchman, George Turner as "Bragg," a henchman, Ted French as "Sneezer," a henchman, Brad Slaven as "Kirk Mason," Steve Clark as "The Sheriff," William Fawcett as "Doc Talbert" (unaccredited), Eddie Parker as "Posse Rider" (unaccredited), Matty Roubert as "Stagecoach Guard" (unaccredited), The Sunshine Boys (Eddie Wallace, M. H. Richman, Freddie Daniel, and J. D. Sumner) as musicians.

Margie Rodgers (Helen Mowery) owns a stagecoach line that is plagued with a string of robberies of the gold shipments she carries, thereby driving her insurance premiums to an unaffordable level. Unbeknownst to Margie, her uncle, Henry Rodgers, is the person surreptitiously orchestrating these robberies so he can take over his niece's stage line.

Led by Lash Taggert (Bob Duncan) and his three henchmen, Kyle (Bill Hammond), Bragg (George Turner), and Sneezer (Ted French), the outlaws attempt to hold up the stage driven by Margie. Riding as a passenger on the stage is the Yucca County Sheriff (Steve Clark), who with the stagecoach guard, fire back at the outlaws during the chase. Eddie, wearing a black cowboy hat, and Soapy arrive on the scene just in time to thwart the robbery attempt.

The sheriff is wounded in the battle and Eddie suggests that Soapy be made acting sheriff. Margie tells Eddie that her stagecoach has been held up each time it carries a gold shipment, and that her uncle says it is proof that the bandits are receiving advance information about the gold.

Eddie pretends to turn outlaw so the bandits will think he is on their side. His scheme is unsuccessful, but he does learn that Margie's uncle is the person tipping off the outlaws. Eddie breaks into Rodger's office at the bank but is caught by Rodgers. Rodgers shoots Eddie believing that he has killed him, when in reality the bullet just scratched him. Eddie hits the floor pretending to be dead.

Eddie and Soapy later intercept a message from Rodgers tipping off Taggert of the next gold shipment. Eddie and Soapy foil the hold up and prove the connection to Rodgers.

Eddie sings two Dean-Hal Blair collaborations beginning with the film's hauntingly beautiful standard "Range Beyond the Blue," and later on with "The Pony With the Uncombed Hair," a jaunty novelty piece.

Pete Gates' composition of "West of the Pecos" is also added and is nicely showcased by Eddie.

Eddie's leading lady in *Range Beyond the Blue*, Helen Mowery, got her start as an actress performing in B-movie roles for Columbia Pictures. Born in 1922, the Wyoming native did not have an extensive acting career but starred opposite the company's leading cowboy hero, Charles Starrett, three times in *The Fighting Frontiersmen* (1946), *Across the Badlands* (1950), and *The Kid From Broken Gun* (1952).

She later did television guest-starring roles on such shows as *Science Fiction Theater*, *Perry Mason* (1957), *M-Squad*, *Men into Space*, *Sea Hunt*, and *Lock Up*. Mowery is currently ninety-two years old.

Another supporting cast member in this film was Ted French, who worked in a number of Eddie's movies, mostly as a henchman and stuntman. Ted was the father of actor Victor French, who is probably best remembered for his roles with Michael Landon in TVs *Little House on the Prairie* and *Highway to Heaven* during the 1970s and 1980s. The senior French died in 1978, while the younger French died in 1989, due to advanced lung cancer. He was fifty-four.

Because of budget constraints at PRC, the studio often cut costs by using and reusing stock footage from other films to fill in the story line on any given picture. Such stock footage could be of cattle or horse stampede scenes, outlaw chases, shoot out scenes in town, or even Indian warpath scenes. It saved the studio time, man power, and of course, expenses to "cut and paste," if you will, such scenes into the current production.

Range Beyond the Blue was the recipient of the "cut and paste" method used in the film. There were three stagecoach chase scenes in the film. In the first chase scene the stagecoach was occupied by Mowery as the driver, Matty Roubert as the stagecoach guard, and Steve Clark as the sheriff sitting inside the coach itself. When the outlaws came upon them, Mowery gave the horses a furious "giddy-op" while Roubert fired on the bandits as did Clark by sticking his rifle out the stagecoach window.

In the third and final chase scene, the only personnel on the stagecoach were Mowery and Roubert. Yet when the cameras did a long view pan of the chase scene, earlier film footage of the first chase scene was incorporated as the sheriff's rifle can be seen sticking out the window firing at the bandits.

Another uncorrected mistake was when Bob Duncan and his outlaws take the strongbox from Helen Mowery's stagecoach. It is not the same strongbox they forced open when they reached their hideout.

Released on March 17, 1947, *Range Beyond the Blue* was one of the more action-packed flicks Eddie made, mistakes and all.

(11) *West to Glory* (1947)

West to Glory would be Eddie's eleventh film for PRC. It was produced by Jerry Thomas and directed by Ray Taylor. Orchestration was once again done by Walter Greene. The original screenplay was written by Elmer Clifton and Robert B. Churchill.

Clifton, born in Chicago in 1890, began acting on stage at age seventeen, and worked with pioneering movie director D. W. Griffith in various capacities between 1913 to 1922, including appearances in *The Birth of a Nation* (1915) and *Intolerance: Love's Struggle Throughout the Ages* (1916).[8]

Clifton got his directing start with the big-budget whaling epic *Down to the Sea in Ships* (1922), probably his most best-known production, which brought Clara Bow to the attention of audiences.

Clifton's career began to wane in the late 1920s, and although he worked occasionally for major studios such as Columbia and RKO, he spent most of his remaining career writing and directing low budget B-Westerns and thrillers for low-rent studios such as PRC.[9]

Clifton died of a cerebral hemorrhage in October 1949, in Los Angeles. He was fifty-nine.

Robert Busey Churchill, another native of Chicago, had written two screenplays for Hollywood before being tapped to join Elmer Clifton with the production of *West to Glory*. After this, he wrote an original screenplay for Lash La Rue in *The Fighting Vigilantes* (PRC 1947). In the 1980s, he produced *Curious George* and *Frog and Toad* cartoons.[10]

Churchill died in December 1997 in Los Angeles, at age eighty-six.

Eddie and Flash are joined by Roscoe Ates as "Soapy Jones," and leading lady Dolores Castle, making her screen debut as Maria," in solving murder and a diamond and gold theft. Support cast include Gregg Barton as "Jim Barrett," Jimmy Martin as "Cory," Zon Murray as "Bill Avery," Alex Montoya as "Juan," Harry Vejar as "Don Lopez," Casey MacGregor as a henchman, Bill Hammond as a henchman, Ted French as a henchman, Carl Mathews as "Vincente," Slim Whitaker (uncredited), and The Sunshine Boys (Eddie Wallace, J.D. Sumner, J. O. Smith, M. H. Richman, bass player, and Freddie Daniel) as singing and musical ranch hands. This would also be the last Eddie Dean film in which The Sunshine Boys would appear.

Two con-men Jim Barrett (Gregg Barton) and his friend Cory (Jimmy Martin) from the East come out West to join up with Bill Avery (Zon Murray) in a plan to steal the fabulous and well-known Lopez Diamond from its owner, Don Lopez (Harry Vejar). As a result of the drought on his land, Lopez has sold all of his other jewels for gold so that he can take his people to a better place to live and work.

Eddie and his partner, Soapy Jones, attend a fiesta at the home of Don Lopez who, in accordance with his custom, displays a valuable diamond necklace to his guests. He has Maria, one of his guests, wear it.

Barrett offers to buy the necklace but Don Lopez declines to sell. Barrett, with his henchmen Cory and Bill Avery (Zon Murray), plan to steal the Lopez Diamond. Maria, to Eddie's surprise, appears to be working with the outlaws. But, as Eddie's investigation proceeds, it develops that Barrett's gang has also robbed Don Lopez of his gold, and that Maria is a representative of the Mexican government, sent to protect the gem.

Through a last minute fluke, Soapy discovers the stolen Lopez gold stuffed inside the head of the buffalo that is mounted on the wall of the cantina.

What made *West to Glory* so unusual, so different, was in the story line. Clifton and Churchill had written a brief silent dream sequence in the film depicting Eddie and Soapy reversing their hero/sidekick roles. Eddie and Soapy are doing a stake out at the Lopez Rancho hoping to catch the bandits when Soapy wanders off near the well and falls unconscious after hitting his head on the handle of the wheel that brings water up from the well.

During his unconscious state, Soapy dreams he is the hero and is dressed just like Eddie, with black hat, bib buttoned shirt with a neckerchief tied smartly under the collar and toting two six guns. Eddie is dressed exactly like Soapy wearing his pancake hat, checkered shirt, and vest all covered with "X's" in the pattern, while displaying an insipid look on his face á la Stan Laurel, complete with large, "puppy dog-eyes." In some respects, Eddie loosely resembled Mortimer, the character he played in *Down Missouri Way*. This scene once again showed the diversity in how Eddie could play different characters with opposite personas with ease.

However, as usual, Soapy gums up the works as the hero in his own clumsy but loveable way, and the two-and-a-half-minute silent dream sequence concludes with Soapy chasing Barrett on foot out of the saloon and managing to fall face first in the horse trough. Or that's what audiences *thought* happened.

Eddie told writer David Rothel in 1984 what really happened in that scene:

"Our producer, Jerry Thomas, didn't go for it even though they shot it. I was the one who ended in the horse trough. The dream was in the film when released, but they didn't complete the sequence where I ran out, like Roscoe would do, and fell in the horse trough, which I really did. Jerry Thomas said 'People out there have a lot of respect for you, Eddie, and we don't want to lose that.'"[11]

Bad guy Gregg Barton vividly remembered a snafu he experienced during the filming of that same dream sequence:

"I was fortunate, freshly out of World War II, to have worked in one of Eddie's Westerns. I was very impressed by his friendliness and I'm sure he could see I was new and very nervous. He helped me greatly while we were filming *West to Glory*. In the comedy dream sequence, his sidekick, Roscoe Ates, wants to stop me, the heavy, from moving in on his girl (Dolores Castle); it almost became a disaster! The girl is on my lap. I have a drink shot out of my hand so I fling the girl practically through the bar. I angrily kick back the chair but it gets hung up on my spurs. I reach for my gun, which I can't get because my long coat covers it. Finally, I get my gun, which I press too hard and cock (to make me look fast) and it fires, still secure in the holster, with the blast hitting me in the leg. The crew roared with laughter and Ray Taylor, our director, had a stunt man straighten me out. We made it in the next take."[12]

In the film, Eddie sings a pair of tunes he and Hal Blair composed. The first was "Cry, Cry, Cry," a jaunty novelty piece about a man who was dissed by his love and who now has the satisfaction of knowing that she is experiencing the same treatment from another that she originally gave him, as it's her turn now to "cry, cry, cry." The Sunshine Boys provide the engaging musical back up.

The second tune is the film's closing number, "West to Glory," an anthem of inspiration and hope sung by Eddie in a powerful Broadway musical style.

The film's middle song, composed by Pete Gates, is a romantic ballad sung by Eddie to Dolores Castle in a private moment outside the grounds of the local mission church.

Not much is known about Dolores Castle, Eddie's leading lady in *West to Glory,* but the attractive Hispanic actress had a brief career in B-films from the latter part of the 1940s that concluded with appearances on a handful of television Western shows such as *The Adventures of Kit Carson* and *The Cisco Kid* (1952).[13]

Released on April 12, 1947, *West to Glory* has an engaging story line but is marred by the dream sequence. It could have easily been removed from its final release.

(12) *Black Hills* (1947)

Black Hills was Eddie's twelfth PRC film and his fourth for 1947. Production was once again under the auspices of Jerry Thomas while Ray Taylor supervised the cast from the director's chair. Musical supervision was overseen by Dick Carruth with original music scored by Walter Greene.

Original screenplay was written by Joseph F. Poland. Born in 1892, in Waterbury, CT, Poland wrote for 136 films between 1913 and 1962. After making a successful transition from silent films to talkies, he wrote original screenplays for Gene Autry and other B-Western features, as well as for numerous cliffhanger serials including *The Adventures of Captain Marvel* (1941), *Dick Tracy vs. Crime, Inc.*(1941), *Spy Smasher* (1942), *Zorro's Black Whip* (1944), *Superman* (1948), *Batman and Robin* (1949), and *Atom Man vs. Superman* (1950).[14]

Poland also assimilated well in to television having written for *The Lone Ranger* TV series in 1950, and for *The Range Rider* show (1953).

Poland died in 1962 in Los Angeles. He was sixty-nine.

In this film Eddie, introduces his audience to some new co-stars. The first is Eddie's new horse White Cloud, a four-year-old golden palomino stallion that succeeded Flash. Eddie rode the film range on White Cloud in four of his flicks.

According to a motion picture trade magazine article, since the day White Cloud was born, Eddie had been training him for the time when he would make his movie debut.

"Hours of patient work have been devoted to teaching him a series of tricks which, Dean believes, will delight all thrill-lovers," the article was quoted as saying.

The piece went on to say that in some ways Eddie hated to retire Flash, but he was getting past the age where he could fulfill the script demands. "Unfortunately, horses are not like actors, and when they slow down they cannot be graduated to character roles," Eddie said in the article. Eddie was also quoted as saying that he looks forward to making many films with White Cloud. "He is smart, photographs beautifully, and seems to like appearing before the camera," Eddie said.[15]

The other new co-stars are Eddie's back up vocal/musical group, Andy Parker and the Plainsmen, who had one of the smoothest sounds in the history of Western music.

Born in Magnum, Oklahoma, on March 17, 1913, Andy Parker was reared on a ranch. He started singing professionally at age sixteen on various radio stations in Oklahoma, then in Kansas and Missouri.

Parker married Helene Hudson from Wichita, Kansas, on August 14, 1937. He moved to San Francisco two months later to assume the role of a singing cowboy on *Death Valley Days* radio show on NBC. He also did personal appearances until war broke his group up in 1941.[16]

The Parkers were the parents of three children. The oldest, Joseph Andrew, was born in 1939. Next was a daughter, Andrea Susanne, who passed away in 2010 from cancer. She was sixty-seven. The youngest Parker sibling was Phillip Dennis, who passed away in 2012, at age sixty-one, after suffering for several years from Alzheimer's disease.

Parker worked at defense plants throughout the war and became associated with Dude Martin's *Round-Up* in the fall of 1943. Parker, Hank Caldwell (also of Dude Martin's *Round-Up*) along with Charlie Morgan formed the Plainsmen in 1944, and relocated to Los Angeles.

In 1946, the Plainsmen were featured in an unaccredited role in *Cowboy Blues*, with Ken Curtis, and they were recording on Coast Records. By this time George Bamby, Earl "Joaquin" Murphey, and fiddle player Harry Simms joined the group. Deuce Spriggins, a Spade Cooley alumnus, was a Plainsmen for a brief period before returning to Cooley. Later that year, the Plainsmen were signed on as regulars on CBS' weekly *Hollywood Barn Dance* radio show as well as local shows on KNX and KMPC.[17]

In February 1947, original member Hank Caldwell left and was replaced by Paul "Clem" Smith, another Dude Martin alumnus. With this manifestation of the group they were known as "Andy Parker and the Plainsmen."

Parker and The Plainsmen were featured on *The Hollywood Barn Dance* from 1946 to 1947 and on Hank Larabee's Western radio show from July 5, 1946, until February 7, 1948.

In April 1947, Parker signed a contract with PRC Productions for a series of eight pictures starring Eddie Dean. Parker and the Plainsmen signed on with Capitol Records in December 1947.

The "how" of the Plainsmen's first meeting with Eddie is unknown, but Joe Parker, the son of Andy Parker, said, "By 1947, the Plainsmen were fast becoming a very popular group on Hollywood's Western music scene, and having already recorded with Rusty Draper, Ozzie Waters, (among several other Coast Records artists), as well as Jack Rivers, Ken Curtis and Deuce Spriggins. They very likely had worked with Eddie, on radio, and/or in public appearances. Since there seemed to be a very good rapport between the Plainsmen and Eddie, it's not hard to imagine them being signed to do their first picture with Eddie in *Black Hills*, which was released in October 1947."[18]

Subsequent Eddie Dean flicks that Andy Parker and the Plainsmen appeared in were *Shadow Valley, Check Your Guns, Tornado Range, The Westward Trail, The Hawk of Powder River,* and *The Tioga Kid.*

Between June and July 1947, Andy Parker and the Plainsmen backed up Eddie on eight sides for Majestic Records, just about the time *Black Hills* would have been filming for its October release.[19]

Within the next five years, the group recorded over 200 transcriptions on Capitol Records and backed up a variety of artists including Tex Ritter and Gordon MacRae.

In 1949, the Plainsmen were also featured on KTLA television with Carolina Cotton and other Western stars. Murphey soon left the group as did Bamby.

Parker and the Plainsmen worked with Eddie again on the short-lived TV series, *The Marshal of Gunsight Pass*, broadcast live for ABC in 1950.

"While doing some research on *The Marshal Of Gunsight Pass*, the IMBb website indicates the first episode as having been televised 'live' from the Iverson Ranch, but with Russell Hayden as the Marshal," Joe Parker said. "Eddie Dean became Marshal Number 2 in subsequent episodes. My dad's diary shows the Plainsmen did a total of nine episodes, between March 2 and April 27, 1950. As far as I can tell, they were televised 'live' from ABC's new television studios in Hollywood, at Prospect and Talmadge, (ABC having purchased the old Vitagraph studios in 1949, which had originally been built 1912). I remember my dad taking me to watch an episode being televised at the ABC studios, and seeing how 'cheap,' the sets were."[20]

Andy Parker and the Plainsmen were also on Leo Carrillo's *Dude Ranch Varieties*, which ended in 1952.

During the early 1950s, the Plainsmen were dropped from Capitol Records, but they continued to appear at California clubs and were regulars on radio KHJ in Los Angeles. Music director Ken Darby had Parker and Morgan sing the title song with Marilyn Monroe for the film, *River of No Return* (20th-Century-Fox, 1954), also starring Robert Mitchum.[21]

Two years later Morgan left the Plainsmen and Parker retired the group. Parker died on October 2, 1977, in Pleasant Hill, CA. He was sixty-four.

Charlie Morgan, an original Plainsmen, was born in Denison, Texas, son of a vaudeville family, The Morgan Family. He is the brother of songstress and game show star Jaye P. Morgan. Morgan spent his boyhood between ranch life of Northern Texas and Central Colorado and the country's vaudeville circuit. Morgan joined the Plainsmen to sing as a baritone solo, play rhythm and solo guitar, and sing second tenor in the vocal combinations.[22]

Paul "Clem" Smith was born in Perry, Oklahoma, the son of an Oklahoma farmer-rancher, where he spent most of his boyhood. Smith started his professional career as a member of Glen Rice's "Original Beverly-Hill-Billies" in 1935. He emigrated to California that same year and was associated with some of the best known Western groups around San Francisco. He spent over three years in the Army during World War II as a radar operator attached to the Western Air Wing. Smith joined the Plainsmen shortly after his discharge in 1946. He played bass and string guitar and sang baritone in vocal combos.[23]

George Bamby was born in Detroit and came to Los Angeles as a child. He studied accordion under Gallo-Rini and became one the best known and most accomplished accordionists ever to be associated with Western music. Bamby joined the Plainsmen in 1946 after a long successful association with Spade Cooley. Bamby sang bass with the vocal group and did all instrumental arrangements for the band.[24]

Earl "Joaquin" Murphey was born in 1923 and reared in Los Angeles. He was nicknamed "Joaquin" due to his personality. He has been acclaimed by professionals as the finest steel guitarist in the business and was hailed as an innovative and influential steel guitarist who helped define the soundof Western Swing.[25]

He started his professional career in 1943 working for Spade Cooley and stayed with him for three years. Murphey joined the Plainsmen in 1943. He was best known for his "violin tone" solos and wild jazz choruses which helped developed the style of the Plainsmen.[26]

After leaving the Plainsmen in 1950, Murphey recorded and performed extensively with a myriad of other Western music stars.

Murphey passed away on October 25, 1999, in Los Angeles from complications from metastatic cancer. He was seventy-five.

Other cast members in *Black Hills* joining Eddie Dean and White Cloud were Roscoe Ates as "Soapy Jones," Shirley Patterson, who returned for her final Eddie Dean film as a leading lady as "Janet Hadley," Terry Frost as "Dan Kirby," Steve Drake as "Larry Hadley," Nina Bara as "Chiquita," William

Fawcett as "Clerk Tuttle," Lane Bradford as henchman "Al Cooper," Lee Morgan as "The Sheriff," George Chesebro as Land Agent "Harvey Allen," Steve Clark as "John Hadley,"(unaccredited), Eddie Parker as "Al Quillan," a henchman (unaccredited), and Andy Parker and the Plainsmen (Charlie Morgan, George Bamby, Earl Murphey, and Paul "Clem" Smith), as singing and musical cowhands.

John Hadley (Steve Clark) discovers a rich vein of gold ore in an abandoned and well-hidden cave on his ranch but doesn't tell his daughter, Janet (Shirley Patterson), or his son Larry (Steve Drake). Dan Kirby (Terry Frost), a local saloon owner, and his henchman, Al Cooper (Lane Bradford), spot Hadley at the mine and learning that his gold discovery is still a secret, kill him and then set dynamite to the cave to cover the evidence. Unable to find their missing father, Larry and Janet are forced to borrow payroll money from Harvey Allen (George Chesebro), local land-company head, promising to pay it off after the spring roundup. On the way home, Larry is robbed by Kirby and his henchmen.

Eddie and his sidekick, Soapy Jones (Roscoe Ates) ride in just as the robbers are making a getaway. They give chase and shoot the one carrying the money. The money is retrieved by the young Hadley.

One of the outlaws not directly involved in the hold up on young Hadley attempts to ambush Eddie and Soapy in a gun battle. The outlaw retreats and in so doing, loses his hat. Eddie retrieves the hat finds the initial "A. Q." in the hat band. Larry Hadley suggests the hat belongs to Al Quillan, one of Kirby's men.

When Eddie confronts Quillan (Eddie Parker) about the hat at Kirby's saloon, a fight ensues between Eddie and Quillan. Eddie wins the fight and leaves.

Back at the Hadley Ranch, Eddie is asked by Janet and Larry to stay on as ranch foreman. Eddie agrees to do so. Allen goes away on a business trip and Kirby has Tuttle (William Fawcett), who has accumulated a lot of IOU's gambling at Kirby's saloon, to forge a document so he can buy the Hadley mortgage. Kirby then plans to kill Allen by intercepting the stagecoach on which he is returning.

Eddie learns of this, meets the stagecoach out of town, and warns Allen of the plot. Eddie lends Allen his horse and tells him to hide out in the hills until dark and that he will meet him at Allen's office later that evening. Eddie then rides shotgun on the stagecoach back into town. But Kirby changes his plan, has Cooper kill Allen in Allen's office with Eddie's gun and places the blame on Eddie.

After Eddie and the Sheriff trick Kirby in confessing to the murder, a brief gunfight ensues with Kirby's men. Kirby hi-tails it out of town with Eddie and Soapy giving chase. Eddie corners Kirby in a fight and Eddie brings Kirby to justice.

Eddie sings the hauntingly beautiful title song, "Black Hills," a collaboration between he and Hal Blair. At camp during the evening of a cattle drive, Eddie, Soapy, and Andy Parker and the Plainsmen all join in singing the humorous "Punchinello," a Pete Gates offering, about a loveable, well-meaning, but not too bright cowhand who by sheer dumb luck ultimately becomes "the pride of the Tenderfoot Trail."

Eddie then brings the film to a close by singing to Shirley Patterson the lively and light-hearted "Let's Go Sparkin'," another Dean-Blair composition. There are even some rather sensuous close ups scenes between Eddie and Patterson while Parker and his crew swing out during the song's bridge.

There were a number of scenes in *Black Hills* that were later utilized in Eddie's *The Hawk of Powder River*.

Steve Clark is seen riding to what appears to be an abandon cave whose entrance is hidden with tree limbs and leaves. Removing the foliage, he enters the cave. He is watched by Terry Frost and Eddie Parker who investigate and come up on Clark. Clark claims he's discovered a huge gold vain in the cave but hadn't told his children about it as yet. Frost and Parker kill Clark and then blow up the cave to seal its entrance and to hide the *corpus delicti*.

In *The Hawk of Powder River*, Jennifer Holt and her henchmen rendez-vous at the same cave after making a raid and Holt uses the cave to change from her "Hawk" outfit. Later on, Clark happens to ride by seeing a number of hoof prints leading to the cave. He investigates, is caught by Frost and

Eddie Parker while discovering the "Hawk's" clothing with the smell of perfume on them and then is shot dead by Frost and Parker and left in the cave to rot.

When Eddie and Roscoe are first introduced in the *Black Hills* film they are seen leisurely riding their horses in a walking gate while on the trail. Eddie is singing "Black Hills" while Roscoe is shuffling a deck of cards, anxious to demonstrate his slight-of-hand card tricks to anyone gullible enough to engage him. This same scene is used in the opening of *The Hawk of Powder River*.

Another scene from *Black Hills* is at night during the cattle drive, where Eddie, Roscoe, Shirley Patterson, Steve Drake and Andy Parker and the Plainsmen sing "Punchinello." The camera does a long pan of the camp and periodically shows close ups of Eddie, Roscoe, Shirley Patterson and Andy Parker and the Plainsmen either singing or smiling while enjoying the singing. This same scene is used in *The Hawk of Powder River* with the long pan scene of the camp fire and Patterson's silhouette are used with occasional close ups of Jennifer Holt smiling while enjoying the camp fire entertainment.

Finally, *Black Hills* marks the beginning of showing the same town in the remainder of Eddie's series. There is a church at one end of the town that seems to be the main entrance into the town and whenever there is a ranch house used in the films, it's usually the same one where there are lots of tall flowers growing in the front and the hitching post is off to the side.

Released on October 26, 1947, and filmed at Corriganville, in Simi Valley, CA, *Black Hills* was also released to German-speaking audiences in Austria in 1949 under the title *Cowboy Serenade*.

Since many of Eddie's Westerns were filmed at Corriganville, and had became a noted place to film Westerns, Tom Corrigan, son of the late Ray "Crash" Corrigan, recounted how his father bought the ranch in Simi Valley, CA, that became Corriganville.

"In the mid-1930s my father was in a couple of movies that were filmed in the area. The owner was running a few head of cattle at the time. My father asked him if he was interested in selling. He said yes, and wanted

$12,000, but in cash. My father told him he would give him $5,000 a month for three consecutive months, and if he missed a payment or was late by one day, he would lose the property."[27]

Eddie remembered that event well. He recalled as to how he and Crash toured the country to raise the funds for the final payment and how they returned in the nick of time to make the final payment on the property.

"I think it was in 1937. Crash asked me to do some personal appearances with him. Crash did not have much stage experience at that time so I was the M. C. and did the singing while Crash would tell about the stunts that were used in the movies. Crash had a Packard touring car that we drove across country doing three to six shows a day at one night stands. I remember one incident that happened in Joplin, Missouri. We did not know that we were to do a matinee. We had just arrived in the motel and got to sleep when the phone rang. The people at the theater said we had fifteen minutes before we to put on the first show. We dressed and ran to the theater, not having time to wash our faces or to look over the stage. I entered from the right side of the stage and did my part but when I left I forgot and went off the left side. Well, there weren't any steps on that side, so I fell about ten feet on to a concrete walkway that led to the basement. Fortunately, I wasn't hurt, but I did get some bruises. I was lucky that I was in pretty good shape.

"We finished up the tour in Virginia. The reason for the tour was so Crash could make enough money to make the last payment on the property that became Corriganville. When we finished the tour time was running short before time would be up on Crash's agreement. We took turns driving back. We drove day and night. We got back the night before the note was due. We burned up the engine in that Packard getting back. The roads in those days were bad, one lane each way. I'll never forget that trip across country in that Packard."[28]

Ray "Crash" Corrigan passed away on August 10, 1976, at the age of seventy-three.

(13) *Shadow Valley* (1947)

Shadow Valley was the thirteenth Western Eddie made for PRC. In the opening film credits something different took place. The film was introduced as "The New PRC Presents," as Eagle Lion replaced PRC as the studio's official name. But for purposes of continuity and consistency, the name PRC was still retained on the credits.

Once again, Jerry Thomas was at the helm of *Shadow Valley's* production department, while Ray Taylor directed the project. Musical supervision was done by Dick Carruth with Walter Greene assisting in providing incidental music.

Eddie and his horse White Cloud ride into action in *Shadow Valley* with Roscoe Ates as "Soapy Jones," Jennifer Holt as "Mary Ann Jarvis," George Chesebro as "Ben Gunnison," Eddie Parker as "Barney Foster," Lee Morgan as "The Sheriff," Lane Bradford as "Bob," a cowhand, Carl Mathews as a henchman, Budd Buster as "Judd Grims," Andy Parker and the Plainsmen (George Bamby, Charlie Morgan, Earl Murphey, Paul "Clem" Smith) as cowhands/musicians, Forrest Taylor as "Pop Jarvis"(unaccredited), Bob Woodward as "Walt Jarvis" (unaccredited), and Wally West as a henchman (unaccredited).

Eddie and his sidekick Soapy Jones (Roscoe Ates) get involved in crooked lawyer Ben Gunnison's (George Chesebro) attempt to acquire the Jarvis Ranch. Gunnison knows there is gold there and having already killed Mary Ann Jarvis' (Jennifer Holt) father (Forrest Taylor) and uncle (Bob Woodward), he now tries to persuade her to leave so he can buy the property. But Eddie gets her to stay and then starts his search for the killer.

In *Shadow Valley* Eddie sings three musical offerings by Pete Gates: the romantic "Rose Anne of San Jose," the melancholy but easy-flowing "I'm Gonna Hang My Heart on the Hitching Post," and the film's closer as he rides away singing the jaunty and light-hearted "Corn Bread Country" with accompaniment on the chorus refrain by Andy Parker and the Plainsmen.

Released on November 29, 1947, at least ten percent of this fifty-eight-minute Western is comprised of stock shots from earlier Eddie Dean films.

Actor George Chesebro, who played Ben Gunnison, the crooked lawyer in *Shadow Valley*, often played dual roles in his film career as either the good guy or the bad guy. However, he is mostly recognized for his litany of portrayals as "the heavy."

Born in 1888 in Minneapolis, MN, Chesebro's Hollywood film career began in 1915, doing early features and serials. Starting in the 1930s, Chesebro became one of the most recognized bad guys of B-Westerns and serials. It has been estimated that Chesebro appeared in approximately 400 films between 1915-1954, including 300 Westerns and 34 cliffhangers. He also played unaccredited cowboy henchman roles in a few Three Stooges shorts. His film work at Republic Pictures, from 1935-1953, includes seventy movies, mostly Westerns and serials.[29]

Chesebro died in Los Angeles, CA, on May 28, 1959. He was seventy.

Bob Woodward was a regular in Eddie's films, playing unaccredited minor supportive roles, mostly as a gang member. Woodward was also stunt man who worked as Eddie's double in his films.[30] According to Eddie's son, Edgar Glosup Jr., Bob was not only a great guy but also a great cowboy.

As 1947 came to a close, it was no surprise that Eddie once again made the list of the "Top Ten Money Making Western Stars," for the second year in a row. Eddie still anchored the #10 position, while other Western stars who also made the list ahead of him were as follows, in their respective order: Roy Rogers, Gene Autry, William Boyd, "Wild Bill" Elliot, Gabby Hayes, Charles Starrett, Smiley Burnette, Johnny Mack Brown, and Dale Evans. It is interesting to note that a third of the Western stars on this list – Gabby Hayes, Smiley Burnette, and Dale Evans – were not lead actors in their own right.

As Eddie moved in to 1948 with high hopes and popularity, production changes in some of Eddie's films loomed on the horizon from PRC having to do with budget constraints. As a consequence, most of his films from that year suffered from less-than stellar production quality, having to utilize film footage from Eddie's previous movies to fill in the gaps of a given story line.

Eddie christened 1948 with a bang with the release of a fine "shoot-'em up" drama entitled *Check Your Guns,* one of Eddie's personal favorites.

(14) *Check Your Guns* (1948)

Check Your Guns was Eddie's fourteenth film of his Western series for PRC, or as the film credits listed the studio as "The New PRC Pictures, Inc." Produced by Jerry Thomas and directed by Ray Taylor, the original screenplay was written by Joseph O'Donnell.

Born in 1891 in New York City, O'Donnell had a long and distinguished career in motion pictures as a screenwriter. Most of his career was spent writing for B-movies. In addition to *Check Your Guns*, some of his more memorable works include *Murder By Television* starring Bela Lugosi (1935), and serials *Spy Smasher* (1942), *The Master Key* and *Secret Agent X-9* (both from 1945), as well as a number of Lash La Rue and Buster Crabbe Westerns for PRC.[31]

O'Donnell died in December 1963, in Woodland Hills, CA. He was seventy-two.

Released on January 24, 1948, the fifty-five-minute *Check Your Guns* was filmed at the Iverson Ranch in Chatsworth, CA.

In this action-packed Western, Eddie and his horse White Cloud are joined by Roscoe Ates as "Soapy Jones," Nancy Gates as "Cathy Jordan," George Chesebro as "Banker Farrell," I. Stanford Jolley as "Brad Taggert," Mikel Conrad as "Ace Banyon," a Taggert henchman, Lane Bradford as "Slim Grogan," a Taggert henchman, Terry Frost as "Sloane," a Taggert henchman, William Fawcett as "Judge Hammond," Ed Cassidy as "Sheriff Dave Clark" (unaccredited), Steve Clark as "Judge Dick Walsh" (unaccredited), Wally West (aka Mason Wynn), a henchman, Dee Cooper, a henchman, Russell Arms and Carl Mathews, as hired gunmen, Andy Parker as "Deputy Jeff/ musician" and The Plainsmen (George Bamby, Charlie Morgan, Earl Murphey, and Paul "Clem" Smith), as ranch hands/musicians.

Eddie arrives in the frontier town of Red Gap and finds that a corrupt judge (William Fawcett) and a gang of hired henchman working for Brad Taggert (I. Stanford Jolley), control the town. Eddie is appointed sheriff after the town sheriff is shot (Ed Cassidy). Aided by his sidekick Soapy Jones

(Roscoe Ates), Andy Parker and the Plainsmen, and Cathy Jordan (Nancy Gates), daughter of a rancher murdered by the Taggert gang, set out to restore law and order to Red Gap.

To do that, Eddie demands that everyone check their guns while inside the town limits. Those who refuse must pay the price. Cleaning up Red Gap is not as easy as first believed. There are twists and turns along the way that make room for plenty of shoot-outs, gun plays, and one memorable fisticuffs scene in the saloon between Eddie and Ace Banyon that actually looks real with Eddie almost being beaten up by Banyon. But our hero takes a brief moment to recover from the blow his adversary had given him, kicks away a chair that is in his path and with one punch knocks out Banyon.

According to Edgar Glosup Jr., Eddie's son, a portion of that fight scene was real as Mikel Conrad made a mistake and inadvertently socked Eddie in the jaw, stunning him. Eddie, in reality, needed to take that brief pause to recover from Conrad's blow so as to continue with the fight.

Taggert hires a pair of outside gunslingers (Russell Arms and Carl Mathews) to do away with Eddie but are killed by Eddie in a brief gun fight. Cathy Jordan writes a family friend, Judge Walsh (Steve Clark), a legitimate circuit judge, about the goings on in Red Gap and pleads for him to come to Red Gap to dispense justice.

Taggert and Banker Farrell (George Chesebro), a Taggert crony, plan to kill Eddie in an unfair gunfight on the streets of Red Gap with Taggert hiding on a side street using a pocket mirror to reflect the sun in order to momentary blind Eddie so Farrell can shoot him dead. Eddie proved to be quicker on the draw and kills both men with a bullet apiece. Taggert's men are rounded up and brought to justice while law and order are once again restored to Red Gap.

Eddie warbles three songs in this film, the first of which is a novelty piece composed by Eddie and Hal Blair called "A Miserable 'Onery Coyote," in which Eddie is joined by Ates and Andy Parker and the Plainsmen, while the remaining two songs come from the pen of Pete Gates, Nancy

Gates' brother. There's the pretty ballad tune, "God's Little Lanterns," and the film's closer, "Moseyin' Along," an engaging and adorable duet piece between Eddie and Gates.

Born in 1926, in Denton, Texas, Nancy Jane Gates started her career in show business as a teenager singing with Texas area bands and on radio in the late 1930 and early 1940s. In 1941, she was called to Hollywood to do a screen test and was signed to RKO Pictures.

Gates' screen credits include playing Marjorie, the niece of Throckmorton P. Gildersleeve (Hal Peary), in *The Great Gildersleeve* (RKO 1942) and *Gildersleeve's Bad Day* (RKO 1943), a number of B-Westerns, *The Greatest Show on Earth* (1952), directed by Cecil B. DeMille and starring Charlton Heston, James Stewart, Cornel Wilde, Betty Hutton, and Dorothy Lamour, and the 1954 thriller *Suddenly!* opposite Frank Sinatra and Sterling Hayden.[32]

Gates starred or co-starred in thirty-four films and made fifty-five television appearances including *Perry Mason, Maverick, Wagon Train,* and *Alfred Hitchcock Presents.*

In 1948, Gates married American Airlines Captain Bill Hayes in 1948 and became the parents of four children, including Hollywood producers Jeffrey M. Hayes and Chip Hayes. She retired from acting in 1969.

Russell Arms, who played a hired outlaw in *Check Your Guns* and who also appeared in *Tornado Range* as "Dorgan," a killer henchman, recalled Eddie as a very gracious and helpful individual.

"I was fairly new to Western movies when I worked with Eddie Dean and it was a very good introduction to a whole new world for me," Arms said. "Eddie was a gentleman in best sense of the word. I never saw him get angry on the set. He was aware and appreciative of both his cast and crew. He was also aware of his shortcomings as an actor and even went so far as to ask for my help on one of the scenes we had together. He knew of my theater background and thought I might be able to help make the scene play better. As a newcomer, I was impressed by this, as that was a rare thing for a star to do! He didn't have to be a perfect actor because his warmth and down-to-earth qualities, plus his very good singing voice made his series very successful. I truly enjoyed working with him. This was at the time of the singing cowboy and I thought he was right up there with (Gene) Autry and (Roy) Rogers and all the rest. To me he embodied a real Western star!"[33]

While Eddie wore a white cowboy hat in this film, Red Gap was created by utilizing the same town props and the same ranch house as previously shown in Eddie's flicks. To even show that film editing wasn't always what it should be, for a quick second evidence of horse droppings can even be seen behind some horses tied to the hitching post in town.

(15) *Tornado Range* (1948)

In *Tornado Range*, Eddie debuts his new film mount, Copper, a rust-colored five-year-old gelding quarter horse with a light mane and tail. The announcement of Copper's introduction to motion pictures came by way of a small article published in a movie trade magazine from 1948 which stated, in part: "The sterling way in which Copper responded to direction and carried out his assignments during the filming of his first picture (*Tornado Range*) seems to indicate that there will be a rush on the part of movie cowboys to remount themselves on quarter horses and even now many are asking themselves why they hadn't thought to use one of these hard-working, sure-footed ponies in films before this."[34]

Jerry Thomas produced this film while Ray Taylor was its director. Musical supervision was by Dick Carruth with film editing by Joseph Gluck. Original screenplay was written by William Lively.

William Edison Lively was born in Charleston, West Virginia, twelve days before Eddie. Lively had written over sixty-five screenplays including a number of B-Westerns and action adventures, the Bowery Boys, serials such as *Spy Smasher, Dick Tracy vs. Crime, Inc., G-Men vs. the Black Dragon, King of the Rocket Men*, and a variety of television series including *Dick Tracy, Ramar of the Jungle, Hopalong Cassidy, Captain Midnight, The Roy Rogers Show, Sergeant Preston of the Yukon*, and *Sky King*.[35]

Lively died in 1973 in Los Angeles at age sixty-six.

Filmed on location at the Iverson Ranch in Chatsworth, CA, the fifty-six-minute *Tornado Range* was released to American theaters on February 21, 1948.

Eddie and Copper are joined by supporting cast members Roscoe Ates as "Soapy Jones," Jennifer Holt as "Mary King," George Chesebro as "Lance King," Terry Frost as "Quirt Thayer," Brad Slaven as "Jebby Sawyer," Marshall Reed as "Sam Wilson," Lane Bradford as "Thorne," a henchman, Russell Arms as "Dorgan," Steve Clark as "Pop Sawyer," and Andy Parker and the Plainsmen (George Bamby, Charlie Morgan, Earl Murphey, Paul "Clem" Smith) as musicians.

Eddie, under orders as a U.S. Land Office agent, tries to prevent a range war from being started between homesteaders and ranchers when a caravan of the so-called "nesters" begin to take over land acquired by the homesteaders through a government lease.

Quirt Thayer (Terry Frost), working both sides against the middle, has his gang pretend to join with the ranchers in seeking revenge against the settlers for raids on the ranchers by Thayer's henchmen. When Thayer henchman Dorgan (Russell Arms) kills Pop Sawyer (Steve Clark), a would be "nester," Sawyer's son, Jebby Sawyer (Brad Slaven), seeks revenge. When Eddie tries to stop him, Dorgan shoots leading rancher Lance King (George Chesebro) and Eddie and Jebby Sawyer are accused and sentenced to hang for the attempted murder of King.

Eddie uses his friendship with Mary King (Jennifer Holt), daughter of rancher Lance King, to bring the real culprits to justice.

Eddie sings two songs in *Tornado Range*, leading off with the gently flowing ballad, "Little Ranch Upon the Hill," an original by the Massey Brothers, Curt and Alan, and the film's closing number, the stirring yet march-like, "Song of the Range," composed by Eddie himself.

Brad Slaven, who worked with Eddie in two films, stated that he thought Eddie was more like a real cowboy than some of his movie contemporaries.

"Of all the Western actors I worked with, I liked Eddie the best," Slaven said. "He seemed more like a real cowboy. He had a great singing voice. I grew up singing although I never sang in movies. If we went up to the Circle J Dude Ranch where PRC would put us up while we shot the movies at Monogram Ranch, we'd sing different things in the evening. I used to write parodies on songs and Eddie enjoyed those."[36]

Bad guy Terry Frost got his professional start in theatrics reciting poetry at houses of prostitution in Oregon, Washington, and Minnesota as a way of entertaining waiting "johns" while the girls they were soliciting were kept busy. Born in Minnesota in 1906, Frost later became involved with stock companies and vaudeville shows.[37]

He and his wife settled down in Los Angeles to pursue an acting career. He also opened a restaurant, Terry Gene's, on Wilshire Boulevard.

Frost's agent got work for him in B-Westerns. Throughout the 1940s and 1950s, Frost had freelanced in over 120 movies and series and over 150 television shows. He played mostly bad guys, which he liked. He appeared in four of Eddie's films, three of which he played the "heavy." He was also a regular on the 1950s TV series *Highway Patrol* starring Broderick Crawford.[38]

During the 1960s, Frost turned to teaching a drama course at Patricia Stevens Career College in Pasadena for a year. After that he worked for a travel agency as a tour director for nine years, traveling to all parts of the world. Frost also became an author, writing a handbook for aspiring actors entitled *Actors Only*. In later years, he was a frequent guest at Western film festivals.[39]

He died of congestive heart failure on March 1, 1993, in Los Angeles. He was eighty-six.

Tornado Range had a boo boo in it when Roscoe Ates' name changed from "Toby" to "Soapy" about mid-way through the picture. One has to wonder why no one in production noticed it, or if they did, why no one bothered to correct it before releasing the picture. The answer to this enigma lies in the budget. These were low-budget films and re-shooting the scene to make such necessary corrections would have cost PRC more money than it was willing to spend.

(16) *The Westward Trail* (1948)

The Westward Trail was Eddie's sixteenth film for PRC, and his second film (and last film) with his horse Copper. Filmed at the Iverson Ranch in Chatsworth, CA, the fifty-eight-minute film was released on March 13, 1948.

Produced by Jerry Thomas and directed by Ray Taylor, musical supervision was under the direction of Dick Carruth with incidental music composed and directed by Walter Greene. Original screenplay was written by Robert Alan Miller.

Eddie and Copper are joined in this film with Roscoe Ates as "Soapy Jones," Phyllis Planchard as "Ann Howard," Eileen Hardin as "Benson's daughter," Steve Drake as "Tom Howard," Bob Duncan as "Larson," Carl Mathews as "Art Hardin," a henchman, Lee Morgan as "Sheriff Buck Mc-Neal," Bob Woodward as the stagecoach driver, Budd Buster as "Benson," Charles "Slim" Whitaker as the bartender, Frank Ellis as "Taggart," the stableman, and Andy Parker and the Plainsmen (George Bamby, Charlie Morgan, Earl Murphey, and Paul "Clem" Smith) as musicians.

Ann Howard (Phyllis Planchard) and Tom (Steve Drake), her arrogant and delinquent brother, purchase a ranch in Prairie City, but unknown to them a rich vein of silver ore runs through the property and a gang of outlaws, led by Larson (Bob Duncan), the town's the local saloon proprietor turned crooked sheriff, plot to get the land. Tom, is none too thrilled with the wild west and wants to return to Chicago.

Larson talks Tom into forging his sister's name to a deed which he thinks he can sell to the sheriff. But the sheriff has other plans, takes the deed, refuses to pay Tom for it and is holding the forged document as a blackmail threat. Eddie, an undercover federal agent, and his partner, Soapy Jones, learn of the underhanded deal and decide to straighten things out by making sure that Larson is brought to justice but also teaches young Tom the honest Western way of life.

In this film, Eddie sings a pair of compositions by Pete Gates and a tune he and Hal Blair wrote together. The first Gates song is "Cathy," a reflective ballad piece sung in reverie about a one-time lost love. The film's second song, "It's Courtin' Time," by Dean and Blair, is directed at Planchard in an attempt at *détente* in their misunderstood yet strained relationship. The final Gates ditty comes at the end of the picture which features Roscoe Ates demonstrating a variety of musical instruments in "When Shorty Plays the Schottische." Andy Parker and the Plainsmen provide musical accompaniment. There is a pair of tragic postscripts concerning two of the cast members from *The Westward Trail*.

The first story deals with leading lady Phyllis Planchard. Born in 1923, she had a brief B-movie career until the mid-1950s. Some of the other films she appeared in include *Heartaches* (1947), *Dancing in the Dark* (1949), *Roadblock* (1951), and *Women's Prison* (1955). She also appeared for one episode on the *Dragnet* television series in 1956.[40]

Faded in to obscurity, Planchard became the subject of media attention in May 2000 when sadly, she became a ward of Los Angeles County due to her declining mental capabilities.

Eight years later the following news item recounted her most current debilitating situation resulting in a court-ordered change in her guardianship:

"A B-movie actress and model in the 1940s, Phyllis Planchard always loved to dress in stylish clothes. A poetry lover, she collected the works of Robert Frost and Shelley. She cherished a 1920s maple bedroom set that once belonged to her parents. Planchard, then 77, was placed in the public guardian's hands in May 2000 after exhibiting signs of confusion and mental decline. She owned a house in North Hollywood, but police found her living in her car. She was taken to a Burbank hospital, then discharged to a nursing home in Glendale. After becoming her conservator, the public guardian moved her possessions to a county warehouse in Pico Rivera. Attorney Lisa MacCarley, appointed to represent Planchard, said in court filings that she had asked that at least a few personal items, particularly clothes, be brought to the nursing home. On photos from her acting days, Planchard wrote across the bottom: 'A beautiful Phyllis loves clothes!'

"But for seven months, Planchard lived in an almost bare room. She wore used clothing – even underwear – donated by her care home, mostly from patients who had died. 'It's about human dignity. She was aware she had clothing and it wasn't brought to her,' MacCarley said.

"Planchard's nursing home complained about her treatment to professional conservator Dan Stubbs, who asked a probate court to remove the public guardian from the case. Agency officials said an employee eventually brought Planchard some belongings and ordered her new clothes. Nonetheless, in 2001 a judge decided Planchard was better off out of the public guardian's hands. The court named Stubbs as her caretaker."[41]

Planchard died in Los Angeles in 2011. She was eighty-eight.

The other story is about Steve Drake, the young man who played Tom, Planchard's wayward brother. He also played Larry Hadley in *Black Hills* and in *The Hawk of Powder River* (an unaccredited role of previous film footage from *Black Hills*). He was killed in an automobile accident nine months after *The Westward Trail* was released.

Drake's real name was Dale Laurence Fink, but he went by the stage name of Steve Drake.

According to one report, Drake had developed his muscles "driving an ice route back in Tulsa, Oklahoma."

"It was Steve's intention to carry on his father's ice business," the story continued, "but he learned, during a Hollywood vacation one summer, that there was a future for good-looking young men and made new plans."[42] Unfortunately, there wasn't to be any future for the handsome newcomer.

A local San Fernando Valley newspaper reported the terrible news on December 20, 1948:

"Death today ended the meteoric career of young actor Steve Drake, who died from injuries suffered in an early morning automobile crash. The 25-year-old's car ran out of control at a corner in the San Fernando Valley near Sherman Oaks, where he lived with his parents at 4135 Allott Boulevard. His car left the pavement and overturned early in the morning on Sunday as he drove south of Balboa Boulevard at Victory Boulevard. He died [at Burbank's St. Joseph Hospital] a few hours later."[43]

(17) *The Hawk of Powder River* (1948)

In the litany of Eddie's films, *The Hawk of Powder River* was released on April 10, 1948, and is listed as his seventeenth production. In actuality, it was produced during the preceding year. This was the final film in which Eddie rode White Cloud.

Produced by Jerry Thomas and directed by Ray Taylor, musical supervision for *The Hawk of Powder River* was once again done by Dick Carruth with Walter Greene providing the incidental music. The original screenplay was written by George Smith who was creative yet audacious in his approach in having a female as the secretive murderous leader of a gang of outlaws. Portrayed as the antagonist in this story, she was calculating and ruthless, letting nothing get in her way of what she wanted.

Joseph Gluck did a creative piece of film editing, judiciously using Western stock footage of hold up scenes, chase scenes, explosive gunfight scenes and previous film footage from Eddie's pictures to bring the story to life without breaking the PRC bank. Much of the story's plot evolved around reprising the actual film footage from *Black Hills*. (See *Black Hills* synopsis).

That is why Eddie can be seen riding White Cloud for this picture when his last two production releases featured Copper. All of Eddie's non-equine scenes were filmed for this new picture. Whenever Eddie needed to been seen riding White Cloud, film footage from *Black Hills* was used.

However, there is a major film editing blunder that is inexcusable. During the closing moments of the film, June Carlson is biding goodbye to Eddie and Soapy and Eddie rides away not on White Cloud, but on a black horse, presumably Flash. Viewers then see Eddie and Soapy jogging effortlessly along the trail as Eddie is riding Flash singing "Wild Country," which is the exact same scene lifted from Eddie's 1947 movie of the same name and inserted as the closer for this "cut-and-paste" production.

Joining Eddie as a deputy marshal and his horse White Cloud on this exciting and most unusual adventure were Roscoe Ates as "Soapy Jones," Jennifer Holt as "Vivian Chambers, aka, The Hawk," June Carlson as "Carole Chambers," Eddie Parker as "Mike Cochrane, lawyer," Terry Frost as

"Mitchell," a henchman, Lane Bradford as "Cooper," a henchman, Ted French as "Carson," a henchman, Carl Mathews as a henchman, Steve Clark as "Bill Chambers," Steve Drake as "Larry Hadley" (unaccredited from previous footage), Andy Parker as "Charlie," and the Plainsmen (George Bamby, Charlie Morgan, Earl Murphey, and Paul "Clem" Smith), as cowhands/musicians.

Vivian Chambers (Jennifer Holt) is the secret leader of an outlaw gang. Known as "The Hawk," she and her henchmen terrorize the area. Bill Chambers (Steve Clark), owner of the Bar-X-2 Ranch,does not know that his niece, Vivian, is the Hawk and is using his ranch as headquarters. She wants the Chambers Ranch for herself.

When a local newspaper editor begins a crusade against the Hawk's reign of terror, Vivian has her henchmen murder him.

When Bill Chambers accidentally discovers the gang's hideout, he, too, is killed by the Hawk's henchman, attorney Mike Cochrane (Eddie Parker) and Mitchell (Terry Frost). Next in line to inherit the Chambers Ranch is Vivian's cousin, Carole Chambers (June Carlson). Vivian sends her men to kill Carole who is arriving on the stage. She is saved in the nick of time by cowboys Eddie and Soapy (Roscoe Ates), who decide to get to the bottom of the fearful goings-on.

Eddie has Carole Chambers sequestered for her safety at an old line shack until the reading of her father's will. Soapy and Andy Parker and the Plainsmen are helping to guard her. The Hawk and her gang find out about it, and ride out to attack the cabin. *The Hawk of Powder River* ends in a shootout during which Vivian is shot and killed by Eddie.

Many B-Western film aficionados have argued that this was Eddie's best Western – and certainly the balladeer's most unusual as Eddie didn't give a second thought at shooting and subsequently killing a female desperado.

Eddie sings four songs in this picture, all reprised from his previous films and edited into the final production. Two are a collaboration between Eddie and Hal Blair on "Black Hills" and "Wild Country," while the creativity of Pete Gates is once again spotlighted on "Rose Anne of San Jose" and "Punchinello."

The film's "heavy" was lovely Jennifer Holt who stated publicly that this was her favorite movie because she got to play the villainess instead of the pure, sweet heroine.

She was born Elizabeth Marshall Holt in Hollywood, CA, in 1920, to actor Jack Holt and his wife, Margaret Woods. Her older brother was RKO cowboy hero Tim Holt. She made her film debut in the 1941 Hopalong Cassidy Western, *Stick to Your Guns* (Paramount). She went on to make forty-seven films during the 1940s, all but eight were Westerns. She also played the female lead in a pair of serials, *The Adventures of the Flying Cadets* (Universal, 1943) and *Hop Harrigan* (Columbia, 1946).[44]

Holt was Eddie's most frequent leading lady in his films appearing five times in that capacity. In addition to *The Hawk of Powder River*, she was in *Song of Old Wyoming*, (1945), *Shadow Valley* (1947), *Tornado Range* (1948), and *The Tioga Kid* (1948).

Holt made her final film in 1949 and in 1950 she co-hosted *Panhandle Pete and Jennifer*, a television show which ran for one season. Throughout the 1950s she made guest appearances on various television Western series such as *Tales of Wells Fargo*. She also participated in several television programs that originated from Chicago, including the fifteen-minute *The Adventures of Uncle Mistletoe*, which broadcast locally over the ABC network. On the show, Holt played "Aunt Judy" opposite "Uncle Mistletoe," a puppet. Beginning in the 1970s, Holt occasionally participated as a guest star at Western film festivals.[45]

Holt had several marriages, lived in the United States, Mexico, and England. She resided in England at the time of her death on September 21, 1997. She was seventy-six.

The Hawk of Powder River also rates as one of Eddie's favorites from his series of Westerns.

(18) *Prairie Outlaws* (1948)

Prairie Outlaws isn't a new Eddie Dean movie. It's in reality, *Wild West*, first filmed in 1946, and the last of Eddie's Cinecolor productions. This version of the flick was edited, shortened, and released in a Black and White version under a new title, *Prairie Outlaws*. The film does contain new footage of Eddie and Roscoe Ates at the start of the movie conferring with the captain of the Texas Rangers at its headquarters that is not in *Wild West*, while the earlier romantic scene with the two sisters is edited out and two of Eddie's songs removed. For the sake of completeness to Eddie's canon of his films, it is listed here as his eighteenth Western flick that was released. (For a film synopsis, see *Wild West* in Chapter Nine.)

Prairie Outlaws was released as a public relations ploy to bolster the rising stardom of PRC's new Western star Al La Rue, who had co-starred with Eddie in *Wild West* (as he did in *Song of Old Wyoming* and *The Caravan Trail*, respectively). By the time *Prairie Outlaws* was released, La Rue was known to Western fans as "Lash" La Rue, the bullwhip welding hero, who by this time had eight films of his own starring series for PRC under his belt. He would go on to make a dozen more flicks for producer-director Ron Ormond and his Western Adventure production company.

(19) *The Tioga Kid* (1948)

The Tioga Kid is the nineteenth and final flick in the series of Westerns Eddie made for PRC. *The Tioga Kid* is a remake of *Driftin' River* (PRC 1946) with only slight plot changes.

Produced by Jerry Thomas and directed by Ray Taylor, musical supervision was under the auspices of Dick Carruth with incidental music provided by Walter Greene. The original story of *Driftin' River* was by PRC producer-director Robert Emmett Tansey (unaccredited). Original screenplay was written by Ed Earl Repp. Production for this film began in October 1947.

Edward Earl Repp, born in May 1901, in Pittsburgh, Pennsylvania, was a newspaper reporter, screenwriter, and novelist who also wrote occasionally under the pen name of Bradnor Buckner. Repp's stories appeared in several of the early pulp fiction magazines between 1929 and 1945, including *Air Wonder Stories, Science Wonder Stories,* and *Amazing Stories.* During the late 1930s, he began working as a screen-writer for several Western movies starring Tim Holt, Rod Cameron, Johnny Mack Brown, Dick Foran, Russell Hayden, Charles Starrett, among others. Repp died in February 1979, in Butte City, CA. He was seventy-seven.[46]

Eddie plays a dual role as "Texas Ranger Eddie Dean" and outlaw "Clip Mason," aka, "The Tioga Kid," Roscoe Ates as "Soapy Jones," Jennifer Holt as "Jenny Morgan," Dennis Moore as "Joe Moreno," Lee Bennett as "Tucson," a henchman, William Fawcett as "Tennessee," Eddie Parker as "Clem," a henchman, Bob Woodward as "Trigger," a henchman, Wylie Grant as "Sam," a henchman (listed in film credit as Louis J. Corbett), Terry Frost as "Texas Ranger Captain," and Andy Parker as "Texas Ranger Andy" and the Plainsmen (George Bamby, Charlie Morgan, Earl Murphey, and Paul "Clem" Smith) as "Texas Rangers/Musicians" (unaccredited).

Texas Ranger Eddie Dean has an identical twin brother (Clip Mason, aka The Tioga Kid) working with the outlaws of stock footage from the original. All of the songs are recycled, most of the character names are the same, and the main difference is Jennifer Holt is now playing the role that Shirley Patterson had in *Driftin' River* as "Jenny Morgan." Most of the original cast, including Dennis Moore (Joe Moreno), William Fawcett (Tennessee), Lee Bennett (Tucson, a henchman), are also in the film using the same character names, and in some instances, the same footage. All the principals had to shoot minimal new footage with the same or a very close copy to match the majority of stock footage inserted from *Driftin' River.*

Eddie and sidekick Soapy Jones (Roscoe Ates) return some stolen cattle (instead of horses) to Jenny Morgan. Eddie runs off ranch hand Tucson Brown, who is working undercover with the outlaws, led by Joe Moreno. Also in cahoots with the Moreno gang is Clip Mason/The Tioga Kid.

After Jenny sees a wanted poster that makes her think Eddie is the Tioga Kid, Eddie has a hard time convincing her before bringing the gang to justice, aided by the change-of-heart Tioga Kid. In the final shoot out on the street, the Tioga Kid is killed by Moreno and it is then that Eddie discovers that the dead outlaw was in fact, his twin brother who was separated at birth after their parents were killed. Both the Kid and Eddie have matching birth marks on their arms to corroborate their identity.

Much to his credit as an actor, Eddie plays a very convincing bad guy.

Eddie sings three songs in *The Tioga Kid*. He reprises the exact sound track of the beautiful "Driftin' River" from the movie by the same. The piece was composed by Lewis Porter and Robert Tansey.

Eddie, Roscoe Astes, with Andy Parker and the Plainsmen gather around the corral to sing "Way Back in Oklahoma," a novelty piece that Eddie and Johnny Bond composed. Originally, the Sunshine Boys provided the music for this song in *Driftin' River*.

With the final song, "Ain't No Gal Got a Brand On Me," by Pete Gates, Eddie and Andy Parker and the Plainsmen sing to Jennifer Holt in the hopes of warding off any ideas of her wanting to keep Eddie around. The opus provided the perfect exit tune for Eddie and Soapy at the close of the film. The tune was showcased the same way in *Wild Country* when Eddie and Soapy sang it to Peggy Wynn.

The Tioga Kid provides some interesting bit of film trivia. This is the only film of Eddie's in which Terry Frost does not play the bad guy. He is seen at the beginning of the film (during new film footage) as the captain of the Texas Rangers who sends Eddie on assignment to put a stop to the Tioga Kid.

There are some variations to *The Tioga Kid* that slightly differ from *Driftin' River*. Lee Bennett puts a bur under Jennifer Holt's saddle in an attempt to sabotage her success at busting broncos on her ranch.

When Holt confronts Bennett on his deed, Bennett attempts to force his attentions onto Holt. Eddie and Soapy appear on the scene at that moment and Eddie comes to Holt's rescue. In *Driftin' River*, Bennett doesn't act that way toward Shirley Patterson.

Louis Corbett, who played the mercenary outlaw "Whistling Sam" Wade in *Driftin' River*, and who dry gulched William Fawcett as "Tennessee" in the same film, is shown in *The Tioga Kid* doing the same act (from actual previous film footage) to Roscoe Ates, but this time only wounding him.

The horse that the Tioga Kid rode was Copper.

This fifty-four-minute Western drama was released on June 17, 1948.

When Eddie started his series of Westerns, his pictures cost from two to three times more than the average Western, but because Eddie was such a fine singer, the studio tried to put more into the music that he did.

Although Eddie's pictures had plenty of "shoot-em-up" action, he insisted on pulling back on the reigns from having the violent episodes becoming too vicious, he said.

"We had a lot of gunfights and if they got to shooting too many shots, I'd start raising heck about it," Eddie said. "I'd say, 'Look, you see this all the time. Every Western you see you see them shoot, shoot, shoot and never hit anything. When I shoot at something, I either want to hit it or I don't want to shoot.' Consequently, we cut down on a lot of that and a lot of the chases and put more money into the story, the stories were good, and into the music. You can go see any Western and see a guy on horseback chasing someone. I mean how many *thousands* of times have you seen it? So I didn't want too much of that, either, unless it plays a specific important part of the movie."[47]

Eddie always felt that the emphasis in his flicks should be on the story and music as opposed to action, which played an important part in the success of his pictures.

With the conclusion of *The Tioga Kid*, it brought down the final curtain on Eddie's movie career. Television was quickly becoming the main medium for entertainment in America and the life span of the B-Western singing cowboy movies were quickly coming to end. Over the remaining years, he would appear sporadically on television as a guest or in a limited capacity as a lead. All in all, Eddie starred in nineteen Western films. That's about one fourth the films his cowboy contemporaries Roy Rogers and Gene Autry each made during their careers.

When looking back on Eddie's career in films the "what if's" begin to surface. "What if" PRC had continued producing all of Eddie's series of

Westerns in Cinecolor despite the cost? Would it have bolstered his career? "What if" PRC paid more attention to detail in producing Eddie's films, instead of rushing somewhat haphazardly through a time schedule for the sake of financial issues?

Looking at the Black and White Lash La Rue films or even the Buster Crabbe "Billy the Kid" series for PRC, they appear to be of far better quality than those of Eddie's. "What if" Eddie had signed on with Republic Pictures or Monogram Pictures instead of PRC, would he have been showcased the way the movie cowboys from those studios were? Rex Allen, for example, who became a Republic Pictures star two years after Eddie made his last movie, was showcased in a far better way, with better quality film and story lines than Eddie experienced with PRC.

These aforementioned points are just speculation, of course. To dwell on such speculation is futile. What we do know and what we can celebrate is the overwhelming consensus that Eddie had the best and most admired singing voice of all the movie singing cowboys, that he was respected as an individual and as an artist by his peers, that he never had a big star complex, that he left movie buffs with a few well-produced, action-packed films. In addition, he made Western film history by having his initial series of Western movies filmed in color, and because of his popularity he was "legitimized," so to speak, as having been ranked as one of the "Top Ten Money Making Western Stars" for two years in a row.

While his movie career appeared to have faded into the sunset by 1948, Eddie was by no means riding a dead end trail. After his series of Westerns ended, Eddie then focused his attention toward television. His first attempt at the new entertainment medium came in 1950 with *The Marshal of Gunsight Pass*, a live Black and White thirty-minute Western television series that ran for one season (22 episodes) from March 12, 1950 to September 30, 1950 over the ABC network. The show starred Eddie, Russell Hayden, and Riley Hill, who all played the part of the marshal at various times during the program's six-month run.

Roscoe Ates played Deputy Roscoe while Andy Parker played Andy, and Bert Wenland as Bud Glover. The first show was broadcast from a lot at the Iverson Movie Ranch in Chatsworth, CA, with Russell Hayden as the marshal. Eddie became Marshal #2 in subsequent episodes that were then-televised live from ABC's new television studios in Hollywood, at Prospect and Talmadge.

Geared toward a children's audience, the program was telecast live to West Coast stations and viewed via kinescope elsewhere. Even for the year 1950, the production of the program seemed unusually primitive.[48]

Eddie made regular appearances on Leo Carrillo's *Dude Ranch Varieties* TV show, as well as regular TV appearances on *Western Varieties*, a live half-hour weekly Western musical variety show on KTLA Channel 5 from Los Angeles, *Town Hall Party*, and Tex Ritter's *Ranch Party*, all from the 1950s.

Later in the 1950s, Eddie was seen via his films on *The Gabby Hayes Show*, a general purpose Western television series in which the loveable curmudgeon George "Gabby" Hayes" narrated, showed clips from old Westerns, and told tall tales for a primarily children's audience. The first Hayes program ran on NBC at 5:15 p. m. Eastern for fifteen minutes three times per week. It aired from December 11, 1950, to January 1, 1954. The second version was a half-hour broadcast on Saturday mornings, carried for only thirteen weeks from May 12 to July 14, 1956, on ABC.[49]

It was during the second version of the Hayes show that portions of Eddie's films were shown (as were other Western stars) in between Hayes' humorous tales of the exploits of his zany relatives as he happily whittles away. Such viewing allowed Eddie's films to gain greater exposure to a younger audience who didn't grow up watching his films in movie theaters at Saturday matinees.

Eddie's next exertion into television occurred in 1962 with *The Night Rider*, a half-hour TV short starring Johnny Cash, Eddie as Tim Dawson, Wesley Tuttle, Merle Travis, and Johnny Western (who sang "The Ballad of Paladin," the theme song for TV's *Have Gun, Will Travel* starring Richard Boone).

Released on June 1, 1962, *The Night Rider* was a pilot that failed to sell.[50] Tim Dawson (Eddie) is the boss of a trail-herding crew consisting of Kentucky (Merle Travis), a cook who plays the guitar, Joe (Gordon Terry), and Marty (Johnny Western), a young, impressionable cowhand who longs for the glamorous life of a gunfighter. While the four cowhands sing around the campfire, a night-riding gunfighter named Johnny Laredo (Johnny Cash) happens upon their camp and joins them for a cup of coffee. He then rides on, leaving Marty wishing he could go with him.

In the saloon in Bracketville, Johnny Laredo is accosted at the bar by Billy Joe, a drunken young cowboy (Dickie Jones). Roxy (Karen Downes), the saloon singer, shames Billy Joe by calling him a boy, and in an effort to prove himself a man, he draws on Laredo. Laredo is faster and kills Billy Joe, but Laredo's life is immediately changed as he is revolted at what he had to do. He attends the boy's funeral where the service is preached and a hymn sung by the circuit-riding Preacher (Wesley Tuttle). Laredo rides backs to the camp of the trail herders and joins them while trying to come to grips with his past.

Eddie's final television appearances came in 1962 during the first season of *The Beverly Hillbillies.* Eddie plays Sergeant Eddie Dean of the Beverly Hills Police in Episode 19 called "Elly's Animals," which was filmed on November 19 and 29 and aired on January 30, 1963.[51] Granny (Irene Ryan) sets Elly May's (Donna Douglas) dogs and the police on Cousin Pearl (Bea Benaderet) to stop her yodeling, making everyone mad at her. Granny becomes contrite when she thinks she'll get kicked out of the clan for it, until the police find her homemade moonshine still and she thinks Pearl turned her in.

Eddie was paid $200 a day based on union scale for the two days of shooting the episode of "Elly's Animals."[52]

Eddie returned to the sitcom two weeks later again as Sergeant Dean in Episode 21 called "Jed Plays Solomon," which aired on February 13, 1963.[53] Granny can't stand Pearl's yodeling so she reports her to the police. When Sergeant Dean arrives back on the scene to take Pearl out and takes yodeling lessons for himself, Granny thinks she got Pearl in trouble and becomes sad and contrite. Meanwhile, the police find Granny's still, and new trouble results. Eddie was paid the same amount of money per day for appearing in this episode as well.

Not to be counted out entirely, Eddie's film career had the possibility of being resurrected as he was considered to play the lead in a bio-pic about Country singing icon Hank Williams, who died prematurely in 1953, at age twenty-nine. Unfortunately for Eddie, it didn't happen. Eddie himself explains:

"Mr. Marvin Skink, who was President of MGM Pictures, wanted me to play Hank Williams in the film. This about three years after Hank died. He had seen all my pictures, so I went out for an interview and he said I was the guy for the part. But somewhere along the line the talks got bogged down. Maybe Audrey, Hank's first wife, didn't want me to do the part, I don't know. All I know is I had the part cinched, but somebody stopped it.

"The film wasn't made until years later, and Mr. Skink told me that 'As long as I am President of MGM, the picture won't be done at MGM unless (I) do the part.' I have a letter written to me from him stating that. Whenever I'd do a show, people would often tell me that I reminded them so much of Hank."[54]

While Eddie certainly sang differently than Williams, there was quite a discussion between him and Skink as to whether Eddie would use Hank's records and mouth the lyrics during filming or whether Eddie was to do a semi-impersonation.

"I said either way, because I *do* impersonations," Eddie said. "I said I could do it enough like Hank without sounding exactly like him and still have my own identification, if they wanted it that way. Mr. Skink thought that maybe that would be the best thing to do, rather than try to use the records."[55]

The Williams biopic was called *Your Cheatin' Heart* and starred George Hamilton as Williams, Susan Oliver as Audrey Williams, Red Buttons as Shorty Younger, and Arthur O'Connell as Fred Rose. The film was released in December 1964, and was the last MGM musical shot in Black and White.[56]

Hank Williams, Jr., who was fourteen years old at the time, provided the singing voice of his late father in the film.

"Maybe that's what they were waiting for," Eddie said with a laugh.

The one thing Eddie had going for himself that other cowboy actors didn't, was he had his music to carry him through his career. And that's just what he did. He performed, composed, and recorded consistently over the years almost right up to the time of his passing. Although Eddie's movies are part of Western film history, his real and lasting legacy is to be found in his music.

Eddie Dean talks with Henry Hall over his assignment to capture the
outlaw Rip Claxton in *Wild West* (PRC 1947).

Above: Movie poster advertising *Wild Country*,
Eddie Dean's ninth PRC western (1947).

Below: Peggy Wynn, Roscoe Ates, and Eddie Dean on a lobby card
showing the final moments to *Wild Country* (PRC 1947)

Eddie Dean in a publicity photo from 1947.

Eddie Dean loads his six-shooter for a publicity photo from 1947.

Eddie Dean poses with his wife Dearest from 1947.

Above: Eddie Dean shown with Helen Mowrey,
his leading lady, from *Range Beyond the Blue* (PRC 1947).

Below: A lobby card from *West to Glory* (PRC 1947)
showing Roscoe Ates, Eddie Dean and Delores Castle.

Above: A lobby card for *Black Hills*, Eddie Dean's twelfth film for PRC (1947). Pictured is Roscoe Ates and Shirley Patterson. *Black Hills* also introduces movie goers to White Cloud, Eddie's new horse.

Below: Another lobby card for *Black Hills* with Eddie Dean and Roscoe Ates shown with Andy Parker and the Plainsmen.

Above: A scene from *Black Hills* with Charlie Morgan,
Roscoe Ates, Eddie Dean, and Andy Parker (l-r, front), and George Bamby,
Joaquin Murphy, and Clem Smith (l-r, back).

Below: Andy Parker (middle, standing) with The Plainsmen from 1947.
Clockwise, GeorgeBamby, Charlie Morgan, Joaquin Murphey, Clem Smith.

Eddie Dean snuggles closer to Shirley Patterson as he sings "Let's Go Sparkin'" in the final moments of *Black Hills* (PRC 1947). Behind Eddie is his horse White Cloud, a palomino stallion, who made its film debut in the picture.

**Eddie Dean poses for a publicity photo in 1947
with his palomino horse White Cloud.**

Eddie Dean is pictured mounted on White Cloud, his palomino stallion, from a scene from *Shadow Valley*, Eddie's thirteenth production for PRC (1947).

Above: Pressbook cover about Eddie Dean's
latest PRC film, *Shadow Valley*, from 1947.

Below: A lobby card for *Shadow Valley* as Eddie Dean
catches crooked lawyer George Chesebro
red-handed with his hand in the till.

Eddie Dean is ready to get the drop on bad guys George Chesebro and
Eddie Parker in *Shadow Valley* (PRC 1947).

Eddie Dean and Jennifer Holt wonder what Roscoe Ates is
pointing at in *Shadow Valley*. Looking on are Lane Bradford,
Andy Parker (second from left) and the Plainsmen.

Above: Roscoe Ates fiddles while Eddie Dean
wonders in *Shadow Valley* (PRC 1947).

Below: Roscoe Ates (left) fiddles around with Andy Parker (far right)
and the Plainsmen in *Shadow Valley* (PRC 1947).

Above: Eddie Dean takes a moment to pose for a photo with Lee Morgan who plays the sheriff in *Shadow Valley* (PRC 1947).

Below: Eddie Dean croons to Jennifer Holt as they ride the ranch wagon to town in *Shadow Valley* (PRC 1947). Hitched at the rear of the wagon is White Cloud, Eddie's horse.

Above: Eddie Dean duking it out with bad guy
George Chesebro in *Shadow Valley* (PRC 1947).

Below: Roscoe Ates pins the sheriff's badge on Eddie Dean as
George Chesebro, Nancy Gates, and I. Stanford Jolley
watch in *Check Your Guns* (PRC 1947).

Movie poster advertising *Check Your Guns,*
the newest Eddie Dean flick for PRC (1947).

Above: Eddie Dean loads his gun while conferring with his sidekick Roscoe Ates as to their plan for rounding up the bad guys in *Check Your Guns* (PRC 1947).

Below: Eddie Dean with Nancy Gates during the final moments of *Check Your Guns* (PRC 1947).

Sheriff Eddie Dean tries to convince the judge (William Fawcett) that Mikel Conrad as henchman Ace Banyon (to Eddie's right) is guilty of murder in *Check Your Guns* (PRC 1947). Also pictured in front is Nancy Gates, Roscoe Ates and George Chesebro.

Above: An advertisement for *Tornado Range* (PRC 1948).

Below: Eddie Dean proudly shows off his fourth
and newest movie mount, Copper, a quarter horse.
Copper made his debut in *Tornado Range.*

Movie poster for *The Westward Trail* (PRC 1948).

Above: Lobby card for *The Westward Trail* (PRC 1948). Eddie Dean and Phyllis Planchard are covered by a henchman while crooked sheriff Bob Duncan watches.

Below: An ad for *The Westward Trail* (PRC 1948).

Above: Roscoe Ates as Soapy Jones tries to convince
Phyllis Planchard that his pal Eddie Dean is on the
level in a scene from *The Westward Trail* (PRC 1948).

Below: An ad for *The Hawk of Powder River* (PRC 1948).

Above: Film title for *The Hawk of Powder River* (PRC 1948).

Below: Eddie Dean and Roscoe Ates get the drop on
bad guys Eddie Parker, seated, and Terry Frost, standing,
in *The Hawk of Powder River* (PRC 1948).

Above: An ad for *Prairie Outlaws* (PRC 1948).

Below: Lobby card for *Prairie Outlaws* (PRC 1948) showing Roscoe Ates, Lee Bennett, Eddie Dean and Al La Rue with guns drawn ready for a shoot out.

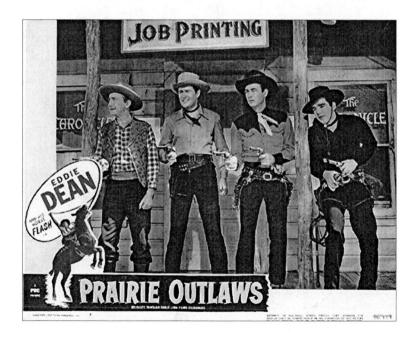

Movie Poster for *Prairie Outlaws* (PRC 1948).

Above: Lobby card for *The Tioga Kid* (PRC 1948).

Below: Eddie Dean knocking out Lee Bennett with a right cross in a scene from *The Tioga Kid* (PRC 1948).

Above: Eddie Dean in a dual role as outlaw Clip Mason, a.k.a
The Tioga Kid, left, and as Texas Ranger Eddie Dean, right,
in a scene from *The Tioga Kid* (PRC 1948).

Below: Jennifer Holt was Eddie Dean's leading lady in five films. She
played the villainess in *The Hawk of Powder River* (PRC 1948).

Poster announcing Eddie Dean as one of the
"Top Ten Money Making Western Stars" of 1946 and 1947.

Poster announcing a public appearance by Eddie Dean.

Eddie Dean in double, 1947.

The Bad Guys We All Loved To Hate

The "Heavies" Who Went Up Against Eddie Dean (And Lost)

George Chesebro

Terry Frost

Bob Duncan

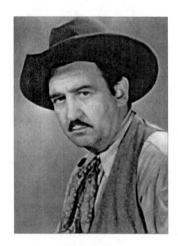

Charlie King

William Fawcett

I. Stanford Jolley

Dennis Moore

Forrest Taylor

12

Music, Music, Music

"It is the best of all trades to make songs,
and the second best to sing them."

\- Hilaire Belloc (1870-1953)

Music has always played a key role in Eddie's life. It was through the gift of music that got him started in the entertainment business and it's what sustained him during and long after his movie career rode into the sunset. Eddie was blessed with the ability to play music along with possessing a fabulous set of pipes that never seemed to tarnish over the years. Touching Gene Autry for luck as Eddie did back in 1938 during a break on the set of *Western Jamboree* must have had efficacy as Eddie had been working steady literally right up to the moment he passed away. However, putting superstition aside, it's probably safer to conclude that he is better remembered and has made more of an impact from his musical artistry than he did from his films.

Eddie recorded over 400 songs and wrote and/or collaborated on over fifty songs throughout his career. Two became hits that have since been solidified to permanent and honored places in the canon of American Western music. The first hit was "One Has My Name, the Other Has My Heart," written with Hal Blair and Dearest Dean. The other chart-topper was "I Dreamed of a Hillbilly Heaven." Eddie composed the music while Hal Southern penned the lyrics.

Eddie also had first dibs to record a number of other fabulous pieces of original material, but was handcuffed from doing so due to artistry categorization from the record companies of which he was signed to at the time. Other recording artists from other labels were then pitched the same material to record and in so doing, became blockbuster hits for them.

After recording eight sides for Bel-Tone Records in 1945, Eddie signed on with Majestic Records the following year. By then, his Western films were gaining great popularity and the label could offer Eddie more commercial success and flexibility.

Majestic Records was based in New York City and the label enjoyed its greatest commercial success in the 1940s, until over-ambitious expansion and an inability to keep distributors supplied with pressings of discs resulted in financial problems, and the label folded in 1948.[1]

For a time in the 1940s bandleader Ben Selvin headed the label's artists and repertory. The company was headed by former New York City mayor Jimmy Walker.

In addition to Eddie, other artists who recorded on Majestic included Louis Prima, Jimmie Lunceford, Eddy Howard, Ray McKinley, Foy Willing and the Riders of the Purple Sage, Georgia Gibbs, Mildred Bailey, The Three Suns, Jane Froman, The Korn Kobblers, The De Marco Sisters, George Olsen, Morton Downey, and Jack Leonard, among others.[2]

Between June 1946 and July 1947, "Eddie Dean and His Boys" recorded sixteen sides for Majestic, portions of which were his own compositions including a reprise of "On the Banks of the Sunny San Juan" (with Glenn Strange), "Spring Has Come to Missouri" (with Hal Blair), "Toodle-Oo My Darling," (with Blair and Tex Ritter), and "It's a Boy," (with Guy and Ormand).[3]

Adding to the Majestic catalog were songs Eddie recorded that were featured in his films such as "There's a Rose That Grows in the Ozarks," from *Down Missouri Way*, "Let's Go Sparkin'" (with Blair) from *Black Hills*, and

"Rose Anne of San Jose," (a Peter Gates composition) from *Shadow Valley* and *The Hawk of Powder* River.

Eddie also did a cover version of "No Vacancy," a Merle Travis-Cliffie Stone offering, that Travis had waxed which became a huge hit. The song laments about the housing shortage World War II veterans faced upon returning home.

As 1948 approached, the musician's union under the leadership of its president James Caesar Petrillo, called for another musicians' union strike to commence January 1. It was the second strike to take place in the decade; the first one lasting from August 1942 until November 1944. This meant that no union musician could set foot into a recording studio to make records. Vocalists were not considered musicians and were therefore exempt from such arbitration.

The basis for the 1948 strike was that the musicians' union claimed that royalties from records played on radio, phonograph records and jukeboxes were being denied to the musicians who made them. The union demanded that record companies pay a percentage of record sales to a union fund set up to help unemployed musicians. Initially the record companies balked at such a proposal, holding out for almost a year.

The 1948 strike was shorter in duration, lasting to December 14 of that year, with record companies capitulating to union demands.

This was the back drop as to how "One Has My Name, the Other Has My Heart" came to be created and recorded.

By December 1947 and with time running out, the record companies were scrambling to get as many artists recorded as possible before the midnight deadline of New Year's Eve. Eddie was in the same lot with Majestic. He had a few songs he wanted to record before the deadline and was waiting for a recording slot to open up.

In the meantime, Eddie and Hal Blair were at Eddie's home studio working on polishing a song the pair composed along with Ethel Girvin called "Wake Me Up in the Morning By the Swanee River," a piece that Eddie said he liked. They had the tape machine running so they could record any musical ideas that might come up as they were working.

Dearest walked into the studio and told Eddie that she had a title for a song that she and Eddie had been discussing for the past five years. Eddie asked her to please wait just a moment until he and Hal finished up what they were doing with "Swanee."

"But I've got the title," Dearest insisted.

"What do you mean?" Eddie asked her. "What title?"

"One Has My Name, the Other Has My Heart," she said.

Eddie and Blair stopped what they were doing and since Eddie had his guitar in hand, he began to instinctively strum some chords and began singing, *"One has my name, the other has my heart."*

Then Blair chimed in with the next line, *"With one I'll remain that's how my heartaches starts."*

During this time, the tape machine was still running.

"Hal and I continued to trade lines and in ten minutes we had that song written," Eddie recalled.

Dearest came back to the studio later and told the boys that she had the perfect ending for the song so that people will understand that it has some moral to it. Her concluding line was, *"If I could live over my life I would change the one who has my heart will also have my name."* [4]

In its finished form, "One Has My Name, the Other Has My Heart," as penned by the triumvirate composers of Eddie Dean, Hal Blair, and Dearest Dean, looked like this:

One has my name, the other has my heart,
With one I'll remain that's when my heartaches start
One has brown eyes, the other's eyes are blue
To one I am tied, but to the other I am true.
One has my love, the other has only me
But what good is love to a heart that can't be free
So I'll go living my life just the same
While one has my heart and the other has my name.
One has my love the other only me

But what good is love to a heart that can't be free
If I could live over my life I would change
The one who has my heart would also have my name.

Eddie knew that he had a hit song on his hands and was anxious to get it waxed prior to the recording deadline. Majestic Records had just finished recording vocalist-bandleader Eddy Howard (the year before Howard recorded his blockbuster hit "To Each His Own" for the label) and the A & R man called Eddie to tell him to be at the recording studio the following day at 2 p. m. as he had a three-hour recording session booked for him.

Ten minutes later the A & R man called Eddie back to tell him the bad news that Majestic Records just went out of business and that the label would not be doing any further recordings. Eddie told him that he had just written a hit song and that it would be in the record company's best interest to record him and the piece. Intrigued, the record exec wanted to hear it.

"I sang it a coppella for him over the phone," Eddie said.

"Gosh! That *is* a hit song if I ever heard one," the A & R man replied.

The record exec called Majestic Records headquarters in New York City and told them that they have to record Eddie with this song. He was told again in no uncertain terms that Majestic Records is no longer in business and that the label will never make another record as far as they were concerned.

Disappointed, the A & R man notified Eddie again with the bad news.

"We didn't know what we were going to do," Eddie lamented. "We knew we had a hit song. I was now in a spot. I didn't have a record company. I didn't have any musicians. All the musicians were taken as well as all the studios as everyone was working frantically up to the last minute to get things done before the strike took effect."

About a half hour after incurring his "pink slip" from Majestic Records, Eddie received a telephone call from Henry Shelb, owner of Crystal Records, a small independent record company in Los Angeles, who invited Eddie to record for him.

"Eddie, I understand Majestic Records isn't recording anymore and I understand that you have some material you want recorded," Shelb said. "Why don't you come here and record them for Crystal Records?"

Shelb had his own studio and pressing plant.

"Do you have musicians?" Eddie asked.

"Yes, I sure do," Shelb replied.

"OK, I'll do it," Eddie said, "only if you promise me that we record this one song that I have as the first song. I don't care what other songs you'd want me to do. I'll do a whole session for you if you want, but I want this one particular song recorded first and pressed tonight as it needs to go out tomorrow."

"Well, I don't care what the song is," Shelb told Eddie. "Just come down here and record and I'll do whatever you say."

Eddie went to see Shelb in his office and handed him the lyrics to "One Has My Name, the Other Has My Heart."

"This is the song I want to do first," Eddie said.

Shelb read the lyrics and told Eddie, "We can't do this."

"Why not?" Eddie asked.

"Because it's too controversial," Shelb shot back.

"You told me I could do anything I wanted to do, now you're going back on your word to me?" Eddie said.

"We can't do this song, Eddie, it's too controversial," Shelb reiterated. "The lyrics . . . they won't play it on the air."

Shelb was correct. He was only telling Eddie the truth. The lyrics were suggestive for that time and its content was perceived as lacking scruples. In essence, the song was considered a slap in the face against the institution of marriage.[5]

Thinking that he wasn't going to get any further with Shelb, Eddie picked up the lyrics and headed out the door.

"Where are you going?" Shelb asked.

"I'm going home."

"Why are you going home? Let's record!"

"No, we're not going to record unless you record this one song, and you get it out tonight, and you get it on the presses as soon as you get the acetate cut, and have it out tomorrow," Eddie insisted.

"Does this song mean that much to you?" Shelb asked.

"It sure does!" Eddie said excitedly. "I've got a hit song and I want to put it out. I don't want to put out junk. I've got a hit song here. I want a hit song! The rest of it you can do what you want to, but this song has got to go!"

"OK, OK, I'll do it," Shelb said, recanting his previous position.

Eddie went into the studio had a quick rehearsal with the studio musicians and immediately recorded "One Has My Name, the Other Has My Heart" a few days before the recording ban would take effect.

The next day Eddie received a copy of the 78 rpm record, and he and Dearest took it to his friend, Cliffie Stone, who hosted a Country Western radio show on KRKD that broadcast from the Arcade Building in downtown Los Angeles.

Stone was in the middle of doing his show. While the engineer working with him was operating the other turntable for broadcast, Stone saw that Eddie had a new record he wanted to plug. Eddie handed Stone the record and he put it on while the other turntable was broadcasting and listened to the first twelve bars. He reached down and took the record off the turntable and said, "I can't play that side. What's on the flip side?"

"This is the side I want you to play," Eddie insisted. "You won't play either side unless you play this side."

"I can't play it," Stone said.

"Why not?" Eddie asked.

"The lyrics," Stone said.

"It's true lyrics," Eddie pleaded. "What are you worrying about the lyrics for?"

"What's the matter with you?" Stone asked of his friend. "You mad or something?"

"No, I'm half mad," Eddie confessed. "I bring you a hit song and you don't want to play it. The man I recorded it for didn't want to record it and now I'm having to battle with you! I just don't want you to play the other side. I want you to play *this* side."

Out of curiosity, Stone asked what the name of the song was on the other side of the record.

"It's called 'Wake Me in the Morning By the Swanee River,'" Eddie replied. "It's a good song, but this is my *hit* song."

"OK, Eddie, if you feel that way, I'll play it," Stone said. "But you'll have to be responsible."

"Alright, I will, no problem," Eddie replied.

Stone played the record on the air and before the song was finished, about 40 calls came in the radio station from listeners who wanted to know where they could get the record.

Lee Gillette, a producer from Capitol Records, also heard the song and liked it and wanted to put it on Capitol, so he called Stone asking him to call Eddie to try to get the master from Henry Shelb.

"I went back to Henry Shelb asking him to let Capitol Records have 'One Has My Name, the Other Has My Heart' so they could make a star out of me," Eddie said. "Capitol had the distribution and the means to really get behind the song. They could make a recording star out of me with this one song. I've been fighting for years for something like this to happen and I finally got a song that's moving."

Now when Shelb learned of all the interest and attention given to Eddie's song, he realized that he was sitting on a gold mine and didn't want to relinquish the song.

"You want me to give up a hit song?" he asked. "You can't take a hit song away from me."

"Well, you didn't want to record it in the first place!" Eddie shot back.

"True, but I did record it," Shelb said.

"Why don't you sell it to Capitol?" Eddie asked once more. "You've got all my other records, you'll come out all right. It'll put you in business." Shelb wouldn't budge.

Lee Gillette called Eddie and of course, there was really nothing they could about it since Shelb legally owned the master.

"Of course Capitol couldn't steal the song like some companies do today with the black market and music piracy," Eddie said. "As long as Shelb was sitting on the piece, my song wasn't going to go anywhere."

The musicians' union strike was well underway as the days progressed further in to1948, and record companies were judiciously releasing their artists' material throughout the year that was recorded before the strike deadline.

While Eddie thought his opportunity for "One Has My Name" went fizzling out like a burned out Roman candle, the miraculous happened. Unbeknownst to Eddie, Jimmy Wakely, with the help of Colleen Summers, got a hold of the song and recorded it. That burned out Roman candle was now burning brighter and more powerful than ever. Wakely's recording turned out to be a huge hit for the cowboy singer and it helped put Eddie's song on the musical map, so to speak.

"I don't know how they did it and I really don't care because they really gave the song a break," Eddie said. "I don't know how they were able to make the record during the strike, whether they had the music prerecorded in Canada or Europe and they dubbed over it. The next thing I know their recording of the song stayed at Number One throughout the nation for 36 weeks. Here I am sitting with a small label with the music and I couldn't do anything."

Some recording artists used that means of having the music prerecorded in another country and then dubbing over the music with their vocals here in the States. Such practices were frowned upon by the musicians' union, but were totally legal within the framework of union guidelines.

Margaret Whiting, in her autobiography, *It Might As Well Be Spring*, confessed this was the means as to how she was able to record her hit song, "A Tree in the Meadow," in 1948.

"One Has My Name, the Other Has My Heart" became so popular that the song was pitched to the networks to broadcast, but every network banned the song because of the lyrics, every one of them. Even the Roman Catholic Church, whom Dearest was a devout member, also took exception to the song's content. By today's standards the lyrics are mild, but in 1948 what it had to say was considered scandalous to the point of being banned by the Catholic Church. The song was definitely a piece of material that was ahead of its time and paved the way for future songs calling attention to similar themes.[6]

It is interesting to note that just a short time later, in early 1949, Jimmy Wakely and Margaret Whiting recorded "Slippin' Around" on Capitol Records, another song of marital infidelity. The song became a big hit for the pair of vocalists.

"Jimmy now had two big hits on his hands in a matter of months: 'One Has My Name' and 'Slippin' Around,'" Eddie observed. "Whether Jimmy wanted to admit it or not, 'One Has My Name' was the one that got him going. It was his first hit song. Without being immodest, 'One Has My Name' really turned things around. That's the song, in my opinion, that did it. I don't know if Floyd Tillman, the composer of 'Slippin' Around,' had his song written before mine or not, but if he had, we were thinking along the same ideas, the same lines, because we knew what was going on; the changes that were coming."

A surprising change that was heading Eddie's way, at least on the surface, was Shelb's desire to see Eddie's attorney at his own request to make arrangements to pay Eddie the money that he owed him for "One Has My Name, the Other Has My Heart."

"I want to pay Eddie," Shelb said to the attorney about his change of heart. "I owe him $6,500 for that one song. I would have to do it by making monthly payments and all I can afford is $25 per month."

Shelb's change of conscience may have been honorable, but in following up on such noble intentions, he failed miserably. Shelb died before ever paying Eddie.

"I don't hold any hate in my heart for the man," Eddie said. "I think if people owe you money, you should be paid. The song was my creation, more or less. I was at least a part of it. It was my record, my singing on it, and then for somebody not to pay you a dime for something that you created and given to them to make the money and put them in the record business and then never paying you is wrong. I don't hate him, I never hated him for it."

In retrospect, Shelb put the screws to Eddie twice: not paying him for the song and by not selling the master recording to Capitol Records.

"In actuality he also put those screws to himself, too," Eddie observed.

"I made a remark about Shelb prior to his passing that to me, he was just a stupid S. O. B. Word got back to him about my remark and he called me and said, 'I understand you said that I was a stupid S. O. B." I said to him, 'If I did to you what you did to me, wouldn't you call me the same thing? I'd come over right now and tell it your face if you want me to. It's just the way I feel, Henry, because I think you're a bad businessman. I just think you did a stupid deal, that's all. You weren't giving anything away because you had nothing before. Everything that was there was given to you. You had everything to gain by releasing my song to Capitol Records."

After getting an earful from Eddie, Shelb hemmed and hawed over the phone and finally had to admit, "Well, you're right, Eddie."

"I didn't dislike Henry Shelb," Eddie confessed. "I just disliked what he didn't do."

In addition to "One Has My Name, the Other Has My Heart" and the jovial "Wake Me Up in the Morning By the Swanee River," Eddie's output at Crystal Records was nominal, recording only six sides with group, "The Frontiersmen," that were made prior to the musicians' union strike deadline.

Most of the sides were original pieces with collaborations with Hal Blair. Roy Barcroft, who usually played the bad guy in dozens of B-Westerns, teamed up with Eddie and Blair to write a "ghoulishly spooky" but lighthearted piece on "Gravedigger's Lament," while Eddie, Dearest, and Blair weaved a melancholy tapestry on "A Million Tears Ago."

Eddie, Dearest, and Hal Blair made their money off "One Has My Name" not through Crystal Records but through the music publishers and from royalties from other artists who recorded the song.

"One Has My Name, the Other Has My Heart" remains one of the big Country Western songs even today with 57 different artists over the years recording it.[7] Eddie's version reached #11. The pantheon of artists include Nat "King" Cole, Al Martino, Vaughn Monroe, Bob Eberley, Pat Boone, Ace Cannon, James Darren, Mickey Gilley, Hank Locklin, Carl Smith, Billy Vaughn, Jerry Wallace, The Johnny Mann Singers, Don Gibson, Willie Nelson, The Morganaires with Russ Morgan and his Orchestra, George Jones and Gene Pitney, and early rocker Jerry Lee Lewis, who had the biggest hit of the song in 1969.

Eddie had been a long-time admirer of Lewis' style with a song, and vice versa. So after Eddie and Dearest went to see Lewis' show at the Palomino Club in North Hollywood, CA, they were invited backstage to talk with "The Killer." Lewis mentioned that he loved "One Has My Name, the Other Has My Heart" and so Eddie told him if he wanted to record it, he could. A few weeks later that's what Lewis did and it became a smash hit for the rock and roll pioneer. His version on Mercury Records reached #3 on the Country chart.[8]

Many of the songs that bear Eddie's name are often seen in collaboration with his wife, Dearest, whom he credits as playing a big part in his career, as well as a man who originally hailed from Kansas City, Missouri: Hal Blair.

"Hal was such a prolific lyricist," Eddie said. "He was one of the best I ever knew."

Born in 1915, Blair came to Los Angeles in 1940 as a member of Cal Shrum and His Rhythm Rangers. Eddie and Blair first met while appearing together in the Tex Ritter film, *Rollin' Home to Texas*. A close friendship ensued between the two men and soon Blair's talents were recognized by Hollywood to provide material for singing cowboy movies of the era.

Blair's closest musical associate without a doubt was Eddie. The pair's musical kinship helped to inspire songs for Eddie's films that included *Black Hills, Check Your Guns, Stars Over Texas, Tornado Range,* and *Wild Country.*

Blair's name was widely recognized on song credits as co-collaborator on many of Eddie's recordings such as "Cry, Cry, Cry," "Spring Has Come Again to Old Missouri," "Boogie Woogie Cowboy" (with Eddie, Gus Snow, Jack Statham), "I Asked a Dream" (with Eddie, Gus Snow, Jack Statham), "You Want to Divorce Me" (with Eddie and Ham Hamilton), "Courtin' Time," "I'm Back in the Game," "Chasing Yesterday," "Institutes and Imitations," "West to Glory," "Song of the Range," "Katmandu," (with Eddie and Dearest. The song was influenced from his service experience in Katmandu from the China-India-Burma Theater during World War II), "I'm Not in

Love, Just Involved" (with Eddie and Dearest Dean), and "One More Time Around" (with Eddie and Howard Barnes), among others.

But it's safe to say Blair's most significant collaborative effort occurred with Eddie and his wife, Dearest, on "One Has My Name, the Other Has My Heart."

In addition to his song writing talents with Eddie, Blair also was part of Eddie's live stage appearances wearing many hats from playing the villain role to being Master of Ceremonies.

"When Hal came out of the service, he had nothing going for him and I knew Hal was a good writer and I took him on the road with me," Eddie said. "When he got back to the States, he was under a lot of stress, nervous stress, because he'd been through a lot in India. He was all the way over to Katmandu, the capitol of Nepal. In fact we wrote a song together called "Katmandu" after he got back. I wanted to help Hal because I'd known him before he went and he was a young man. I couldn't afford to pay him probably what he was worth, but I paid him all I could as I always thought Hal was a very fine writer.

"He went along and he'd M.C. my shows and we'd do some judo stuff and things like that, fight on stage. He acted more like my road manager. While we'd ride from job to job at night I'd come up with an idea for a title song for one of my pictures and we'd share ideas and write it down. I'd then send it back to the studio to get it orchestrated. I figure we wrote half the songs together."

From the mid-1950s to 1967, Blair had thirteen of his songs recorded by Elvis Presley including "I Was the One" (recorded January 10, 1956) which was on the flip side of "Heartbreak Hotel," Presley's first #1 million-selling pop recording for RCA-Victor Records.

Also during this period Blair teamed up with songwriter Don Robertson (who had a chart-topper in 1956 with "The Happy Whistler") to contribute songs to most of Presley's films, including "No More," from *Blue Hawaii*, "I Think I'm Gonna Like It Here," from *Fun in Acapulco* (1963), "I'm Yours," a single from *Tickle Me* that reached #11 (1965), and "What Now, What Next, Where To?" from *Double Trouble* (1967).

Other well known Blair-Robertson collaborations recorded by other artists include "Please Help Me I'm Falling" (Hank Locklin), "Ninety Miles an Hour Down a Dead End Street" (Hank Snow), "Not One Minute More" (Della Reese), "I Was Born to Love You" (Eddy Arnold), "My Lips Are Sealed (Jim Reeves), and "Ringo" (Lorne Greene), from 1964 which reached #1 on the music charts.[9]

In his later years, Blair and his second wife, Joan, settled in Biggs, CA, where in addition to writing lyrics, he was an avid fisherman at nearby Lake Oroville, where he also made hand crafted fly casting fishing rods. The music world lost a very creative and innovative lyricist when Blair passed away on February 2, 2001, in Biggs, at age eighty-five.

After his disastrous experience with Crystal Records and after the musicians' union strike of 1948 ended, Eddie signed on with Mercury Records. Founded in 1945, Mercury's artist roster boasted of some heavy hitters including Frankie Laine, Patti Page, Vic Damone, and A & R man Mitch Miller, as well as jazz great saxophonist Lester Young and jazz producer Norman Granz, among others.

When Majestic Records folded, Mercury Records purchased the label's catalog. From January 1949 to March 1950, Eddie waxed thirteen sides for Mercury. Eddie's impact on the label was hardly felt although he made some fine recordings of the popular "Careless Hands," "Call of the Outlaw," and "Devil's Desert Land." He also cut some original material in "I Asked a Dream" (with Hal Blair, Gus Snow and Jack Statham) and another controversial piece, "You Want to Divorce Me" (with Hal Blair and Ham Hamilton). In addition, Mercury re-released Eddie's recording of "On the Banks of the Sunny Juan" that he made with Majestic Records which was pressed on the flip side to "One You Must Choose." In March 1950, Eddie recorded an updated version of "On the Banks of the Sunny San Juan," one of the last things he did for Mercury.

Eddie's experiences with record companies can best be described as frustrating, and rightly so. He was given free rein to record many of his own compositions, but for most of his recording career, he was handcuffed by record executives prohibiting him from expanding outside the musical genre box. Such restrictions by categorizing him in only one musical genre cost him opportunities to record other material that turned out to be huge hits for other artists.

One such example was "Jezebel," composed by Wayne Shanklin, in 1950. His other hits during that decade included "Chanson D'Amour (Song of Love)" made famous in 1958 by Art and Dotty Todd, and "Primrose Lane" recorded in 1959 by Jerry Wallace.

Shanklin and Hal Blair were working on some projects together. Blair brought Eddie the original copy of "Jezebel" because Shanklin wanted someone who could do the song justice, so Blair recommended Eddie.[10]

"When Hal brought me this song, I flipped over it," Eddie said. "I really flipped over it and said I really want to do this song."

Eddie was in the final year of his two-year contract with Mercury Records at the time and he wasn't doing too well with them. The record execs had him categorized as a Country artist and therefore stalemated him to record material only in the Country music genre.

"For some reason, I never could convince anyone that I was qualified to do other things besides Country Western material," Eddie said. "It's funny how people will type you. For instance, the actors and actresses in Hollywood have so much talent that you never hear about, that they could succeed in another phase of show business. But because they are typed, you never hear about it. I was a singer for years, and when I made my series of pictures, all of sudden, as far as Hollywood was concerned, I wasn't a singer any more, even though I sang in my pictures. I was an actor and they wouldn't say that I was a singer and an actor or vice-versa. I'm probably a very poor actor, but I was accepted so I guess I couldn't have been too bad, you know. Maybe it was something else and had nothing to do with my acting. The Hollywood people always felt that my singing was a little high-class for country people. But you know, country people like good music."

Murray Nash was Eddie's A&R man in the Country music division at Mercury Records. Eddie expressed to Nash his desire of wanting to record

"Jezebel." Nash wouldn't let Eddie do it because the song didn't fit the perimeters of a Country song.

"I loved Murray Nash and I thought he was just fabulous, but we got stalemated," Eddie said. "Because he was my A&R man in the Country field there was no way that he would let me do material outside of Country music. Murray said to me, 'Eddie, I just don't think you should sing that song.' And I said, 'You don't think I should or you don't think I *can*?' He said, 'Oh, you sing it just great, just great!'

So I said, 'Then why in the hell can't I record it?' He said, 'We've got you in a category.' I told him, 'I'm not interested in categories! I'm interested in selling records! I'm interested in Eddie Dean being a record seller!'

"To me, it didn't make any difference whether I sang Country music or what as long as I could make a record that would sell. This was the most important thing if I was going to make record. I was a different voice and a different person and I wanted to be my own person. But the powers-that-be didn't see it that way. This is always the way it's been – category, category."

Having gotten wind of Eddie's discontent at Mercury, Ken Nelson, the Country music A&R man from Capitol Records, came to see Eddie three different times wanting him to come on board to Capitol Records.

"I told Ken I was ready but that I was tied up," Eddie said. "So I finally said to him, 'I'll go with Capitol Records if you'll let me do one song.' He asked 'What is it?' I answered, 'Well, it just happensto be . . . it'll be a big song for you. 'You can do anything you want to do,' was his reply. I said, 'Fine.'

The interaction between Eddie and Nelson was almost an identical set up as Eddie had with Henry Shelb of Crystal Records.

"The song I want to do is called 'Jezebel,'" Eddie told Nelson.

"That's a great title," Nelson observed.

"It's a great song!" Eddie exclaimed. "If you'll let me do this song, I'll go with Capitol and I can get out of Mercury because we're not compatible any more. We're just not moving."

"Fine, you can do the song," Nelson assured Eddie.

"Okay," Eddie said, "it's a deal."

The two men shook hands on it. A contract was then drawn up an signed. Nelson then submitted "Jezebel" for Eddie to record, but the higher execs at Capitol turned it down stating that Nelson was an A&R man strictly for Country singers and the song that was submitted was not a Country song. Nelson then informed Eddie of the bad news.

"Ken, you might as well release me now because we're starting off badly," Eddie told his boss. "I was promised something and now I'm not going to get to do it."

"I'll tell you one thing, Eddie," Nelson told his new singer, "and I'll stick to this . . . if they don't let you do the song, no one else will do it on Capitol Records."

Nelson remained true to his word.

However, Eddie learned that the real reason why Nash was stalemating him in not doing "Jezebel"was that he wanted to get the song for Frankie Laine, whose contract was due to expire with Mercury on March 31, 1951. In the five-and-a-half-years Laine was with Mercury, he chalked up eight gold records on his resume. He was to start a very fruitful association with Columbia Records beginning on the first day of April.

"So here's Frankie Laine, a big recording star and I'm struggling to get a break with material because I know that the song is the thing," Eddie said. "Murray kept after me wanting the copy of the song, so when I found out that I wasn't going to get to do it on Capitol – and they wouldn't release my contract because I had nothing in writing to that effect – it was only a handshake between Ken Nelson and me, which to me was a contract, more than writing. But to the execs it wasn't because they didn't know what Ken said to me and they didn't know what I said to Ken. So anyway, I knew that I wasn't going to get to do the song on Capitol, so I gave Murray Nash the copy and he got the copy to Frankie Laine and Frankie left Mercury and went Columbia."

So on April 2, 1951, Eddie received a phone and the voice on the other end said, "Eddie, Frankie Laine just recorded 'Jezebel' today."

"I said, 'Thank you very much,'" Eddie recalled.

Eddie got in his car and drove to the Capitol Records office looking for Ken Nelson. He was told Nelson was over at the Capitol Recording Studio at 5515 Melrose Avenue in Hollywood recording Country and Rockabilly artist Skeets McDonald. Ken Nelson was surprised to see Eddie when he walked into the control room.

"What are you doing here, Eddie?" Nelson asked.

"I was told Frankie Laine just recorded 'Jezebel,'" Eddie replied.

"Oh, no!" Nelson responded in dismay.

"This just makes me sick, Ken," Eddie said. "I just don't understand it."

"Well, if it's any consolation to you, it makes me sick, too," Nelson said. "I think I will just cancel this session right now even though it's just getting started. Yeah, I think we'll cancel this one, bring you the band, and we'll do 'Jezebel.'"

"Now you're talking!" an enthusiastic Eddie shot back.

Nelson then started pacing back and forth in the control room second guessing his impulsive comment and its possible ramifications.

"When are you going to call?" Eddie asked. "When are you going to cancel it? Let's get on the ball and do this thing!"

"Eddie, if I do it, I'll get fired," Nelson said regrettably. "I know they'll fire me because they told me not to do this song."

"Alright, let them fire you," Eddie said. "So we're both fired. We've got a hit record on our hands!"

A long ten minutes went by and finally Nelson said to Eddie, "No. I just can't do it. I know I've got a job with Capitol for as long as I want it and I'm not going to jeopardize it by having you record 'Jezebel.'"

For Eddie, that was the end of that. Frankie Laine went on to have the big hit with "Jezebel."

"As far as I was concerned, I had no chance with Capitol Records," Eddie said, "but I did go ahead and record. Ken did record me on several songs and none of them sold. Songs would come my way and I'd take the songs over to the execs and other artists would get to do it. Finally, I went to Ken and asked him, 'Why don't you just release me? Let's don't get mixed up over this any further.' That was the end of the 'Jezebel' thing and Frankie Laine had the hit on it and evidently that was the way it was supposed to be.

"I had everything I could have done on all the material that I had. I did everything I could do without having to fight; you know, really literally having to get out and wanting to hate people in order to be a recording star. I wouldn't put myself in such a position. It's like my wife said one time, 'You know, if you fist fight somebody, you are no different than they are. If you get drunk, you are no different from any other drunk. If the President gets drunk, he's still a drunk just like the other drunk.' It makes a lot of sense, right? It's a philosophy and there's a lot of truth in it. I didn't want to fight and I didn't want people to hate me. I think Ken Nelson is one of the finest guys that I know. He's been very successful, but things just never worked out for Eddie Dean with Capitol. The only place it really worked out was on Majestic where those old records sold well."

From December 21, 1950, through October 20, 1951, Eddie waxed eighteen sides for Capitol Records. As with Mercury, his output hardly caused a stir, although he recorded a pair of fine duet pieces with Margie McPeters: "I'm Not in Love, Just Involved" and "Blue Wedding Bells," (credited on the latter piece as Marge Mack); as well as some compelling single offerings in "Roses Remind Me of You," "Cold Yellow Gold," and "Tears on My Guitar;" and a reverent yet compelling solo interpretation of "The Lord's Prayer."

Eddie would once again see his name on the Capitol label having recorded four songs independently and selling the masters to Ken Nelson for later distribution. From a September 1962 recording session the songs were "Run, Jimmy, Run," "Don't Take Advantage of Me," "Stop Me (If You've Heard This One Before)," and "She Doesn't Know I'm Alive." Capitol delayed in releasing "Run, Jimmy, Run" and "Don't Take Advantage of Me" for almost a year, while the other pair of songs were not issued, being later released in 1966 on Commerce Records.

Eddie's release was doing well and got down to 23rd on the chart when as (sour) luck would have it, America was suddenly invaded by four young men from England who would revolutionize the face of rock music forever.

They were called The Beatles. The British "Fab Four" were signed on to Capitol Records, and suddenly the label realized they were holding a tiger by the tail. They were hot property. Capitol put all their interest and money in recording and promoting The Beatles.

"When The Beatles came out, Capitol didn't press another record for a long time," Eddie said. "Not even any of Nat 'King' Cole's albums. Nobody! Here I am on the chart and everything comes to a grinding halt. Ken Nelson wrote me a letter, one of the nicest letters I ever received from a man. In it he stated that he personally thought I was one of the finest singers in the business and that he felt so sad about not being able to press my records. That's how things were suppose to be at the time, I guess."

From his first round with Capitol, Eddie signed on briefly with Coral Records recording a pair of songs in the early spring of 1952, before heading over to Ode Records to document four sides in November 1953.

This set the scene for Eddie helping bring to fruition his second big hit song of his career: "I Dreamed of a Hillbilly Heaven."

After completing his obligations to Ode Records in 1953, Eddie once again found himself without a recording contract and a little bit disillusioned with the recording industry. In early September of 1954, he received a telephone call from Hi "Hi-Pockets" Busse, an accordionist/singer, who left an indelible mark on American Western music and was one of its unsung champions. He led the Western trio, "The Frontiersmen," who backed up Eddie on his Crystal Records recording of "One Has My Name, the Other Has My Heart."

"Eddie, have you have a recording contract?" Busse asked over the phone.

"No, Hi, I don't," Eddie replied.

"Why don't you record some things with us?" Busse asked. "We're cutting some stuff over at a little place called . . . well, I don't know what he is going to call his label, but he's got a small office in an upstairs building on Hollywood Boulevard near Capitol Records. Come over."

"I don't have any material right now," Eddie confessed. "I've lost interest."

"Well, Hal Southern is here and he said he had a dream that would make a good idea for a song," Busse said. "Why don't we come over and you and he can finish up the song together and record it?"

"Alright, come over," Eddie said.

Busse and Southern came over to Eddie's home. Eddie and Southern never met, so after the three men visited for a while, Eddie said to Southern, "Let's hear this piece you got."

Southern handed Eddie some lyrics calling the piece "I Dreamed of a Hillbilly Heaven." He then played a simple tune on the piano that he worked out to go with the words. Southern claimed that a dream inspired the song and that the name of the song is derived from the nickname, "Hillbilly Heaven," that "Squeakin'" Deacon Moore, a West Coast disc jockey, had given to Bell Gardens, California, because of its considerable number of Country music fans.[11]

"I liked the idea of the song, the *idea*," Eddie said. "I thought we had a good piece of material. I worked with Hal on the words, the names and things, and tightened up the music, sort of helping put things together. We went to the Radio Recorders Studio on Santa Monica Boulevard in Hollywood the next morning to record it."

After recording "Hillbilly Heaven" and what would be the record's flip side piece, "Stealing," with "The Frontiersmen," Woody Fleanor, the owner of the record label, came in the studio to introduce himself to Eddie as the two men had never met, and asked how things were going.

"I think you have a hit record," Eddie said.

"Really?" Fleanor asked.

"Yes, sir, I do," Eddie said.

"I would love to hear it," Fleanor said. "May I?"

Eddie asked the engineer to play the recording back for Fleanor.

He listened to the play back and asked, "Do you really think this a hit?"

"Yes, and if you don't get it out right away, somebody's going to steal it!" Eddie cautioned. "They'll beat you to it. You have to get it out right quick."

"I'll have it out tomorrow," Fleanor promised.

"Or," Eddie added, "you have an alternative. You can try to sell it to a major record label."

"No," Fleanor said. "I'll put it out."

In actuality, Fleanor didn't have a record company per se, as he rented studios that were used primarily for making commercials and jingles for various products. But with "Hillbilly Heaven" he now had a legitimate record company, calling it Sage and Sand Records. For the fifteen years it was in existence, Sage and Sand operated its affairs from that same small upstairs office on Hollywood Boulevard.[12]

Fleanor put Eddie's record out and it hit. However, with Sage and Sand being a small label, it didn't have the distribution capabilities as that of a major label, so Fleanor had a hard time getting distribution, but the record hit well enough, bigger than he realized it would, even though he got bogged down with distribution issues.

The day after "Hillbilly Heaven" was recorded, Eddie "tested the waters" by performing the song as part of his concert program at the Hollywood Bowl with the orchestra conducted by Robert Armbruster.

"The audience really liked the song," Eddie said. "I knew they would."

After "Hillbilly Heaven" was released and enjoyed some success, it would be some years later that it would be resurrected, furnishing greater success for Eddie and Hal Southern as well as for another artist: Tex Ritter.

Eddie got the idea about Tex Ritter thinking he would be the perfect artist to reprise this song. Ritter had been one of the original Western artists to record for the newly-formed Capitol Records when songwriter Johnny Mercer, songwriter, and film producer Buddy DeSylva, and businessman Glenn Wallichs formed the label in 1942, creating the first major West Coast label.

"I called Tex and he came over to the house and picked up the record and he took it over to Capitol Records where he was under contract and they turned it down," Eddie said. "He kept after them and kept after them but they kept turning him down. So about six years go by and I got an idea. Tex called me up and said, 'I'd sure like to do that 'Hillbilly Heaven,' but I just can't get through to them up there. I don't know what's wrong. I'm doing an album and I would like to do the song on this album but I can't seem to get them to see it my way."

"Let me see what I can do," Eddie told his friend.

Eddie called Lee Gillette requesting an appointment to see him. On the day of the appointment, Eddie grabbed some of his old material, some old songs and acetates that he had made and brought them with him.

"I really sort of framed Lee because I didn't go over there to sell myself at," Eddie confessed.

Gillette sat down and listened to what Eddie brought and then he said to him, "You know, Eddie, those are really good songs. You have some real good material here."

"Thanks," Eddie said. "I just wanted you to have a listen."

"May I keep them?" Gillette asked.

"Sure, you may keep them," Eddie said. "Maybe if you decide somebody can do them, I can get a record."

"Let me just keep them and see what happens," Gillette said.

Eddie then conveniently and somewhat surreptitiously picked up his record copy of "Hillbilly Heaven" along with the other material he brought.

Gillette noticed it and asked, "What do you have there?"

"I don't know how this happened to get in the bunch," Eddie admitted. "I don't think you'd be interested in this one."

Gillette looked at it and said, "You know, this is a terrific song."

He played the record and Eddie said, "Why don't you do this song on Capitol?"

"I don't have anybody to do it." Gillette replied.

"I think he was expecting me to say, 'Why don't you let me do it on Capitol?'" Eddie said. "I'd been with Capitol already and I didn't want to get involved at that time, really I didn't."

At that moment, Eddie saw a window of opportunity to do what he came to see Gillette about, and he struck while the iron was hot.

"You've got one of the greatest artists in the world who can do this song and he's on Capitol's roster."

"Who is that," Gillette asked.

"Tex Ritter," Eddie said.

Gillette swung around his swivel chair two or three times and said, "We'll do it."

"I don't think Tex ever believed I went over and talked with Lee Gillette," Eddie mused. "I told him that I did, but I don't think he ever believed it because he had worked so hard on it himself. I think I talked to Lee just at the right time and with the way I said, that I convinced him that Tex Ritter should do 'Hillbilly Heaven.' Well, the rest they say is history. I'm sure glad Tex did it because he sang it so beautifully; he sang it so great."

In 1961, Ritter finally got to record "I Dreamed of a Hillbilly Heaven" using the same format as Eddie recorded six years earlier, but putting his own unique stamp of individuality on the piece while adding the names of Country stars that had recently entered "Hillbilly Heaven."

Eddie's association with Sage and Sand Records was his longest and most amiable of his recording career, staying with the independent label for four years from 1954 to 1958 while recording over fifty-six sides. A number of them later appeared on LP albums put out by Crown Records. He returned briefly to Sage and Sand from 1960 to 1961 to record eight sides.

During the recording session for "Hillbilly Heaven," Eddie also waxed a song his nineteen-year-son composed called "Impatient Blues." The grooving, bouncy blues piece would later appear on Eddie's albums for Crown Records and Sutton Records. Eddie' son, Edgar Glosup, explains how his composition came about:

"I wrote that when I was about sixteen or so. You know how those 'kid' romances go. I always seemed to be the loser on breaking up. I never broke up with anyone and I just started writing about the girls I liked. Again these were young people and no serious love affairs, just wishes. I wrote a couple of other songs but didn't get them recorded. 'Impatient Blues' is based on the typical cowboy sorrow theme of 'Here's Love, Here's Life, I've Lost Again.' I thought 'Impatient Blues' was a great title but I didn't get very far with the rest of the lyrics."

Eddie also stated that he had another hit song slip through his fingers not because of musical genre type-casting by record execs but by pure thievery. In late 1956, Eddie came across "Walkin' After Midnight," a piece composed by Donn Hecht and Alan Block. Eddie worked on the song by himself in his studio at his Burbank home fixing it to his specifications and satisfaction. He dubbed in all the background music playing the guitar, mandolin, and whistle. He borrowed Cliffie Stone's bass fiddle (he's the only man Stone would allow to borrow his bass, according to Eddie). He also had it fixed to where he could get an echo sound, spending two weeks on perfecting it complete with a delay on it, as well.

"I wanted to create the mood based on the title of the song," Eddie said. "I could hear my footsteps. It sounded like I was in the middle of a big city like New York or Chicago and the big buildings around me creating a little echo of me being lonesome walking after midnight. I thought it was one of the best things I ever did. I knew this was a hit song for me. I just knew it"

Eddie took his completed work over to Woody Fleanor at Sage and Sand Records and Fleanor suggested to Eddie that he give the work to a man to redo it as he thought it sounded corny. That individual grabbed Eddie's version and gave it to Patsy Cline, who was just breaking into show business at the time, according to Eddie.

Cline's big break came when she won on the Arthur Godfrey Talent program on January 21, 1957, singing "Walkin' After Midnight." Days later, she recorded the song. "Walkin' After Midnight" became a huge hit for the twenty-five-year-old Cline, reaching #2 on the Country chart and #12 on the Pop chart.[13]

"This set me back a long ways in show business because I love show business but I couldn't believe anyone calling the piece corny and who would do that," Eddie said. "I have nothing against Patsy Cline. I was the one in front of the audience all the time knowing what they wanted to hear. I was the performer. Woody was behind the desk. He only looked at the money that certain things generated. I looked at the public that wanted something new, something different. Every time I hear 'Walkin' After Midnight' I think why did this man do this to me because there wasn't any competition between a male singer to a female singer on a record."

A short time later after Cline recorded the song, Eddie got to record his version of "Walkin' After Midnight" on Sage and Sand backed by the Cletro Combo (Eddie Cletro, guitar, Bill Flynn, bass, Tex Atwater, drums, and Eddie Carver, accordion).

By 1959, Eddie recorded some standard cowboy tunes called *Musical Heritage of the Golden West*, as part of a children's record series for Cricket Records. Later that year, he recorded *Eddie Dean Sings a Tribute to Hank Williams*, a very popular and critically acclaimed album for Design Records.

Eddie continued to record singles throughout the 1960s for smaller independent labels including Crown, Commerce and Mosrite, with Crown Records producing a number of LP albums.

Throughout the 1970s and 1980s Eddie recorded a number of artistically fine albums on Jimmy Wakely's Shasta Records including *The Very Best of Eddie Dean; Sincerely, Eddie Dean; A Cowboy Sings Country;* and *Dean of the West.*

During the mid-1970s, Eddie recorded "My Elusive Dream," with Karen Scales, his granddaughter. The song appears on the Shasta album, *Eddie Dean: A Cowboy Sings Country.* The piece is about a man who laments chasing after a litany of big and somewhat unrealistic dreams that goes bust while his long-suffering wife tags along.

"Karen has somewhat of a Joni Mitchell-type singing style," Eddie said. "She did a great job on the song."

In 1985, Ed Jr. produced *Eddie Dean in Concert*, recorded live as an outdoor concert on the grounds of Andy Griffith's old home in Toluca Lake (located within the cities of Burbank and Los Angeles). This album is highly acclaimed as Eddie that evening was in tremendous voice, robust and full of verve, giving a high-energy concert that even wowed guest stars Roy Rogers and Dale Evans, Pat Buttram, Jock Mahoney, and Iron Eyes Cody, who were in attendance.

One of the last things Eddie recorded was "Cold Texas Beer" in the

1990s on the Bradley Brothers record label. The song reflected Eddie's West Texas roots. The song was written especially for him by Hall of Fame guitarist Bill Aken, the adopted son of actors Frank and Lupe Mayorga who had worked in a few films with Eddie in the 1940s. Eddie had asked Aken to write him a new song and "Cold Texas Beer" was written in less than two days and tailored specifically to Eddie's vocal style.[14]

In recent years, European labels, such as Cattle Compact and BACM, as well as American labels of Soundies and Allegro, have released previously recorded material of Eddie's, both commercial recordings as well as transcription recordings.

Edgar Glosup Jr., who later produced many of his father's recordings and live shows, confessed that he regretted not having his dad record two theme albums: a Christmas album and a Gospel album.

"Dad would have done a beautiful job on both types of projects," Glosup said.

Eddie continued to perform on a regular basis literally right up to his passing in 1999. Over the years, when many Western stars faded into the sunset, he was still creating and still in the public eye actively expressing himself through music with his magnificent voice belying his age. He was very fortunate. He was also very blessed.

Eddie performed a song in his live shows called, "What Would I Do Without My Music?" Thank goodness Eddie never had to come to grips with answering that question since it would have been a disastrous, unthinkable one. Music was his life, and his life was in his music. Music and the man were inseparable. Music was the DNA of his legacy.

The sheet music to "One Has My Name, The Other Has My Heart,"
the controversial song composed by Eddie, his wife, Dearest,
and Hal Blair. It was Eddie's first hit song.

The sheet music for "I Dreamed of a Hill-Billy Heaven," composed by
Eddie with Hal Southern and recorded by Eddie in 1954 on Sage and Sand
Records. It was Eddie's second major hit song.

Above: Sage and Sand Records label of
"I Dreamed of a Hill-billy Heaven," from 1954.

Below: Crystal Records label from late 1947 of
Eddie's recording of "Baby You Should Live So Long."

Above: Eddie shaking hands with Hal Blair (left) during the
mid-1940s. Eddie and Blair had a musical kinship like no other
and the two collaborated on many songs together.

Below: Hal Blair later in life during the 1990s. He died in 2001, at the age of 85.

**Eddie and leading lady Shirley Patterson
on tour for Majestic Records in early 1947.**

Eddie and Shirley Patterson on tour for Majestic Records in 1947. It looks like
Eddie is about to sharpen his shooting skills using Majestic platters as targets.

A collage of recording artists adorns *The 1946 Majestic Records Billboard Music Yearbook.*
Eddie is pictured in the lower left corner while his brother, Jimmie Dean, is pictured
with Foy Willing and the Riders of the Purple Sage in the upper right corner.

Eddie whittles some wood as he poses for a
publicity photo for Capitol Records in 1950.

Above: A Capitol Records release of "I'm Not in Love, Just Involved" from June 1951.

Below: Eddie on Commerce Records from 1966.

Above: Eddie's 1959 critically acclaimed tribute
album to Hank Williams on Design Records.

Below: A sample of a children's record that Eddie
made in 1959 on Cricket Records.

Above: Shasta Records album cover of *Dean of the West* from the early 1970s of which Eddie sings songs from his western movies.

Below: Another one of Eddie's Shasta Records albums from the 1970s.

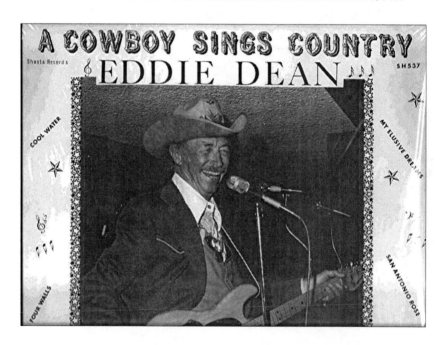

Above: "The Golden Cowboy" striking an enthusiastic
pose for his Crown Records album.

Below: Eddie on a 45 RPM single for
Mosrite Records from 1966.

Eddie Dean LP albums from Castle Records, above, and Shasta Records, below.

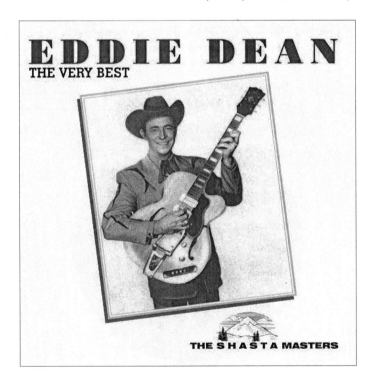

13

Home On The Range

There was more to Eddie than just what was portrayed in movies and what was heard on recordings. Off screen and off stage, while "home on the range," he was just a regular person, an extraordinary husband and father, and a devoted family man without pretensions. He treated celebrities or fans the same gracious way.

The following vignettes, in no particular order, seek to illustrate Eddie's family dedication, the avid outdoorsman, and the gifted artist who enjoyed creating and sharing in the visual arts. They also show the civic-minded individual who sought the well-being of his community and profession, and how he responded to fan adulation. Most of the following sketches come from him, from Edgar Glosup Jr.'s recollections, and from appreciative fans.

Dearest Dean, Eddie's wife, was an enthusiastic and constant companion on his tours, concert dates, and social gatherings. She was very proactive in her husband's career and assisted in a variety of practical ways, from music collaborator to management and marketing specialist to bookkeeper. On many levels, she was his anchor in life.

Dearest was insightful, sharp, creative, engaging, and gracious. She and Eddie were married for sixty-seven happy years. That's quite a testimony that not all Hollywood marriages fail and end in divorce. She was also a loving and caring mother, grandmother, and great-grandmother. She was definitely matriarchal in her approach to family.

Eddie's daughter, Donna Lee Glosup, upon graduation from Our Lady of Corvallis High School, went to Woodbury College in Los Angeles, where she met her husband, Dick Scales. Their marriage only lasted about thirteen years. The couple had four children: Shellee, Debra, Jeff, and Karen.

Shellee has three daughters: Jade, Rosalynn, and Leah. Jade has a son, Kyle. Rosalynn has a girl, Audrey, and a boy, Ian. Leah doesn't have any children.

Jeff Scales has a son, Jeff.

Debra Richardson doesn't have any children. Debra danced in the adult show, *Lindo de Paris*, in Las Vegas.

Karen has a daughter, Olivia.

Donna remarried to Ted Knorr and lived in Newport Beach, CA, and eventually moved to Westlake Village, CA, to care for her folks after Eddie had his heart attack. She was an untiring nurse for them both until her folks died.

"Donna was a great gal," Ed Jr., said of his sister. "We were very close. She always had time for me whenever I needed to talk. She was probably the most understanding woman I have ever known. There were so many fond memories when we were kids. She was a kick and very talented. She could dance and sing, but as you can well imagine, there was only room for *one* star in our family. Sad, but true . . . "

Donna Lee Knorr died on August 30, 2011, at the age of seventy-nine.

Ed Glosup Jr., married out of college in 1953. The couple had three children, Dean, Jeff, and Gina.

Dean Glosup (born in 1954) has two daughters, Paige Glosup and Angelica Glosup.

Jeff Glosup has a son, Casey Glosup, who currently serves in the United States Air Force. Casey has two sons: Luke Glosup and Bradley Glosup.

Gina Glosup does not have any children, but her vivacious personality makes her a wonderful aunt and stepmother to two boys and their four grand-children, according to Ed Jr.

Ed Jr. has another son by a previous marriage, Charles Glosup, a lighting technician who owns his own company. His company has provided lighting expertise on such television shows as *Tool Time, Girlfriends,* and *Reba.* He is currently working on new show for CBS called *Mom.*

Charles has a son, Ethan Glosup, age seventeen.

Ed Jr. is currently married to Barbara Sardo since 1974. Through that marriage, Ed Jr. gained two step-sons: Gary and Greg. Gary is the father of two sons: Michael and Christopher; while Greg is the father of James and Natalie.

According to Ed Jr., Barbara is "the best thing to have happened to him," and in their nearly forty years of marriage, stating "we are still on our honeymoon."

After Ed Jr. graduated from college, he engaged himself in community affairs and service clubs. He was past president of the California Kiwanis and the Jaycees, also serving in both organizations as their California State Chairman. He was active in Young Republicans, the Exchange Club of Burbank (he even presented his father the coveted "Book of Golden Deeds," the Exchange Club's highest honor in 1969), and the NOVA Opportunity Center (a program started to hire and train mentally and physically challenged individuals). He was appointed to the Burbank Park and Recreation Board and the Burbank Civil Service Board. He was a Republican Committee member for many Republican candidates, legislative and judicial. He even threw his hat in ring vying to be elected to be a member of the Burbank City Council, but lost.

"My life (growing up) was very full and busy," Ed Jr. said. "My Dad was my hero. He was the kindest, most understanding man I knew. He hardly ever got mad. My mom was the greatest and very understanding of my growing up. She was all ways there for me when needed. I was also fortunate to meet so many people with whom they were associated."

Ed Jr. worked for some years in the airline business which overhauled planes for the major airlines. He then worked in the industrial plastics field retiring in 1994. He and his wife Barbara reside in Shingle Springs, CA, just outside Sacramento.

One individual who Ed Jr. said was like a second father to him was

Glenn Strange. He was an actor, musician, and hunter like Eddie. The 6-foot 5-inch tall Strange is remembered for playing the nemesis roles in Westerns as well as monster roles (he was the Frankenstein monster three times for Universal Pictures during the 1940s and a werewolf-like creature in *The Mad Monster* [PRC, 1942]). He also played Sam Noonan, the bartender, on CBS's *Gunsmoke* television series.

Ed Jr. recalled that his first hunting trip for pigeons as a boy was with his dad and Strange.

"Glenn taught me how to shoot a shotgun, how to load it with all the safety aspects," Ed Jr. said. "He gave me his old shotgun, a Model 97, with a hammer and a pump."

Eddie and Strange also composed music together, some of which were in Eddie's movies.

Strange died of lung cancer on September 20, 1973, in Los Angeles. He was seventy-four. As a final tribute to his dear friend, Eddie sang at his funeral service at Forest Lawn-Hollywood Hills Cemetery.

While Eddie shunned off-screen drama that is often closely associated with Hollywood, he became very close friends with individuals in the entertainment business, often spending time together as families for Sunday afternoon barbeque gatherings, camping, hunting, and fishing trips. One such family he became close to was that of Max Terhune.

Terhune's two sons, Rolltaire and Bob, although physically twice as big as Ed Jr. all played well together. Terhune's wife would make special sandwiches to eat while Terhune himself often entertained the families with his feats of prestidigitation and legerdemain (magic). Terhune's daughter would also gather the kids together outside at night and tell ghost stories. Bob Terhune went on to become a preacher who also worked in the entertainment business.

"They were a fabulous family," Ed Jr. said.

Another great family friend was actor Rocky Cameron, aka, Gene Alsace, who worked with Eddie in *Harmony Trail* and had a few minor roles in some of Eddie's movies. He gave Ed Jr. his first .22 rifle, a bolt action Marlin that he still has to this day.

"(Gene) was another hero of mine and a real cowboy," Ed Jr. said.

Another special friend of Eddie's was Tex Ritter. Eddie and Ritter became friends during the filming of Ritter's 1940 film, *Rolling Home to Texas*, in which Eddie had a singing part. Ritter was the firstWestern star to record on the newly formed Capitol Records in Los Angeles in 1942. In August of that year, the musicians' union strike took effect and lasted for Decca and Capitol until November 1943 (other major labels such as Columbia and RCA-Victor held out for another year). Ritter was ready and eager to resume recording on Capitol and asked Eddie for his help in selecting the right material.

The 78 rpm records at that time were made with shellac, and shellac was in scarce quantities as it was utilized for the war effort. Capitol Records somehow had gotten two truckloads of shellac to make records after they capitulated to musician union demands.

"I need your help in picking out some good material as well as something the company and myself can make some money with," Ritter said to Eddie.

Ritter arrived at Eddie's house about eight in the evening with a stack of songs that Eddie claimed was two feet high! Ritter stayed until five in the morning as both men spent the entire evening going over song after song, trying to find the best four that brawny-voiced cowboy could record on his next recording session.

Finally, Eddie picked four songs out of the group that he liked. They were "Have I Stayed Away Too Long?," "There's New Moon Over My Shoulder," "I'm Wastin' My Tears Over You," and "There's a Gold Star in Her Window."

"The material pertained to the mood of the war that was going on," Eddie said. "All the guys were going away, and some were coming back."

Ritter was appreciative of Eddie's help, but within a few days called Eddie back asking to meet with him again, because he was, as he said, "still disturbed about the songs."

Ritter came over and the two cowboys went over the same stack of material concluding with Eddie picking the same four songs as before.

"You know, that's funny," Ritter confessed. "You've picked every one of the songs that the studio picked, except one."

It seems that the studio wanted to nix "Have I Stayed Away Too Long?" and replace it with another song.

Eddie encouraged Ritter to keep that song in the recording session.

"Tex, I would keep this song," Eddie said. "because a guy could be writing home asking his sweetheart, 'Honey, have I been away too long?' People can connect with this song."

Ritter agreed. He was able to keep the song in his next recording session on November 24, 1943, even though he was slated to record only two songs. The other song recorded on the flip side was "There's a Gold Star in Her Window" (Capitol 147). Ritter would record "There's a New Moon Over My Shoulder," and "I'm Wastin' My Tears On You" on his very next recording session for Capitol on March 9, 1944 (Capitol 174).

"I was glad to be a part of Tex's career and I was glad I helped him," Eddie reflected "I wish I could have had somebody to help me like that. Really. Because I don't think you can pick out your own material all the time. Somebody's got to help you."

It would be almost thirty years later that Eddie once again helped his friend Ritter career-wise (as well as helping himself) when he got Lee Gillette at Capitol to agree to have Ritter record Eddie's version of his hit song, "I Dreamed of a Hillbilly Heaven."

Even outside the professional arena the Deans and the Ritters were close family friends. Ed Jr. explains:

"Dad and Tex were great friends. Tex was a very special guy. His wife, Dorothy Fay Southworth, a former actress herself (she appeared in four of Ritter's films, as well as played the heroine in the serials *The Green Archer* starring Victor Jory [1940] and *White Eagle* [1941], before retiring to marry Ritter in June 1941) actually taught me how to whistle with four fingers in my mouth. Dad used to whistle to call Donna and me to dinner and we'd come running. That's how I called my kids and my dog today. Thank you, Auntie Fay!

"We'd go visit them at their house in the San Fernando Valley and Tex had a train yard out on the side of his house for the kids. The tracks ran through rocks and trees. It was a great train. They had a brand new son at the time, Tommy. John wasn't born yet. Tommy became a very successful attorney, even though he has Multiple Sclerosis. (Note: John Ritter of TV's *Three's Company* fame, passed away unexpectedly at the age of fifty-four on September 11, 2003, and Dorothy Fay Southworth Ritter passed away at the age of eighty-eight on November 5, 2003.)

"One year Dad and I went with Tex and a couple of other guys duck hunting at the Salton Sea. Tex always took his little dog, Ditty Boo. While we were sitting in the hotel room, Tex was telling me all the dangers of hunting out of a boat. I was very interested in what he had to say. As a boy of twelve, I took it all in. We both had little boats to row out to some trees to hunt; Tex and his partner, Dad and me. When it got close to sundown, Dad and I returned to the hotel, but no Tex. We were just about to call the sheriff and in comes Tex, soaking wet and head bowed down. We asked what happened and he said, 'I stood up to take a shot, slipped and blew a hole in the boat and down she went.' Now the Salton Sea is only about four feet deep where we were hunting, thank heaven, or Tex may not have made it back. He said, 'See what happens when you stand up in a boat. Make sure you learned a lesson.' We all just cracked up. What a guy! He came to the hospital when all three of my kids were born. That's special."

Other times, Eddie and Ed Jr. would hunt with Roy Rogers and once with his son, Dusty.

"Roy and his wife, Dale Evans, were two very special people," Ed Jr. said. "They were friendly, congenial, and always interested in talking to you. They made great eye contact and showed so much interest to whom they were speaking. We saw a lot of them in the '80's and '90's, but not nearly enough."

Some of Eddie's other pals included character actor Dub Taylor, who played "Newly O'Brien" on TV's *Gunsmoke*, and his son Buck.

"Dub used to come to the house (in Burbank), grab Dad, and go crow hunting in the San Fernando Valley," Ed Jr. recalled. "We ran into him a few times down by the Colorado River when Dad, Glen, and I would go hunting. Dub loved to pot shoot by finding ducks in a pond, flushing them out and getting them."

One of Eddie's best friends was Hal Blair.

"Dad and Hal wrote so many songs together," Ed Jr. said. "Many of those songs were in Dad's films. Hal helped Dad build his studio behind our house in Burbank. That's where 'One Has My Name' was penned. It's amazing what a short time it took Dearest, Hal, and Dad to composed that song. Hal and his (first) wife, Doris, used to baby sit Donna and me when the folks would go on the road. He was a hoot and she was beautiful. She had a likeness similar to Ava Gardner. Hal was a soldier and a great patriot. We really missed him."

Eddie and family were very close friends of the Hoosier Hot Shots, Paul "Hezzy" Trietsch, Ken Trietsch, Charles "Gabe" Ward and Frank Kettering, who eventually emigrated to Hollywood.

"Ken, Dad and I played a lot of golf together," Ed Jr. said. "He kind of adopted me as he didn't have any children. He later moved to Westlake Village and were neighbors to my parents."

Some of the memories Ed Jr. had as a youngster was going with his father on location to shoot his movies at Corriganville, Iverson Ranch, and Melody Ranch, all within twenty miles of each other.

"I traveled a lot with Dad on location," Ed Jr. recalled. "He didn't want a single horse, so he had quite a few. One was Flash, whose real name was Black Diamond (the same Black Diamond that Lash La Rue rode). I would always get on him with his black saddle and all that silver, I was king. I had only to bring him back when they were ready to shoot, and not wore out or sweaty. I obliged.

"I also remember one time at Corriganville, Crash Corrigan had a lunch truck on the property like you see today on the streets. On this lunch truck was a nickel slot machine. I had some nickels in my pocket and proceeded to play the machine. On the third nickel, 'Bingo,' I hit the jackpot. It paid $5. Dad told me I wasn't allowed to play the machine, but Crash said it was my nickel and I should be allowed to keep the money. He was a pretty honest guy. Thanks, Crash. We were pretty close or as long as his dog were concerned. He had a Chow-Chow and when I showed my friend how the dog's skin was gray like his fur, his dog objected and gave me a lesson I would never forget, plus about four stitches!"

Ed Jr. also recalled going on the road in 1947 to promote one of Eddie's movies:

"Most call it these days as going on tour, and we did – Donna, me, Dearest, Dad and the Sunshine Boys. We spent three months during the summer of driving, working, seeing the country and towns in Ohio, Kentucky, Texas, etc. While Dad was entertaining, Dearest, Donna, and I would set up a sales area for pictures in the lobby. Donna and I were the sales people and sold tons of pictures of Dad for twenty-five-cents apiece. There were lots and lots of quarters to count later on as we poured them on the bed in our motel room. After a while the Sunshine Boys talked to Dad and said that we were cutting in on their income. Donna and I had no idea they also wanted to sell photos. We wanted to give some of the money to them but hey said no and that they would handle it in the future. It was all good, they were happy. They were terrific guys.

"I didn't know it was so hard on Dad to do all the driving, singing, doing a gun act on stage with hardly any rest between shows. What a guy. He never offered any complaints and even made time to go fishing with me in Zanesville, Ohio. Of course, we didn't have a fishing license and the game warden who visited us on the river was pretty lenient when he saw who it was. Thank heaven! I hated to see the headlines in the local newspaper, 'There's Something Fishy About Our Cowboy!'"

In later years Ed Jr. traveled with his dad whenever he played a nightclub or rodeo throughout California, Nevada and Arizona.

"I remember when Dad broke records every time he played the Golden Nugget in Las Vegas," Ed Jr. said proudly. "It was pretty exciting."

Eddie loved working for W. E. Greene, who owned the Golden Nugget in Las Vegas. He always treated Eddie very well and paid him well, too. Eddie agreed to perform at the hotel-casino's cocktail lounge for a two-week stint from April 2 through April 15, 1970, for a fee of $2,800 per week.[1]

When Eddie was doing the *Judy Canova Show*, the program that immediately followed was *The Harry James Show*, which featured the trumpet-playing bandleader Harry James broadcasting from various locations from around the country. This particular time James and crew were in Hollywood and did a broadcast from the same radio studio as the *Canova Show*, on Vine Street.

"Wow, to meet Betty Grable and Harry James was magic to a young guy at twelve!" Ed Jr. said. "It was just one of my unforgettable moments."

Back in the late 1940s, Eddie was approached by the Republican Central Committee about running for Governor of Texas.

"I had good name recognition at the time," Eddie said, "and another singer had been elected Governor of Louisiana. That was Jimmie Davis (who composed the song, "You Are My Sunshine." A Democrat, he served from 1944-1948 and again from 1960-1964). I met with the Committee and told them if I ran I would be my own man and not a puppet politician. They agreed and they still wanted me to run. I believe I would have had a good chance of winning, but I decided not to run. That may have been the biggest mistake of my life."[2]

However, Eddie's political aspirations were not totally shot down from that fateful decision. In July 1954, Sulphur Springs, Texas's, most famous son was bestowed the title of Honorary Mayor and Honorary Judge of Sulphur Springs, as part of the Sulphur Spring Centennial celebration.

Other ceremonial titles bestowed on Eddie over the years include Honorary Mayor of Pacoima, CA (1954), Honorary Admiral in the Mythical Texas Navy, Honorary Marshall of Dodge City, KS (1954), Honorary Colonel of Oklahoma on Governor's Staff, Honorary Optimist (1953) from the Optimist Club, and Honorary Jaycee (1967) from that service organization.

On an average, Eddie performed in over twenty charity benefits a year including March of Dimes, NOVA Opportunity Center, Goodwill Industries, The Heart Fun, the American Cancer Society, Little People International, the American Heart Association, the Los Angeles Police Memorial Foundation, the City of Hope, the John Tracy Clinic, the Los Angeles Children's Hospital, the Arthritis Foundation, the American Lung Association, and the Alicia Ann Burn Foundation.

Eddie was also the recipient of numerous awards for benefits and contributions he made over the years which include "Rap City in Blue" West Valley "PALS" from the Los Angeles Police Department (1984), "The Los Angeles Police Memorial Foundation Award," "Lifetime Member Award" from the Newhall/Saugus/Valencia Chamber of Commerce (1979), the "Hollywood Press Club Award" for promoting the Hollywood Press Club ideals, honored at "Eddie Dean Day" in Yankton, SD (1947), "Haven on Earth Ranch Award" (1979) for handicapped children, special guest at the Memphis Film Festival (1981), Western Walk of Fame (1982) in Newhall, CA, "Golden Mask Award" from the Hollywood Appreciation Society (1982), "Golden Jubilee Award" (1983), "Burbank Optimists' Award" (1974), "Country Music Award" (1983), "Heritage Award" from the National Film Society (1981), "Award of Merit" from the National lung Association (1982), "American Heart Association Award" (1977), "Certificate of Appreciation for Distinguished Service" from the Burbank Elks Lodge(1985), "Golden Boot Award" (1983), and the "March of Dimes Award" (1977 through 1984, for seven consecutive years).

In 1985, Eddie was nominated by family and friends for a star to be installed on the Hollywood Walk of Fame for his motion picture contributions. Because of the extenuated application process and the politics involved, Eddie's application for a star never materialized, even though the $3,000 sponsorship fee at the time was secured.

"For my fans to be able to walk along and see my name would be a real joy me," Eddie confessed. "It's history, and I'm a part of show biz history."[3]

"Getting that star to become a reality was a major headache," Ed Jr. said. "I often suspected that Johnny Grant, who headed up the Hollywood Walk of Fame, for some reason kept the family on the hook."

Eddie also received various proclamations from city, county, state and federal politicians from Los Angeles County Supervisor Baxter Ward (1979), Congressman Barry Goldwater, Jr. (1979), California Assemblyman Robert Cline (1979), California State Senator Lou Cusonavitch (1979), United States Senator from California S.I. Hayakawa (1979), Los

Angeles County Supervisor Michael Antonovich (1982), a Resolution from California Assemblywoman Cathie Wright (1982), County of Los Angeles from Supervisor Baxter Ward (1982), California State Legislature from Assemblywoman Marion La Follette (1982), and a Resolution by the Los Angeles City Council declaring "Eddie Dean Day" (1994). The latter resolution erroneously mentions "Topper" as Eddie Dean's horse. Topper was William Boyd's (Hopalong Cassidy) magnificent white steed.[4]

Eddie had also accepted invitations to be Grand Marshall in over fifty parades and rodeos across the United States, including the 13th Annual Cherry Festival in Beaumont, CA, in May 1947. In addition, he rode in the Tournament of Roses Parade in Pasadena on the "Cinecolor Float" and in the Santa Claus Lane Parade in Hollywood during the 1940s and 1950s.

Eddie was a very popular performer with his "Rodeo Revelers" on the rodeo and state fair circuits throughout the 1950s. Venues on the circuit included the Snake River Stampede in Nampa, ID, the Salt Lake City County Fair in Salt Lake City, UT, the Nebraska State Fair in Lincoln, NE, the Oklahoma Free State Fair in Muskogee, OK, various rodeos in Texas, Kansas and Alabama, the Louisiana State Fair Rodeo in Shreveport, LA, among others. One of biggest rodeo production companies that loved having Eddie perform was headed by Tommy Steiner.

Eddie would be booked for these events through Music Corporation of America (MCA) at venues anywhere from three to seven days for fees ranging from $1,000 to $2,000.[5]

Many G. I.'s remember being entertained by Eddie in wartime and in peacetime in Korea, Taiwan, Japan, the Philippines, Germany and many United States service camps such as Camp Pendleton and El Toro Marine Base, Vandenberg Air Force Base (CA), and Almandorf Air Force Base, Alaska.

When Bullhead City, AZ, was being built up as a resort community in 1960, Eddie was booked to perform there. Bullhead City is located roughly ninety miles south of Las Vegas and directly across the Colorado River from Laughlin, NV. Eddie did his show outside along the Colorado River from the back end of a large flatbed truck complete with microphones and electrical sound equipment.

Eddie took Dean Glosup, his six-year-old grandson, with him. The man in charge of the concert owned a home right on the bank of Colorado River and his back deck extended over the river. It was a great place to go fishing.

"Dean liked to fish so we out on the back deck of this man's house to do a little fishing," Eddie said. "I was showing him how to cast his line and he got a nibble on his line. All of sudden, before he realized what was happening, here comes an osprey flying overhead and it dove into the water right where Dean's line was and plucked that fish right out of the water! It was amazing. Needless to say, Dean wasn't too thrilled about having his fish stolen by a bird!"

Every movie singing cowboy was given a moniker by which they were known. Roy Rogers, for example, was known as "The King of the Cowboys." Gene Autry was tagged as "America's Favorite Cowboy." Tex Ritter was recognized as "America's Most Beloved Cowboy." Rex Allen was "The Arizona Cowboy." Eddie was dubbed "The Golden Cowboy," for his smooth yet "golden" singing voice, but that appellation came later in his career.

The individual who christened Eddie with that title was Colonel Tom Parker, the entertainment impresario known best as the manager of Elvis Presley. Parker, whose real name was Andreas Cornelis van Kuijk, was born in 1909, the seventh of eleven children of a Jewish family in Breda, the Netherlands. Parker's alleged dubious past in the Netherlands and his alleged illegal immigration to America have often remained a dark and unexplainable secret part of his life.[6]

In 1948, Parker received the rank of colonel in the Louisiana State Militia from Jimmie Davis, the governor of Louisiana and a former Country singer, in return for work Parker did on Davis' election campaign. Parker used the title throughout his life, becoming known simply as "The Colonel" to many acquaintances.[7]

Parker was often criticized for extracting more than the industry's customary 15 to 20 percent fee managers receive from those whom they represent. He would often command 25 percent as his clients became more successful. Parker displayed a ruthless devotion to Presley's interests and took up to 50-percent of "The King of Rock and Roll's" earnings toward the end of his life.[8]

Parker possessed a keen but shrewd mind for talent management, first working with popular singer Gene Austin when his career was on the skids, then managing Country artists Eddy Arnold and Hank Snow, then pop teen-idol Tommy Sands.

Parker expressed an interest in managing Eddie's career around early 1955.

"(Parker) was very interested in handling me," Eddie said. "He told me, 'Eddie, go get yourself a gold outfit, a gold suit, and we'll call you 'The Golden Voice' or 'The Golden Cowboy,' as I'd like to handle you.'"

Eddie made a date to have lunch with Parker in Las Vegas in the hopes of discussing how his career could be taken to a new and more dynamic level. However, that meeting turned out to be a bust as Parker expressed a last minute interest in handling another client.

"Eddie, I've got some sad news for you," Parker said. "I just found a guy I really want. His name is Elvis Presley."

"I was disappointed, to be sure, but the Colonel made the right choice," Eddie said. "Elvis was a rare and exciting talent and Parker was behind the scenes making Elvis a huge success. Elvis even publicly credited Parker for making him a big star."

Eddie's rejection by Parker almost parallels a similar encounter he had with Art Satherly, who wanted to devote energy in promoting Gene Autry.

By the time Eddie met with Parker, he had the publicity out on his name and new byname as well. In addition, he had already ordered the gold suits from Nudie Cohn, who designed and manufactured his own brand of individually created Western wear for all the Western stars in Hollywood.

Cohn was born Nuta Kotlyarenko on December 15, 1902, in Kiev in the Ukraine. To escape the pogroms of Czarist Russia, his parents sent him at age eleven with his brother, Julius, to America. Cohn learned the garment business and he and his wife, Helen "Bobbie" Kruger, moved from New York to the Los Angeles area and began designing and manufacturing clothing from their garage.[9]

As their creations gained a following, the Cohns opened "Nudie's of Hollywood" on the corner of Victory and Vineland in North Hollywood, dealing exclusively in Western wear, a style very much in fashion at the time.

Nudie's designs brought the already-flamboyant Western style to a new level of ostentation with the liberal use of rhinestones and themed images in chain stitch embroidery. Many of Cohn's designs, called "Nudie Suits," became signature looks for their owners. Among his most famous creations was Elvis Presley's $10,000 gold lamé suit.[10]

In 1963, the Cohn's relocated their business to a larger facility on Lankershim Boulevard in North Hollywood and renamed it "Nudie's Rodeo Tailors."

In addition, Cohn was equally famous for his garishly-decorated automobiles. He customized eighteen vehicles, mostly white Pontiac Bonneville convertibles, with silver-dollar-studded dashboards, pistol door handles and gear shifts, extended rear bumpers, and enormous long horn steer horn hood ornaments. They were called "Nudie Mobiles." The nine remaining cars are considered valued collector's items.[11]

Cohn died in May 9, 1984 at the age of eighty-one.

"I was usually kind of conservative in my dress," Eddie remarked. "There wasn't one singing cowboy that dressed conservatively. Not one. Gene Autry dressed loud. Roy Rogers dressed loud. Finally Nudie talked me into a lot of the loud clothes that I wear. The women like them and if you can please the other sex with your nice clothes and that you look nice, then that makes me very happy.

"A man doesn't usually care how I would dress. I can walk on the stage with Levi's and old dirty shirt and an old dirty hat, and they wouldn't care. I mean 90 percent of them would accept you as a man, as long as you sing well and entertain well, fine. But I think women like to see a man dressed up.

They like to see a guy neat. I think a man in the business owes it to his public to dress nice on stage. I have all solid gold suits with rhinestones and then I have suits of red and green with gold trim and rhinestones. I have blue suits with rhinestones, all different ones. As long as you look neat that's the main thing. Clean and neat. I think that's the most important thing."

During one of Eddie's visits to Bakersfield, CA, where he was quite popular, Nudie Cohn accompanied him, where they experienced the ugly affects of racism.

"Nudie wanted me to drive one of his 'Nudie Mobiles' to see a performance in Bakersfield, which is about a two-hour drive away," Eddie recalled. "We were driving down 'the Grapevine' on I-5. It's the main route between Northern and Southern California. It has a very long 6 percent steep grade. Nudie was feeling a little bold and said to me, 'Let's see how fast this thing will go.' I said, 'You mean it?' 'Yeah,' Nudie said. 'This thing has never been driven over 65 miles per hour.' I stepped on it and got it to about 110 mph. Nudie suddenly got panicky and I finally slowed down, easing on the brakes. 'Boy, I'm glad I wasn't driving,' Nudie said wiping the sweat from his forehead with a handkerchief, looking a little pale, 'I wouldn't know what to do.'"

Eddie and Nudie arrived safely in Bakersfield, checked into a motel, and then went to the club where Bonnie Owens, the wife of Buck Owens, was entertaining that night.

While Eddie and Nudie were eating dinner prior to the show, in walks a military man dressed in civilian clothes accompanied by a black man. The bouncer at the door stopped the two men and nicely told them that in this area they might run in to trouble and politely advised them to watch what they do and say.

The pair sat down minding their own business. A little while later the police came in as someone complained about the presence of a black man in the club. When the police confronted the two men about the complaint, the military man flew into a rage.

"Nudie and I were sitting next to them and the guy who blew his stack starts to throw a punch at me," Eddie said. "I got in a judo position to defend myself and he backed off. He then grabbed his black friend and ran out."

After dinner, Cohn went out to fill up his car with gas so he wouldn't have to get it the next morning. While he was gone, the club manager asked Eddie if he would play Black Jack in the adjoining area, hoping that when customers would see Eddie playing cards, they would come in to play cards, too. Eddie agreed to do it, and was given $50 to play. A crowd soon gathered around the Black Jack table.

"The dealer wouldn't let me play with the money the manager gave me," Eddie said. "Once a good crowd assembled, I went to the manager and gave him back the money."

In the meantime, Cohn drove to a nearby gas station and there at that filling station was the same black man who was at the club, now with his face completely cut open!

"When Nudie told me about it, it made me sick to my stomach," Eddie said. "but there was nothing I could do about it."

Ed Jr. related another hunting story in which Eddie ended up briefly entertaining at a restaurant:

"Dad and I hunted all over. We hunted mainly for quail in California and in Baja Mexico. One night we were driving to San Quintín, a small coastal town on the west coast of Baja California near Ensenada. We stopped at a fine little restaurant called 'Los Cueves de Los Tigres' ('The Caves of the Tigers'). I had stopped there many times in the past, but not with Dad. A man named William was the owner. We sat down and a man was playing a guitar and singing; a wandering minstrel. He came by our table and started to sing "Maria Elena." Dad chimed in and when he was done the man complimented him and asked him if he would sing another Mexican song. He did and brought the restaurant down. There were about fifty people in the restaurant and I bet thirty knew who Dad was. What a great night! That's another reason why my dad is my hero. He never said no to a request, no matter where. He was proud of his singing and *nobody* had a better voice!"

Another story that illustrates Eddie's accommodating his fans comes from a story posted on the Internet by Dave Parker. He wrote:

"When I was a youngster, Eddie Dean was my favorite singing cowboy on the old black and white T.V. In October 1977, while I was a hunting guide on Santa Cruz Island (part of the Channel Islands group in Southern California). I had the pleasure of being guide to Eddie Dean and his son, Eddie, Jr. They flew over to the island for a three-day hunt for wild boar and we had us a time! Each night after dinner I'd talk Eddie into singing with his guitar for us. What a nice man and a damn good shot for being in his seventies. At the end of the hunt, I drove them to the dirt airstrip.

"While waiting for the plane to land, Eddie asked me if I would be his guest at the Lamplighter in Hollywood where he was singing. Being the character I am, I told him I wasn't rightly sure. He asked how come? I told him I reckon I could make it if he would sing my favorite Western song, "Strawberry Roan." Eddie said he hadn't sung it in years and didn't know if he remember all the words. About that time the plane landed and was pulling up to us. After shaking hands, Eddie picked up his guitar out of the jeep and started walking toward the plane. He got about halfway there, stopped, turned around and started playing his guitar and singing, '*I was just hanging 'round town not earning a dime, when a feller steps up and says I suppose you're cowboy by the looks of yer clothes . . . .*' I enthusiastically told Eddie I'd be there!

"Eddie embarrassed the hell out of me at his show. After singing the first song, he stopped and told the audience about what a great wild boar and sheep hunt he just had on Santa Cruz Island. He then went on to tell them how his guide wouldn't show up if he didn't sing 'Strawberry Roan' for him. Eddie sang an honest five-minute version of 'Strawberry Roan!' It had more verses in it than Marty Robbins ever heard of! It was the old original 'cowboy' version Eddie had picked up from different cowboys over the years, while rolling them all into one! It was great and what a night we had!

"I still have the autographed 33-LP, *Eddie Dean: The Album*, that Eddie gave me that night which he inscribed, 'To Dave on the 'Big Hunt,' please don't make me open sooo many gates next time!' The album has all his songs and is covered with his early movie photos. I really treasure it!"

Here's a story about those crazy cowboys. In 1984, Monte Montana, well-known as a rodeo trick rider, actor, stuntman, and cowboy, as well a perennial participant in the Tournament of Roses Parade until his death in 1998 at age eighty-seven, got married to Marilee Young in the San Fernando Valley. It was his third marriage. Eddie and his family were invited to the wedding and it turned out to be quite a ceremony, according to Ed Jr.

Montana's wife-to-be was in a stagecoach about ¼-mile away from the rendezvous point. Monte appeared on top of a hill. As the stagecoach approached the marriage area, Montana came galloping down the hill on his Paint twirling a rope around his head and then lassoed his wife-to-be.

"It was a great wedding and that had excellent showmanship," Ed Jr. recalled. "We later went to his house in Agua Dulce (near Santa Clarita, CA) to a reception. During that time he asked me to open up his sliding den doors when he came riding up. I said, 'Are you sure?' He said, 'This horse owns more of this house than I do.' Monte came riding up and I opened up the door and he rode into the den where there were about a hundred people. He sat there on his horse and said howdy to everyone there."

Hollywood screen legend Mickey Rooney was another person who loved Eddie. Both entertainers lived near each other in Westlake Village. Rooney would call Eddie once or twice a week to play golf.

"I got to play with Mickey a couple of times," Ed Jr. said. "He gave me some great tips. When he was playing in *Sugar Babies* in Hollywood in 1980 (for which he was nominated for a Tony Award), he invited the folks and my sister and me to the play. During intermission, we went back stage to see Mickey and were ushered to his dressing room which was really, really small. His TV was on and he held up his hand and cued us to wait. He was watching a Buddy Rich short on drumming. Mickey was a drummer himself. When it was done he said, 'Buddy is the greatest drummer of all time.' We yacked for about five minutes and said we better get back as the bell had rung. Mickey said, 'Hold on, you've got time. I'll let you know when.' He rules.

After the musical had started, Mickey said, 'In about five minutes I go on, then you can go and sit.' Of course, when we returned, we were seen by everybody trying to get to our seats. Mickey was playing the role of a judge.

He banged his gavel for the person he was judging to hurry up because he had a golf game with Eddie Dean. Well, we all just cracked up how he put that into his dialogue during the play. Everybody applauded."

Eddie played a lot of golf during his life and especially in semi-retirement, he found himself a new home on the golf course range. Ed Jr. was privy to play golf with many celebrities who played along side his father such as Greg Palmer, Ken Toby, Fred MacMurray, Randy Owen of Alabama, and Howard Keel, "one of the nicest guys I've ever met," according to Ed Jr.).

Eddie was also a returning favorite over the years as a celebrity golfer in the annual Tim Conway Celebrity Golf Tournament held at the North Ranch Country Club in Westlake Village. Proceeds raised from the tournament went to the United Cerebral Palsy/Spastic Children's Foundation. It was at this affair in 1987, that the author briefly met Eddie for the first and only time, asking for his autograph, which was graciously given him.

Eddie said that in his life time as a golfer, he hit five holes in one. At one time, he was a six-handicap golfer. In later years, he claimed he was a 17-handicapper.

Eddie wanted to honor many of the West Coast Country and Western artists and musicians and was one of the founding members of the Academy of Country and Western Music, formed in 1967. He served in that organization as its Vice President.

The Academy eventually dropped "and Western" from its title and is known today as the Academy of Country Music (ACM).

In 1978, hit maker Patti Page presented Eddie with the Pioneer Award from the ACM on the nationally televised Academy of Country Music Awards show that year stating that Eddie was "one the best singers around and a fine gentleman." The Pioneer Award was created in 1968 for recognition for outstanding and unprecedented achievement in the field of Country music.

Previous winners since the award's inception include Gene Autry, Tex Ritter, Roy Rogers, Tennessee Ernie Ford, Hank Williams, Bob Wills, Stuart Hamblin, Sons of the Pioneers, Tex Williams, Eddy Arnold, Chet Atkins, Ernest Tubb, and Roy Acuff.

In 1980, Eddie was inducted in the Western Music Association Hall of Fame.

An accomplished oil painter, Eddie was President of the Valley Artists Guild in 1947, and one of his paintings, Front Street in Dodge City, KS, as it looked back in 1878, remains hanging in the Boot Hill Museum in Dodge City.

Eddie's paintings are numerous ranging from still life's to portraits to landscapes. He was also a master wood carver creating exquisite bas relief wooden likenesses of Will Rogers, President Abraham Lincoln, Indian braves, and horses. He also created a detailed likeness of Abraham Lincoln on a pipe that he showed to Gutzon Borglum, the architect-sculptor who gave face to Mount Rushmore.

Eddie also was talented in making a variety of guitars that he used throughout his career. He even made a guitar from the expandable oak table leaf taken from the family dining room table.

Eddie was also an accomplished gunsmith having made the handle and butt of the rifle out of oak to fit a 30/40 Krag rifle used for hunting.

In 1969, Eddie and Dearest sold their home in Burbank and moved to Westlake Village at 32161 Sailview Lane, Westlake Village, CA 91360, residing there until the end of both their lives

Poppa James Franklin Glosup died from cancer on January 25, 1959, at age ninety-one. During the later years of his life he lived with his daughter, Daisy Mae Roby, a school teacher, in Iowa Park, TX, before residing with Eddie and family in Burbank.

Eddie was deeply saddened by his father's passing as he remained in close contact with him over the years.

After Father James passed on, the family farm was not fought over by the children, but discussed a lot with with son Virgil Glosup. Somewhere down the line, Virgil bought out or was given the rights to the farm. He wrote letters asking from the relatives for $5 or $6 to pay taxes. Eddie didn't want to be bothered with the farm anymore and gave his share to Virgil.

Frank Glosup ended up with a part of the farm or maybe all of it. Ed Jr. and his wife, Barb, visited with his Uncle Frank and Aunt Rose in the 1970s and toured the farm.

"Uncle Frank had just purchased a huge barn and had probably fifty acres of alfalfa growing," Ed Jr. said. "When we visited the 'back forty' there was a large pipe coming out of the ground. I asked what that was (knowing quite well what it was), and he answered with much shyness, 'Oh, that's the oil well. Just turn on the valve and out it goes to the refinery.' I think with all the paperwork I read when Dad passed, I think everyone gave their share to Uncle Frank. The paperwork and understanding the lease agreements were just too much for my mom and dad. The debt for the original farm went away. I'm sure the boys took care of Grandpa."

Eddie was a frequent guest performer at The Palomino, a popular Country Western music spot located on Lankershim Blvd. in North Hollywood, CA. Owner Tommy Thomas loved having Eddie perform at his club. Eddie usually got paid $400 for this engagement.[12]

Eddie would often be invited to perform at Knott's Berry Farm in Buena Park, CA, for special Country music shows, as he did on October 18, 1980, when he was part of "Knott's Annual Country Party Saluting Radio KLAC's 10th Birthday." On the bill with Eddie were Tex Williams, Jimmy Wakely, Bill Monroe, Debby Boone, Gail Davis, The Oak Ridge Boys, and Johnny Blankenship and his group Country Sunshine. Tickets for this gala sold for $8.75 per person.

On Sunday, September 25, 1988, Eddie was honored by being invited by Gene and Jackie Autry to sing the National Anthem at Angels Stadium in Anaheim, CA, on the closing day of the California Angels' baseball season. The Angels hosted the Minnesota Twins, losing to them 6-2. For the record, the Angels finished in fourth place that season in the American League West with a record of 75 wins and 87 losses, 29 games behind the first place Oakland Athletics.

Eddie was also very accommodating to his many fans for autographs and pictures. He would be mailed requests for such from all around the world, even as recently prior to his passing. One such request Eddie received was a heart-felt plea from Nina E. Warren, whose husband, Earl Warren, served as the 30th Governor of California (1943-1953) and was currently the 14th Chief Justice of the United States Supreme Court (1953-1969).

Her letter, dated September 27, 1957, was written on official stationery of the Supreme Court of the United States. The letter read:

> "Dear Eddie Dean,
>
> We met a lonely little boy in Scotland this summer whose greatest interest in life is collecting autographed photographs of screen and television stars. You are one of his favorites, and nothing would please him more than to be able to add your picture to his collection. I hope that you will grant his request.
>
> He is the son of our Consul General in Edinburgh, and is the only American boy in his school. Life apparently is rather dismal for him so far away from his friends at times.
>
> Photograph should be addressed to:
> John Kuppinger
> 14 Abercromby Place
> Edinburgh 3,
> Scotland
> With thanks and best wishes,
> Nina E. Warren (Mrs. Earl Warren)"

Naturally, Eddie followed through on Mrs. Warren's request, and needless to say, young John Kuppinger was elated to receive Eddie's autographed photo. Chief Justice Warren died in July 1974 at age eighty-three. Mrs. Warren died in April 1993, at the age of one hundred.

One hardcore cowboy film buff persuaded Dearest to snip him a lock of Eddie's hair when the couple attended a B-Western film festival in Charlotte, NC, in 1985.[13]

"I told this guy that I didn't have enough hair as it is," Eddie jested.

"Sometimes I wonder what it is about me that someone would want to show so much respect and affection."

It's because Eddie was also loyal to his fans who would still attend his club dates and concerts and write him requesting autographed photos and even snippets of his hair is why he is so accommodating. Without his fans, Eddie realized that he would be nothing.[14]

"It's the fans who have helped supported me over the years who made me who I am," Eddie said.

Eddie Dean was a man of faith who believed in Jesus Christ as his Lord and Savior and remained a Baptist his entire life. He allowed Dearest to freely practice Roman Catholicism and never interfered in the religious instruction and education of his children. However, Eddie was not an avid churchgoer for the simple fact of his celebrity status. Early in his career he faithfully attended worship services but was always hounded by requests from the minister or choir director to sing for the congregation. Eddie said he didn't mind doing that on occasion, but the requests for such actions would come more frequently than he liked. He just wanted to be one of the regular worshipers. So, he quit attending church all together so as not to be imposed upon.

Eddie Dean in a relaxed posture in 1947.

Eddie Dean on television during the early 1950s for the March of Dimes.
Eddie was a long-time celebrity spokesperson for the
charitable organization in its fight against polio.

Eddie Dean and Roscoe Ates attempting
to get water out of an old water well pump.

Above: Eddie Dean and a scruffy-looking Roscoe Ates in the early 1950s.

Below: Head shot of Eddie Dean from the mid-1950s.

A publicity photo of Eddie Dean from the 1950s.

Above: Eddie Dean and Shirley Patterson at a western film convention in the late 1970s.

Below: Eddie Dean's good buddy Glenn Strange
shown here as Sam Noonan on TVs *Gunsmoke*.

Eddie Dean, and Eddie's son, Edgar Glosup (age 17),
and Glenn Strange strike a "three-for-all" pose, ca. 1950.

Edgar Glosup Jr., in 2013, posing in front of a
still life painting created by his father, Eddie Dean.

Above: Donna Lee Glosup Knorr, daughter of Eddie
and Dearest Dean, August 9, 1932 – August 30, 2010.

Below: Donna Lee Knorr with mom Dearest Dean, ca. 1980s.

Edgar Glosup, Eddie Dean's son, presents Eddie with "The Book of Golden Deeds" award from the Exchange Club of Burbank, CA, in 1969. It's the service club's highest award for meritorious service to the community.

Eddie Dean displaying some samples of his paintings. Notice the portrait
in the lower right corner of Roscoe Ates, his movie saddle pal.

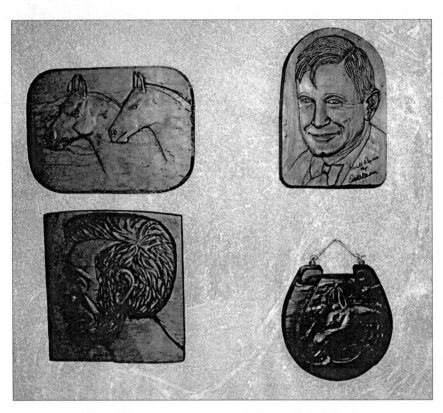

Eddie Dean was also an accomplished wood carver creating
bas reliefs of Will Rogers, Abraham Lincoln, and horse heads.

A painting Eddie Dean made of Front Street in
Dodge City, Kansas, as it looked in 1878.
The painting is on permanent display in
the Boot Hill Museum in Dodge City.

Above: Eddie Dean holding a 30/40 Krag rifle he made out of oak wood.

Below: Eddie Dean singing and strumming at home on an acoustic guitar he made.

One of Eddie Dean's favorite hobbies was golf. He is pictured here
dressed casually wearing a Hawaiian shirt and sandals practicing
his putting inside his home in Burbank, ca. 1949.

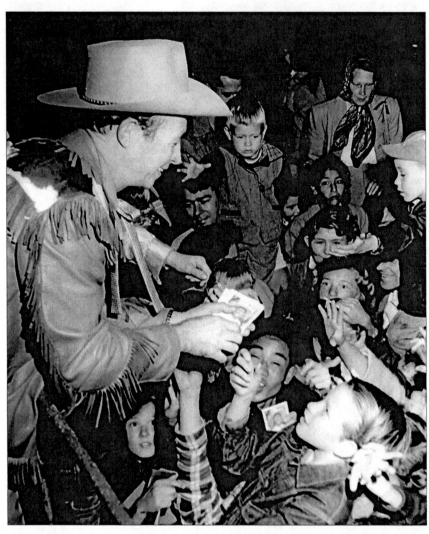

Eddie Dean with a large group of his most enthusiastic fans: kids!

Above: Eddie Dean signing autographs for his young fans
during a tour in Fontana, CA, in the early 1950s.

Below: Eddie Dean is joined by Monte Hale, Patsy Montana,
Gene Autry, and Herb Jeffries at the Gene Autry Museum in 1989.

Cowboy royalty enjoying a fun-filled moment at Nudie's Rodeo Tailors. Pictured above are, standing l-r, Rex Allen, Roy Rogers, unidentified man, Gene Autry, Eddie Dean, and Smokey Rogers. Kneeling in front are Nudie Cohn and Tex Williams.

Above: Eddie and Dearest Dean with Roy Rogers and Dale Evans in the 1990s.

Below: Ad for the "Chuck Wagon Round-Up," an all-star western show
from 1949, location unknown, of which Eddie Dean was a part.
The show was promoted by Ralph Autry, Gene Autry's brother.

Eddie Dean in the 1960s, above, and
Eddie Dean in the 1990s, below.

Eddie Dean is photographed having a casual chat with friend Gene Autry who made an impromptu visit to Eddie's home in Westlake Village, CA, during the spring of 1995. Autry and his driver autographed the photo for Eddie.

14

The Last Roundup

Eddie Dean rode high, wide, and handsome on movie screens and enjoyed a recording, stage, and club popularity that continued long after his movie career ended.

In 1979, at the age of seventy-two, Eddie underwent quintuple-coronary bypass surgery at Cedars-Sinai Medical Center in Los Angeles. While on the operating table, Eddie suffered a heart attack which nearly killed him.

"We almost lost Dad at that moment, but thank God, he pulled through," Ed Jr. said.

The Texas wrangler indeed pulled through and recovered so well that it wasn't long after he was able to resume his normal life style of stage shows, recordings, and golf.

However, part of that normal life style involved smoking cigarettes. Eddie was a life-long smoker. He also often performed in venues throughout his career where smoking was permitted and breathing in all that second-hand smoke also helped to contribute him getting emphysema, he said. During the last couple years of his life he had to have help breathing through a portable oxygen tank with tubes affixed through his nostrils.

Although Eddie was a fairly resilient individual, there were times while wearing his oxygen mask he would be asked if he would entertain by singing a song. He would accommodate that request by removing his oxygen mask and sing that song in typical Eddie Dean style – with his magnificent golden voice that would belie his age and physical condition. Such actions astounded his fans. His phrasing of a song and breath control was remarkably impeccable for a man who was suffering from lung disease.

On February 6, 1999, Eddie attended an affair at Iverson Ranch in Chatsworth, CA, to help raise funds to have his star placed on the Walk of Stars in Palm Springs, CA. His star was added posthumously, two weeks after his passing. In attendance for that fund-raising affair was singer Herb Jeffries, eighty-six, who in the mid-1930s made a handful of singing cowboy movies under the guise of "race films." He was known as "The Bronze Buckaroo," and who later sang with Duke Ellington and his orchestra.

Eddie and Jeffries took a photo together at that event, as Eddie looked thin and frail. It was his last public appearance.

In the days that followed, Eddie's breathing became progressively erratic and extremely difficult as the emphysema continued to destroy the elasticity in the air sacks in his lungs. He knew the end would soon be near but continued to fight and hold on for fear of having to leave Dearest to be all alone.

He was admitted to nearby Los Robles Hospital in Thousand Oaks. While there, he went in to a coma. Dearest, Ed Jr. and his wife Barbara, were constantly at his bedside.

"Dad was in a coma, but if I asked him to, he'd squeeze my hand, so he was aware of what was going on," Ed Jr. said. "We talked with him as he was failing quickly. He wouldn't let go and just hung on because he was worried about Dearest, I'm sure."

"When we convinced Dad that Dearest would be well taken care of, he came to an acceptance of that," Ed Jr. said. "About three minutes later, he just breathed in and out and he was gone. It was hard to believe but we were glad that he wasn't suffering any more. It's hell when you can't get your breath. Dearest asked me a million times, 'Is your Daddy dead?' It was very hard for her to grasp and believe that her major hero was gone. It was hard for me, too."

Death came quietly for Eddie Dean on Thursday, March 4, 1999, at 6:15 p. m. He was ninety-one. The golden voice of "The Golden Cowboy" was silenced and would be no more. The angels joyfully and mercifully ushered in the most recent inductee as well as one of the brightest and arguably one of the most illustrious stars to ever grace "Hillbilly Heaven."

Over 200 people attended Eddie's funeral at the Pierce Brothers Valley Oaks Memorial Park in Westlake Village including Wesley and Marilyn Tuttle, Fred Martin of the Cass County Boys, Dick Jones, Joanne Hale, Doug Green of Riders in the Sky, Tom Corrigan, Ray "Crash" Corrigan's son, Country artist Freddie Hart, Charlie Dierkop, Jon Locke, Rusty Richards, the widows of Hank Penny and Cliffie Stone, Donna Martell and Bill Campbell. Actor Johnny Seven read a message from Dale Robertson. Johnny Blankenship and his group "Chaparral" sang at graveside.[1]

Eddie was laid to rest in the Gethsemane plot of Valley Oaks Memorial Park. Three years later, on July 12, 2002, Dearest Dean died at age eighty-nine, succumbing to the effects of dementia. The headstone on Eddie's and Dearest's grave reads "Glosup" at the top with "Eddie Dean, Husband and Father, 1907-1999" and "Dearest Dean, Wife and Mother, 1911-2002" also etched below it.

Artistically, Eddie left a legacy of his films and his vast array of compositions and recordings, but more importantly, he left an indelible imprint of *himself* that was saturated with integrity and authenticity in all that he did and all with whom he interacted.

Dick Jones, who played in a number of B-Western films and starred in his own television show in the mid-1950s called *Buffalo Bill Jr.* had this to say about Eddie's character:

"Eddie was a beautiful human being. A gentlemen, a gentlemen's gentlemen . . . a good friend and I just loved being around him. Gonna miss him a lot. There are only two singing cowboys I would consider real singers, Eddie Dean and Rex Allen."

Ronnie Pugh, research librarian at the Country Music Foundation and Hall of Fame, evaluated Eddie's legacy accordingly: "Eddie and his brother,

Jimmie, were one of the first brother acts back in the 1930s. Then he was a pioneer of the real smooth singing style. Finally, his enduring contribution to Country music will be his songwriting."[2]

Country music manager Don Bradley said that Eddie's legacy will be "his music. He never had the promotion and marketing that Roy (Rogers) and Gene (Autry) had because he and Dearest always did all of their own business. But Eddie was one of the finest singers the good Lord ever made. And he was a great writer. He wrote 80 percent of all the music in his movies."[3]

In an article published in *Country and Western Variety*, a Nashville, TN, publication, Bradley wrote,

"The roads that Eddie Dean has traveled in the past 60 years would make him a great candidate for a travel agent. He could probably drive a lot of them old Texas highways in his sleep. But he never wasted those days on the road counting Burma Shave signs – he used all those miles to write songs and many of them ended up in his Western movies. When he was at home he didn't waste that time either watching a 700-pound TV with a six-inch picture – he took a chunk of wood and carved it into a guitar, or a piece of raw canvas and turned it into a work of art fit for any gallery. If I was ever sure of anything in my life, I'm absolutely sure that God put a song in Eddie's heart and those songs will still beat in hearts all over the world long after we've gone to 'Hillbilly Heaven.'"

What has been believed throughout folklore concerning the seventh son of a seventh son of a seventh son being endowed with certain noble talent, special abilities, or even extraordinary fortunes definitely applies to Eddie. He was indeed blessed with noble talent, special abilities, and extraordinary fortunes. He utilized these gifts and talents through the medium of the entertainment industry to enrich the lives of many by reflecting their lives through his films and his music. Eddie Dean wasn't bigger than life; he was life itself. He was a man who, in his own way, tried to help all of us to see that life is much more than just about self. And we are all a little better off for it because of him.

Before his departure for "Hillbilly Heaven," Eddie reflected about himself, epitomizing humbleness coupled with an attitude of gratitude that was so in keeping with his character:

"I'm a positive thinker. I love life. My family is very important to me. I've worked hard for what I've done. I know I'm not one of the big stars, but I know I'm one of the top in certain areas. That's a great compliment to anyone. All in all, I've had a beautiful wonderful life, with so many phases to my life that many people never had. If I were to start over, I'd do the same thing, I'd just try to do it a little better."[4]

Publicity photo of Eddie Dean in the mid-1960s.

Eddie Dean was in perfect voice and still performing into the 1990s.

Above: Eddie Dean with Herb Jeffries at Iverson Ranch to help raise money for Eddie's Palm Springs Walk of Fame star on February 6, 1999. Less than a month later, Eddie died.

Below: Headstone marking the grave of Eddie and Dearest Dean in Westlake Village, CA.

Eddie Dean, one of the brightest and most
illustrious stars to ever grace "Hillbilly Heaven."

Eddie Dean Filmography

Non-Starring Roles

(**1938**) - **1.** *Western Jamboree* - Gene Autry and Smiley Burnette * Eddie Dean as "Thompson" (unaccredited)

2. (**1939**) - *The Lone Ranger Rides Again* - Robert Livingstone as The Lone Ranger and Chief Thundercloud as Tonto * Eddie Dean as "Cooper, the settler" (Chapters 1-3, 6-7, 12 - unaccredited)

3. (**1939**) - *Renegade Trail* - William Boyd as Hopalong Cassidy and George "Gabby" Hayes * Eddie Dean as "Red," a singing cowhand

4. (**1939**) - *Range War* - William Boyd as Hopalong Cassidy * Eddie Dean as "Pete," a henchman

5. (**1939**) - *Law of the Pampos* - William Boyd as Hopalong Cassidy and Sidney Toler * Eddie Dean as "Curly Naples," a henchman (credited)

6. (**1939**) - *Rovin' Tumbleweeds* - Gene Autry and Smiley Burnette * Eddie Dean as a singing cowhand (unaccredited)

7. (**1939**) - *The Llano Kid* - Tito Guizar, Gale Sondergaard, Alan Mowbray * Eddie Dean as a gambler (unaccredited)

8.(**1940**) - *Santa Fe Marshall* - William Boyd as Hopalong Cassidy * Eddie Dean as the town marshal

9. (**1940**) - *The Showdown* - William Boyd as Hopalong Cassidy * Eddie Dean as the marshal

10. **(1940) - *The Light of Western Stars* -** Victor Jory, Noah Berry, Jr. Tom Tyler
    * Eddie Dean as "Nels," the Stillwell hand

11. **(1940) - *Hidden Gold* -** William Boyd as Hopalong Cassidy * Eddie Dean as "Logan," the Express Agent

12. **(1940) - *The Golden Trail* -** Tex Ritter * Eddie Dean as "Bart," the henchman

13. **(1940) - *Stagecoach War* -** William Boyd as Hopalong Cassidy * Eddie Dean as "Tom," the henchman

14. **(1940) - *Oklahoma Renegades* -** The Three Mesquiteers (Robert Livingston, Raymond Hatton, Duncan Reynaldo) * Eddie Dean as a veteran

15. **(1940) - *Knights of the Range* -** Victor Jory, Russell Hayden, Jean Parker
    * Eddie Dean as "Skyler," the cowhand (unaccredited)

16. **(1940) - *Rolling Home to Texas* -** Tex Ritter * Eddie Dean as "Sheriff Eddie Dean"

17. **(1941) - *The Trail of the Silver Spurs* -** The Range Busters (Ray "Crash" Corrigan, John "Dusty" King, Max Terhune) * Eddie Dean as "Stoner"

18. **(1941) - *A Man Betrayed* -** John Wayne, Frances Dee, Edward Ellis
    * Eddie Dean as "Elmer," the ice man (unaccredited)

19. **(1941) - *Pals of the Pecos* -** The Three Mesquiteers (Robert Livingston, Bob Steele, Rufe Davis) * Eddie Dean as a slender henchman in a barroom brawl (unaccredited)

20. **(1941) - *Kansas Cyclone* -** Don "Red" Barry * Eddie Dean as "Pete," a henchman

21. **(1941) - *Sunset in Wyoming* -** Gene Autry and Smiley Burnette * Eddie Dean as a cowhand (unaccredited)

22. **(1941) - *Outlaws of Cherokee Trail* -** The Three Mesquiteers (Bob Steele, Tom Tyler, Rufe Davis) * Eddie Dean as a murdered guard (unaccredited)

23. **(1941) - *Down Mexico Way* -** Gene Autry and Smiley Burnette * Eddie Dean as a barbeque guest (unaccredited)

24. **(1941) - *Gauchos of El Dorado* -** The Three Mesquiteers (Bob Steele, Tom Tyler, Rufe Davis) * Eddie Dean as a henchman (unaccredited)

25. **(1941) - *Sierra Sue* -** Gene Autry and Smiley Burnette * Eddie Dean as "Jerry Willis," a pilot

26. (1941) - *Fighting Bill Fargo* - Johnny Mack Brown and Fuzzy Knight
    * Eddie Dean as one of the musicians (unaccredited)

27. (1941) - *West of Cimarron* - The Three Mesquiteers (Bob Steele, Tom Tyler, Rufe Davis) * Eddie Dean as a "Rebel Rider" (unaccredited)

28. (1942) - *The Lone Rider and the Bandit* - George Houston, Al "Fuzzy" St. John, Glenn Strange * Eddie Dean as the first miner

29. (1942) - *Raiders of the West* - Bill "Cowboy Rambler" Boyd, Art Davis, Lee Powell * Eddie Dean as "Pete," a henchman in Duke's office (unaccredited)

30. (1942) - *Stagecoach Express* - Don "Red" Barry, Al "Fuzzy" St. John Eddie Dean as "Randall," a henchman

31. (1942) - *Gang Busters* - Kent Taylor, Robert Armstrong
    * Eddie Dean as "Blair," police lab technician in Chapter 1 (unaccredited)

32. (1942) - *Arizona Stage Coach* - The Range Busters (Ray "Crash" Corrigan, John "Dusty" King, Max Terhune) * Eddie Dean as a henchman (unaccredited)

33. (1943) - *Don Winslow of the Coast Guard* - Don Terry, Walter Sande * Eddie Dean as "Clark," Winslow's aide in Chapters 2, 3, 9, 12, 13 (unaccredited)

34. (1943) - *King of the Cowboys* - Roy Rogers and Smiley Burnette * Eddie Dean as "Tex," a lawman (unaccredited)

35. (1944) - *Harmony Trail* - Ken Maynard, Ruth Roman, Glen Strange, Max Terhune * Eddie Dean as "Marshal Eddie Dean"

36. (1945) - *Wildfire* - Bob Steele, Sterling Holloway * Eddie Dean as "Sheriff Johnny Deal"

Starring Roles

1. (1945) - *Song of Old Wyoming* - Eddie Dean with Emmett Lynn, Al La Rue, Jennifer Holt, Sarah Padden (released October 12, 1945) Cinecolor

2. (1946) - *Romance of the West* - Eddie Dean with Emmett Lynn, Joan Barton (released March 20, 1946) Cinecolor

3. (1946) - *The Caravan Trail* - Eddie Dean with Emmett Lynn, Al La Rue, Jean Carlin (released April 20, 1946) Cinecolor

4. **(1946)** - *Colorado Serenade* - Eddie Dean with Roscoe Ates, David Sharpe, Mary Kenyon, Dennis Moore (released June 30, 1946) Cinecolor

5. **(1946)** - *Wild West* - Eddie Dean with Roscoe Ates, Al La Rue, Lee Bennett, Sarah Padden (released December 1, 1946) *Final Cinecolor film*

6. **(1946)** - *Down Missouri Way* - Eddie Dean, Martha O'Driscoll, John Carradine, Roscoe Ates (released August 15, 1946) Musical comedy, Black and White

7. **(1946)** - *Driftin' River* - Eddie Dean with Roscoe Ates, Shirley Patterson, William Fawcett (released October 1, 1946) Black and White

8. **(1946)** - *Tumbleweed Trail* - Eddie Dean with Roscoe Ates, Shirley Patterson, Johnny McGovern, The Sunshine Boys (released July 10, 1946) Black and White

9. **(1946)** - *Stars Over Texas* - Eddie Dean with Roscoe Ates, Shirley Patterson, Lee Bennett, The Sunshine Boys (released November 18, 1946) Black and White

10. **(1947)** - *Wild Country* - Eddie Dean with Roscoe Ates, Peggy Wynne, I. Stanford Jolley, The Sunshine Boys (released January 17, 1947) Black and White

11. **(1947)** - *Range Beyond the Blue* - Eddie Dean with Roscoe Ates, Helen Mowrey (released March 17, 1947) Black and White

12. **(1947)** - *West to Glory* - Eddie Dean with Roscoe Ates, Delores Castle, The Sunshine Boys (released April 12, 1947) Black and White

13. **(1947)** - *Black Hills* - Eddie Dean with Roscoe Ates, Shirley Patterson, Andy Parker and The Plainsmen (released October 26, 1947) Black and White

14. **(1947)** - *Shadow Valley* - Eddie Dean with Roscoe Ates, Jennifer Holt, Andy Parker and The Plainsmen (released November 29, 1947) Black and White

15. **(1948)** - *Check Your Guns* - Eddie Dean with Roscoe Ates, Nancy Gates, Andy Parker and The Plainsmen (released January 24, 1948) Black and White

16. **(1948)** - *Tornado Range* - Eddie Dean with Roscoe Ates, Jennifer Holt, Andy Parker and The Plainsmen (released February 21, 1948) Black and White

17. **(1948)** - *The Westward Trail* - Eddie Dean with Roscoe Ates, Phyllis Blanchard, Steve Drake, Bob Duncan, Andy Parker and The Plainsmen (released March 13, 1948) Black and White

18. **(1948)** - *Prairie Outlaws* - Eddie Dean with Roscoe Ates, Al LaRue, Lee Bennett, Sarah Padden * Edited and cut Black and White version of *Wild West* minus some songs

19. **(1948)** - *The Hawk of Powder River* - Eddie Dean with Roscoe Ates, Jennifer Holt (released April 10, 1948) Black and White

20. **(1948)** - *The Tioga Kid* - Eddie Dean with Roscoe Ates, Jennifer Holt, Andy Parker and The Plainsmen (released June 17, 1948) Black and White * *The Tioga Kid* is a remake of *Driftin' River* (1946) with only slight plot changes, lots of stock footage, and approximately fifteen minutes of new film footage.

This concludes Eddie Dean's series of Western films for Producers Releasing Corporation. Eddie Dean Westerns are broadcast frequently on the Encore Western Movie cable channel. Many of his Westerns can be purchase on DVD via the Internet at Oldies.com

Eddie Dean Discography

SESSIONS

July 9, 1928 – Chicago, IL – Eddie Dean (solo vcl/gt)

001 C-2042 **Barefoot Days** Vocalion unissued/trial recording

September 10, 1934 – Chicago, IL - Jimmie and Eddie Dean (Jimmie Dean [vcl], Eddie Dean [vcl/gt])

    002 C 9446 **Tell Mother I'll Be There** Decca 5023

    003 C 9447 **(There's) No Disappointment in Heaven** Decca 5023

    004 C 9448 **There Shall Be Showers of Blessings** Decca 5024

    005 C 9449 **Happy in Him** Decca 5024

    006 C 9450-A **There's No Friend Like Jesus** F5340 [GB]

    007 C 9455-A,B **God Will Take Care of You** unissued

November 2, 1934 Furniture Mart Building, 666 Lake Shore Drive, Chicago, IL – Jimmie and Eddie Dean (Jimmie Dean [vcl], Eddie Dean [vcl/glt])

    008 C 776-1 **My Last Moving Day** Banner 33295 Melotone M-13262 Conq. 8438 Oriole 8412

    009 C 777-1 **The Soldier's Story** Perfect 13095

November 13, 1934 Furniture Mart Building, 666 Lake Shore Drive, Chicago, IL – Jimmie and Eddie Dean (Jimmie Dean [vcl], Eddie Dean [vcl/glt])

> 010 C 834-1 **When I Move to That New Range** BA 33295 ME 13262 CQ 8439 PE 13095 OR 8412 RO 5412

> 011 C 835-1 **The Old Mill Wheel** unissued

> 012 C 836-1 **Since My Mother's Dead and Gone** unissued

November 15, 1934 Furniture Mart Building, 666 Lake Shore Drive, Chicago, IL – Jimmie and Eddie Dean (Jimmie Dean [vcl], Eddie Dean [vcl/glt])

> 013 C836-2 **Since My Mother's Dead and Gone** ARC 70257 Conqueror 8439

> 014 C 853-1 **End of the Bandit's Trail** unissued

January 7, 1936 Furniture Mart Building, 666 Lake Shore Drive, Chicago, IL – Jimmie and Eddie Dean (Jimmie Dean [vcl], Eddie Dean [vcl/glt])

> 015 C777-3 **The Soldier's Story** unissued

> 016 C853-3 **End of the Bandit's Trail** unissued

January 24, 1935 Furniture Mart Building, 666 Lake Shore Drive, Chicago, IL – Jimmie and Eddie Dean (Jimmie Dean [vcl], Eddie Dean [vcl/glt])

> 017 C777-4 **The Soldier's Story** Banner 33372 Melotone M-13339 Oriole 8442 Romeo 5442

> 018 C853-4 **End of the Bandit's Trail** Banner 33372 Melotone M-13339 CQ 8471 Perfect 13120 Oriole 8442 5442

October 29, 1935 Furniture Mart Building, 666 Lake Shore Drive, Chicago, IL – Dean Boys (Jimmie Dean [vcl], Eddie Dean [vcl/glt])

> 019 C1123-2 **My Old Herdin' Song** Conqueror 8598

> 020 C1124-1 **Get Along Little Doggie** Conqueror 8598

> 021 C1125-1,2 **Barefoot Days** unissued

October 30, 1935 Furniture Mart Building, 666 Lake Shore Drive, Chicago, IL – Dean Boys (Jimmie Dean [vcl], Eddie Dean [vcl/glt])

> 022 C 1139-2 **That Little Boy of Mine** Conqueror 8597

> 023 C1140-1,2 **Who's That Calling?** Unissued

024 C1141-2 **The Oregon Trail** Conqueror 8596 ARC 60253

025 C1142-1 **We're Saying Goodbye** ARC 60554

026 C1143-1 **Seven More Days** ARC 60554

November 1, 1935 Furniture Mart Building, 666 Lake Shore Drive, Chicago, IL – Dean Boys (Jimmie Dean [vcl], Eddie Dean [vcl/glt])

027 C1147-1 **Red Sails in the Sunset** Conqueror 8599 ARC 60253 Minerva M-14027

028 C1148-2 **There's an Old Family Album in the Parlor** Conqueror 8599 ARC 70257

029 C1149-1 **Roll Along Prairie Moon** Conqueror 8596

030 C1150-2 **Golden Barefoot Days** Conqueror 8597 ARC 61255

September 4, 1941 Los Angeles, CA – Eddie Dean (Gus Snow [gt], Martin Kob [bass], Jack Statham [accordion])

031 DLA 2718-A **Little Grey Home in the West** Decca 6026

032 DLA 2719-A **On the Banks of the Sunny San Juan** Decca 5988

033 DLA 2720-A **It's Harvest Time in Peaceful Valley** Decca 5988

034 DLA 2721-A **Where the Silvery Colorado Wents Its Way** Decca 6026

February 25, 1942 Los Angeles, CA – Eddie Dean (Herb Kratoska [gt], Frank Marvin [steel], Budd Hatch [bass], Paul Sells [piano/accordion])

035 DLA 2914-A **I'm Back in the Saddle Again** Decca 6034

036 DLA 2915-A **Sleepy Time in Carolie** Decca 6034 46135

038 DLA 2917-A **I'm Coming Home, Darlin'** Decca 6086

039 DLA 2918 **The Land Where the Roses Never Fade** Decca [RSA] FM-5518

040 DLA 2919 **Don't Forget That Jesus Loves You** Decca [RSA] FM-5518

Ca. 1945 Hollywood, CA – Eddie Dean (unknown musicians)

043 **Careless Darlin'** Bel-Tone E-0267

044 **This Lonely World** Bel-Tone E-0267 Gold Seal 2829

045 **Born to Be Blue** Bel-Tone E-0268

046 **The Low Road's Good Enough For Me** Bel-Tone E-0268 Gold Seal 2829

047 **Cry, Cry, Cry** Bel-Tone E-0269

048 **For Better Or Worse** Bel-Tone E-0269

049 **1501 Miles of Heaven** Bel-Tone E-0273

050 **Dream Rose** Bel-Tone E-0273

June 1946 Hollywood, CA – Eddie Dean (unknown musicians)

051 T 772 **Missouri** Majestic 11000

052 T 773 **There's a Rose That Grows in the Ozarks** Majestic 1101

053 T 774 **No Vacancy** Majestic 11000/Royale VLP-6087

054 T 775 **I Was Wrong** Majestic 11001

September 1946 Hollywood, CA – Eddie Dean (unknown musicians)

055 T 913 **Rainbow At Midnight** Majestic 11004/Royale VLP-6087

056 T 914 **Kentucky Waltz** Majestic 11004/Royale VLP-6087

057 T 915 **Ain't It a Shame, Love?** Majestic 1107

058 T 916/2602 **I'll Cry on My Pillow Tonight** Majestic 1107

June 1947 Hollywood, CA – Eddie Dean (unknown musicians)

059 T 1231 **The Midnight Train** Majestic 11021

060 T 1232 **Rose Anne of San Jose** Majestic 11021

061 T 1233 **Toodle-Oo My Darling** Majestic 11018

062 T 1234/2601* **On the Banks of the Sunny San Juan** Majestic 11019 Mercury 6195*

July 1947 Hollywood, CA – Eddie Dean (unknown musicians)

063 T 1234 **It's a Boy** Majestic 11019

064 T 1244 **Let's Go Sparkin'** Majestic 11019

065 T 1245 **I'm a Kansas Man** Majestic 11020

066 T 1246 **Spring Has Come to Old Missouri** Majestic 11018

1948 poss. Hollywood, CA – Eddie Dean (Frontiersman)

067 **One Has My Name, The Other Has My Heart** Crystal 132

068 **Wake Me Up in the Morning By the Swanee River** Crystal 132

069 CRS-211 **Baby You Should Live So Long** 148 211

070 **California Waltz** 148 211

071 **Gravedigger's Lament** Crystal 156

072 **A Million Tears Ago** Crystal 156

January or February 1949 Hollywood, CA – Eddie Dean (unknown musicians)

073 2340 **Don't Tell Me Stories** Mercury 6170

074 2341 **Careless Hands** Mercury 6170

075 2342 **Neath Texas Skies** Mercury 6210 – x45

076 2343/PBE-972 **One You Must Choose** Mercury 6195 6210-x45/Wing WC-16297

Ca. September 1949 poss. Radio Recorders, 7000 Santa Monica Blvd., Hollywood, CA – Eddie Dean and His Boys (unknown musicians)

077 2628 **I Wish I Knew** 6219

078 2629 **Fool's Gold** 6219

Ca. February 1950 Hollywood, CA – Eddie Dean (unknown musicians)

079 7500/YW-7564/YW-7583 **Devil's Desert Land** 6251

080 7501/YW-7565/YW-7584 **You Want to Divorce Me** 6251

Ca. March 1950 Hollywood, CA - Eddie Dean (unknown musicians)

081 YW11/YW-7575 **Call of the Outlaw** 6299

082 7512/YW-7576 **Cowboy** 6282

083 7513/YW-7577 **I Asked a Dream** 6299

084 7514/YW-7578 **On the Banks of the Sunny San Juan** 6282

December 21, 1950 [No. 2006] Capitol Recording Studio, 5515 Melrose Ave., Hollywood, CA - Eddie Dean

085 6939-4 **My Life With You** Capitol F1362

086 6940-3 **Will They Open Up That Door?** F1362

087 6941-1 **If I Should Come Back** F1389

088 6942-7 **All That I'm Asking Is Sympathy** F1389

Ca. February 2, 1951 [No. 2047] Capitol Recording Studio, 5515 Melrose Ave., Hollywood, CA - Eddie Dean (Producer: Ken Nelson)

089 7070 **Let Me Hold You** F1590

090 7100 **Please Don't Cry** F1424

091 7101 **I'll Be Back** F1424

092 7102 **My Sweetheart, My Own** F1497

March 27, 1951 [No. 2111] Capitol Recording Studio, 5515 Melrose Ave., Hollywood, CA - Eddie Dean

093 7334-7 **I Married the Girl** F1590

094 7335-3 **I'm the Old Friend** F1497

095 7336-18 **Poor Little Swallow** F2086

March 27, 1951 [No. 2251] Capitol Recording Studio, 5515 Melrose Ave., Hollywood, CA – Eddie Dean

096 7684 **Blue Wedding Bells** F1915

097 7685 **I'm Not in Love, Just Involved** F1729 (duet with Margie McPeters [Margie Mack])

098 7686 **Roses Remind Me of You** F1729

099 7687 **Cold Yellow Gold** F2086

October 20, 1951 [No. 2335] Capitol Recording Studio, 5515 Melrose Ave., Hollywood, CA – Eddie Dean (unknown musicians)

100 9109 **Tears On My Guitar** F1915/Toshiba ECS-50062

101 9110-11 **The Lord's Prayer** F1842

102 9111 **Beloved Enemy** F1842

Toshiba ECS-50062 **Wanted!** (Japan)

April 24, 1952 poss. Hollywood, CA – Eddie Dean

103 82759 **Raindrops** Coral 9-60740

104 82760 **I Understand** Coral 9-60740

November 3, 1953 Universal Recorders, 6757 Hollywood Blvd., Hollywood, CA – Eddie Dean's Golden Cowboys

105 ODE 1701-A-4 **I'm a Stranger in My Home** Ode 1701 Intro 45-6087

106 ODE 1701-B-4 **Put a Little Sweetin' in Your Love** Ode 1701 Intro 45-6087

107 ODE 1710-A-1 **Bimbo** Ode 1710

108 ODE 1710-B-2 **No, No Not Grandma** Ode 1710

Ca. September 1954 poss. Radio Recorders, 7000 Santa Monica Blvd., Hollywood, CA - Eddie Dean and the Frontiersmen

111 **I Dreamed of a Hillbilly Heaven** Sage and Sand 78-180/LP C-16

112 **Stealing** Sage and Sand 78-180

113 **Impatient Blues** 45-188/LP C-16 Crown CST-584

114 **Cry of a Broken Heart** 45-188

Ca. February 1955 poss. Radio Recorders, 7000 Santa Monica Blvd., Hollywood, CA - Eddie Dean and the Frontiersmen

115 **Blessed Are They** 45-199

116 **Walk Beside Me** 45-199/LP C-16 Crown CST-584

117 **An Orphan's Prayer** 45-200

118 **Just-a-While** 45-200

1955 Hollywood, CA – Eddie Dean

119 6221 **The Big Stampede** Bronco 6221/6222

120 6222 **The 66 Stampede** 6221/6222

Ca. September 1955 Hollywood, CA – Eddie Dean and Joannie Hall

121 **Open Up Your Door, Boy** 45-207

122 **Sign on the Door** 45-207

Ca. October 1955 Radio Recorders, 7000 Santa Monica Blvd., Hollywood, CA - Eddie Dean and the Frontiersmen

123 **The First Christmas Bell** 45-208

124 **Somebody Great** 45-208

Ca. January 1956 Radio Recorders, 7000 Santa Monica Blvd., Hollywood, CA - Eddie Dean and the Frontiersmen

125 **Downgrade** 45-215

126 R1101 **Look Homeward Angel** 45-215 Crown CST-586

Ca. August 1956 Hollywood, CA – Eddie Dean & Cletro Combo (Eddie Cletro [gt], ? [gt], Bill Flynn [bass], Tex Atwater [drums], Eddie Carver [accordion], Joe DeRose [fiddle], John Stout [fiddle], ? [sax)

127 R1192 **Rock 'n Roll Cowboy** Sage and Sand 226

128 R1191 **On the Banks of the Old Rio Grande** Sage and Sand 226/ Crown CST-584

CA. 1956 Radio Recorders, 7000 Santa Monica Blvd., Hollywood, CA – Eddie Dean and the Frontiersmen (Eddie Dean [vcl], Hal Southern, [gt], Wayne West [bass], Hi Busse [accordion])

129 **Ridin' Down the Canyon** Sage and Sand C-1 Sound LP-603

130 **Cattle Call** Sage and Sand C-1 Sound LP-603

131 **Ragtime Cowboy Joe** Sage and Sand C-1 Sound LP-603

132 **Wagon Wheels** Sage and Sand C-1 Sound LP-603

133 **Tumbling Tumbleweeds** Sage and Sand C-1 Sound LP-603

134 **Cowboy's Prayer** Sage and Sand C-1 Sound LP-603

135 **Empty Saddles in the Old Corral** Sage and Sand C-1 Sound LP-603

136 **Little Joe the Wrangler** Sage and Sand C-1 Sound LP-603

137 **Whoopi Ti-Yi-Yo** Sage and Sand C-1 Sound LP-203

138 **Cool Water** Sage and Sand C-1 Sound LP-603

139 **There's a Goldmine in the Sky** Sage and Sand C-1 Sound LP-603

140 **Last Roundup** Sage and Sand C-1 Sound LP-603

Ca. January 1957 Hollywood, CA – Eddie Dean and Cletro Combo (Eddie Cletro [gt], ? [gt], Bill Flynn [bass], Tex Atwater [drums], Eddie Carver [accordion])

141 **Walkin' After Midnight** Sage and Sand 231

142 **Fingerprints** Sage and Sand 231

1957 Hollywood, CA – Eddie Dean

143 **Lonesome Guitar** 45-235

144 **Taos** 45-235

145 **Now Ain't That Love** Sage EDLP-C-5HI

146 **Did You Really Mean It** Sage EDLP-C-5HI

147 **How Can We Two Share One Heart** Sage EDLP-C-5HI

148 **Far Away Gal** Sage EDLP-C-5HI

149 **Deep in the Ozark Hills** Sage EDLP-C-5HI

150 **On a Desert Highway** Sage EDLP-C-5HI

151 **Way Out Yonder** Sage ED EP-5/EDLP-C-5HI

152 **Old Fashioned Love Song** Sage EDLP-C-5HI

153 **I Could Cry Over You** Sage ED EP-5/EDLP-C-5HI

154 **High Country** Sage EDLP-C-5HI

155 **Wait For Me (a Little While Longer)** Sage EDLP-C-5HI Crown CST-586

156 **Waggin' Tongues** Sage ED EP-5/EDLP-C-5HI

157 **When I Move to That Range** Sage EDLP-C-5HI

158 **Old Wyoming** Sage ED EP-5/EDLP-C-5HI

159 **I'm Only a Cowboy** Sage EDLP-C-5HI

160 **Raindrop Waltz** Sage EDLP-C-5HI

161 **Home in San Antone** Sage EDLP-C-5HI

162 **I Could Be a Millionaire** Sage EDLP-C-5HI

1957 Hollywood, CA – Eddie Dean

163 **Night Train** 45-236

164 **One Foot Caught in Quicksand** 45-236

165 **Iowa Rose** 45-249/LP C-16

166 **Nothing But Echo** 45-249

Ca. June 1958 Hollywood, CA – Eddie Dean

169 **Whoopi Ti-Yi-Yo** Cricket C 133

170 **Hobble Dehoy** Cricket C 133

171 **Home on the Range** CEP-30

172 **Strawberry Roan** CEP-30

173 **Buffalo Gals** CEP-30

174 **Streets of Laredo** CEP-30

Plus unknown songs for Cricket CR-33

1959 Hollywood, CA – Eddie Dean

181 **Hey, Good Lookin'** Design DLP-89

182 **One Has My Name, The Other Has My Heart** Design DLP-89

183 **Baby, We're Really in Love** Design DLP-89

184 **Teardrops in My Heart** Design DLP-89

185 **Jesus Remembered Me** Design DLP-89

186 **The Bride With the Faded Bouquet** Design DLP-89

187 **Boogie Woogie Cowboy** Design DLP-89

189 **Tell Me** Design DLP-89

190 **There'll Be No Teardrops Tonight** Design DLP-89

191 **From the Crib to the Cross** Design DLP-89

192 **Half As Much** Design DLP-89

Ca. April 1960 Hollywood, CA – Eddie Dean

193 **I Took the Blues Out of Tomorrow** Sage 45-325/LP C-16

194 **Seeds of Doubt** 45-235/LP C-16 Crown CST-584

Ca. September 1960 Hollywood, CA – Eddie Dean

195 **Somewhere Along the Line** 45-332/Crown CST-586

196 **If Dreams Could Come True** 45-332/Crown CST-586

197 **Smoke Signals** 45-338/Crown CST-586

198 **Rocket to Heaven** 45-338/Crown CST-586

Ca. September 1961 Hollywood, CA – Eddie Dean

199 **Sailor Man** 45-342

200 **I Can't Go on Alone** 45-342/Crown CST-586

Between 1955-1961 Hollywood, CA – Eddie Dean

201 **Love the Way You Say It** LP C-16 Crown CST-584

202 **Banks of the Old Rio Grande** LP C-16

203 **Tangled Lies** LP C-16 Crown CST-584

204 **Katmandu** LP C-16 Crown CST-584

205 **Make Believe** LP C-16 Crown CST-584

206 **I Called and I Called** LP C-16 Crown CST-584

207 **Downgrade** Crown CST-586

208 **Release Me** Crown CST-584

September 25, 1962 [No. 10893] Hollywood, CA – Eddie Dean [purchased masters]

209 38570 **Run, Jimmy, Run** Capitol 4900

210 38571 **Stop Me (If You've Heard This One Before)** unissued

211 38572 **Don't Take Advantage of Me** unissued

212 38573 **She Doesn't Know I'm Alive** 4900

1966 Hollywood, CA – Eddie Dean

213 **Don't Take Advantage of Me** Commerce M 559

214 **Stop Me (If You've Heard This One Before)** M 559

1966 Hollywood, CA – Eddie Dean (Producer: Larry Scott)

215 TK3M-2574 **One More Time Around** Mosrite M-270

216 TK3M-2575 **Playing Both Ends Against the Middle** Mosrite M-270

Eddie Dean recorded after 1966. Some info in albums and singles list Discography is incomplete.

Eddie Dean Standard Transcriptions

Standard V-125
1. Old Chuck Wagon

2. I've Got a Cowboy's Song For Sale

3. My Old Herdin' Song

4. When I Move to That New Range

5. Road to Santa Fe

6. Prairie Moonbeams

7. Dry and Dusty

8. Restin' Beside the Trail

Standard V-127
9. Ridin' Down That Utah Trail

10. Moonlight on the Painted Desert

11. We're Brandin' Today

12. I've Sold My Saddle For an Old Guitar

13. Rainbow Over the Range

14. Poor Old Bill

15. On the Banks of the Sunny San Juan

16. Palomino Pal of Mine

Standard R-125

17. I Only Want a Buddy Not a Sweetheart

18. Too Many Others

19. Last Letter

20. Boogie Woogie Cowboy

21. I'll Be Back in a Year, Little Darling

22. Greener Pastures

23. Taos

24. Don't Think Anymore About Me

25. Thoughtlessly

26. So Long Old Pal

Standard R-126

27. Dry Your Eyes

28. Twilight O'er My Cabin

29. Blue Eyed Bonnie

30. Cowboy's Heaven

31. You're My One and Only

32. When the Bluebonnets Bloom

33. Moonlit Hours

34. I Asked a Dream

35. Didn't I

36. Harbor of Home

Standard R-128

37. Keep a Light in Your Window Tonight

38. Dusty Old Saddle

39. Prairie Paradise

40. Grieving Wind

41. Close By the River

42. Our Island Paradise

43. I'll Take You Home Again, Kathleen

44. There's a Reason

45. Whispering Sands

46. Nacona Moon

Standard R-130
47. Try Smilin'

48. Goodnight, Little Cowboy

49. Chiquita

50. I Wonder Where You Are Tonight

51. Pretty Quadroon

52. I Wish All My Children Were Babies Again

53. I'll Never Let You Go, Little Darlin'

54. I'm Coming Home, Darling

55. Molly McGee

56. An Old Enchanted Mesa

Standard R-134
57. I Wonder Why You Said Goodbye

58. Walking the Floor Over You

59. This Little Rosary

60. Rose of Santa Fe

61. How Can You Say You Love Me

62. Cryin' Myself to Sleep

63. Pay Me No Mind

64. I Hung My Head and Cried

65. Someday You'll Know You Did Wrong

66. Promise to Be True While I'm Away

Eddie Dean on radio:

All-Star Western Theatre – September 1, 1946, hosted by Foy Willing and the Riders of the Purple Sage

All-Star Western Theatre – December 15, 1946, hosted by Foy Willing and the Riders of the Purple Sage

Albums

Royale VLP-6087 *Riders Of The Purple Sage* – ca. 1953 with Foy Willing (10-inch LP)

Kentucky Waltz

Darling What More Can I Do

Rainbow at Midnight;

Chained to a Memory

The Midnight Train

No Vacancy

Sometimes

California

Sage & Sand C-1 *Golden Cowboy Sings The Greatest Westerns* – 1956 (reissued on Sound LP-603)

Ridin' Down the Canyon

Cattle Call

Ragtime Cowboy Joe

Wagon Wheels

Tumbling Tumbleweeds

Cowboy's Prayer

Empty Saddles in the Old Corral

Little Joe the Wrangler

Whoopi Ti-Yi-Yo

Cool Water

There's a Goldmine in the Sky

Last Roundup

Sage & Sand EDLP-C-5 *Hi-Country* – ca. 1957

Now Ain't That Love

Did You Really Mean It

How Can We

Two Share One Heart

Faraway Gal

Deep in the Ozark Hills

On a Desert Highway

Way Out Yonder

Old Fashioned Love Song

I Could Cry Over You

High Country

Wait For Me (a Little While Longer)

Waggin' Tongues

When I Move to That Range

Old Wyoming

I'm Only a Cowboy

Raindrop Waltz

Home in San Antone

I Could Be a Millionaire

Design DLP-89 *Eddie Dean Sings A Tribute To Hank Williams* – 1959 (reissued on DFC-1026)

Hey, Good Lookin'

One Has My Name, The Other Has My Heart

Baby, We're Really In Love

Teardrops In My Heart

Jesus Remembered Me

The Bride With the Faded Bouquet

Boogie Woogie Cowboy

Cold, Cold Heart

Tell Me

There'll Be No Teardrops Tonight

From The Crib to the Cross

Half As Much

Cricket CR-33 *Musical Heritage Of The Golden West:* (tracks unknown) – 1959

Sage & Sand LP-C 16 *Hillbilly Heaven* – 1961

I Dreamed of a Hillbilly Heaven

Love the Way You Say It

Banks of the Old Rio Grande

Impatient Blues

Tangles Lies

Iowa Rose

Walk Beside Me

Katmandu

Make Believe

Seeds of Doubt

I Called and I Called

I Took The Blues Out of Tomorrow

(reissued on **Crown CLP-5258/CST-258** in 1963 and on **CLP-5434/CST 434 Eddie Dean Sings.** Also reissued on Sutton SU-333 **I Dreamed of a Hillbilly Heaven** with two songs omitted)

Crown CLP-5320/CST-320 The Golden Cowboy – 1963

Green Grass

Your Wayward Heart

Smoke Signals

Rocket to Heaven

I Can't Go on Alone

Wait For Me

Downgrade

Look Homeward Angel

If Dreams Could Come True

Somewhere Along the Line

(reissued in 1965 on **CST-583 Eddie Dean Sings Country & Western**)

Sutton SU-333 I Dreamed of a Hillbilly Heaven – 196? (all tracks from **LP-C-16**)

Hillbilly Heaven

Love the Way You Say It

Banks of the Old Rio Grande

Impatient Blues

Tangles Lies

Iowa Rose

Walk Beside Me

Katmandu

Make Believe

Seeds of Doubt

Crown CLP-5578/CST-578 *Eddie Dean Sings Little Green Apples* – ca. 1967

A Heart Will Not Be Silent Long

You Walked Out of My Heart

Banks of the Old Rio Grande

Little Green Apples

Wing Ding Tonight

Country Maggie

The Crawdad Song

You Try a Lot

John Henry

The Cavern

Crown CLP-5581/CST-581 *Release Me* – ca. 1967

Release Me

Love the Way You Say It

Banks of the Old Rio Grande

Impatient Blues

Tangled Lies

Katmandu

Walk Beside Me

Make Believe

Seeds of Doubt

I Called and I Called

Tiara TST-562 *Saddle Up!! With Eddie Dean and Cort Johnson* – 196?
    (sampler, all tracks from **C-16**)

[Eddie Dean]

    Hillbilly Heaven

    Love the Way You Say It

    Banks of the Old Rio Grande

    Impatient Blues

    Tangled Lies

[Cort Johnson]

    Jes' Talkin'

    I'm a Poor Boy

    Down in the Valley

    On the Banks of the Arkansas

    The Fox

Tiara TMT 7563 *In Person* – 196?
    (sampler, all tracks from **C-16**)

[Eddie Dean]

    I Called and I Called

    I Took the Blues Out of Tomorrow

    Iowa Rose

    Walk Beside Me

    Katmandu

[Cort Johnson]

    Black Is the Color of My True Love's Hair

    The Three Foolish Piglets

    Fly into Mount Zion

Amber Tresses Tied in Blue

I Wonder As I Wander

Passaro 3326 *Eddie Dean* (tracks unknown)

Showcase SSH 103/4 *Eddie Dean* (tracks unknown)

Shasta SHLP-513 *Sincerely Eddie Dean* – 1974

One Has My Name, The Other Has My Heart

Release Me

Tumbling Tumbleweeds

I Fall to Pieces

Make the World Go Away

That Silver-Haired Daddy of Mine

Green, Green Grass of Home

Born to Lose

Old Shep

Just a Closer Walk With Thee

Hillbilly Heaven

Shasta SH-LP-537 *A Cowboy Sings Country* – 1976

San Antonio Rose

All I Have to Offer

Foggy River

Can't Help Falling in Love

Cool Water

Your Cheating Heart

Four Walls

I Can't Stop Loving You

Today I Started Loving You Again

My Elusive Dream (with Karen Scales)

(reissued in 1997 on **KRB 5149-2**)

Western Film Collector WFC-61576 *Dean Of The West* – June 15, 1976 (probably recorded in 1974)

Hills of Old Wyoming

Wagon Wheels

Courtin' Time

Tumbleweed Trail

Black Hills

Driftin' River

Ain't No Gal Got a Brand on Me

Stars Over Texas

Way Back in Oklahoma

On The Banks of the Sunny San Juan

Castle [UK] LP-8106 *I Dreamed of a Hillbilly Heaven* - 1981

I Dreamed of a Hillbilly Heaven

Stealing

Cold Yellow Gold

Roses Remind Me of You

I'm Not in Love, Just Involved

Poor Little Swallow

Orphan's Prayer

Just Awhile

Sign on the Door

All That I'm Asking Is Sympathy

If I Should Come Back

Careless Darlin'

This Lonely World

Gravedigger's Lament

Branson Gold BGR 6353-2 *Eddie Dean in Concert* - 1985

San Antonio Rose

One Has My Name, The Other Has My Heart

The Days That End in "Y"

Wabash Cannonball

Medley: Back in the Saddle/Rye Whiskey/Together Again/Crawdad Song

Release Me

Medley: Tumbling Tumbleweeds/Cool Water/Wagon Wheels

For the Good Times

Old Man River

What Would I Do Without My Music?

Simitar 5569-2 *Collector's Edition* – February 24, 1998

Hey, Good Lookin'

One Has My Name, The Other Has My Heart

Half As Much

Teardrops in My Heart

The Streets of Laredo

Ain't No Gal Got a Brand on Me

The Bride With the Faded Bouquet

Boogie Woogie Cowboy

Cold, Cold Heart

There'll Be No Teardrops Tonight

Baby, We're Really in Love

A Cowboy's Dream

Cattle Compact [GER] CCD-214 *The Late and Great Eddie Dean: (1944-1945)* –
1998 (transcriptions)

Boogie Woogie Cowboy

There's a Reason

Try Smilin'

Rose f Santa Fe

How Can You Say You Love Me

Pay Me No Mind

I Hung My Head And Cried

Someday You'll Know You Did Wrong

Promise to Be True While I'm Away

I've Sold My Saddle For an Old Guitar

Poor Old Bill

Rainbow Over the Range

Too Many Others

Taos

Don't Think Anymore About Me

Thoughtlessly

You're My One and Only

When the Bluebonnets Bloom

I Asked a Dream

Walking the Floor Over You

I Wonder Why You Said Goodbye

I'll Never Let You Go (Little Darlin')

I'm Coming Home Darling

Keep a Light in Your Window

Soundies SCD-4116 *On The Banks Of the Sunny San Juan* – January 25, 2001 (transcriptions)

I Wonder Why You Said Goodbye

Walking the Floor Over You

This Little Rosary

Rose of Santa Fe

How Can You Say You Love Me?

Cryin' Myself to Sleep

Pay Me No Mind

I Hung My Head and Cried

Someday You'll Know You Did Wrong

Promise to Be True While I'm Away

On the Banks of the Sunny San Juan

Palomino Pal of Mine

Ridin' Down That Utah Trail

Moonlight on the Painted Desert

We're Brandin' Today

I've Sold My Saddle For an Old Guitar

Rainbow Over the Range

Poor Old Bill

The Old Chuck Wagon

I've Got a Cowboy's Song For Sale

My Old Herding Song

The Road to Santa Fe

Prairie Moonbeams

Dry and Dusty

Restin' Beside the Trail

When I Move to That New Range

Varese Vintage 302 066136-2 *The Very Best of Eddie Dean* – July 2000 (Shasta recordings)

I Dreamed of a Hillbilly Heaven

One Has My Name, The Other Has My Heart

Release Me

I Fall to Pieces

That Silver-Haired Daddy of Mine

Green, Green Grass of Home

Born to Lose

Somewhere, My Love

Cool Water

I Can't Help Falling in Love

Four Walls

Tumbling Tumbleweeds (with Karen Scales)

My Whole Life Was You

Shenandoah

On the Banks of the Sunny San Juan

Allegro 11004 *1501 Miles of Heaven* – May 2001 (double)

Sleepy Time in Caroline

How Can You Say That You Love Me

This Lonely World

Spring Has Come Again to Old Missouri

Red Sails in the Sunset

Oregon Trail

I'm a Stranger in My Home

I Was Wrong

One You Must Choose

Careless Darlin'

Dream Rose

1501 Miles of Heaven

Put a Little Sweetin' in Your Love

Fool's Gold

Where the Silvery Colorado Winds Its Way

Wake Me in the Morning By the Swanee River

Careless Hands

Gravedigger's Lament

The Low Road's Good Enough For Me

A Million Tears Ago

Don't Tell Me Stories

One Has My Name, The Other Has My Heart

Rose of Santa Fe

I Wonder Why You Said Goodbye

Promise to Be True While I'm Away

Walking the Floor Over You

Someday You'll Know I Did Wrong

Whoopee Ti Yi Yo

Cattle Compact [GER] CCD-233 *The Golden Age of Eddie Dean* – 2001

I'm a Stranger in My Home

Put a Little Sweetin' in Your Love

Careless Darlin'

This Lonely World

Gravedigger's Lament

A Million Tears Ago

One You Must Choose

Spring Has Come Again to Old Missouri

Wake Me in the Morning By the Swanee River

One Has My Name, The Other Has My Heart

Born to Be Blue

The Low Road's Good Enough For Me

1501 Miles of Heaven

Dream Rose

The Midnight Train (of Lonesome Valley)

Careless Hands

Don't Tell Me Stories

Prairie Paradise

Close By the River

Our Island Paradise

Chiquita

I Wish All My Babies Were Children Again

Dry Your Eyes

Didn't I

BACM [UK] CD D 066 *Dusty Old Saddle* – 2005 (transcriptions)

I've Got a Cowboy's Song For Sale

My Old Herding Song

Dusty Old Saddle

When I Move to That New Range

Road to Santa Fe

Prairie Moonbeams

Dusty and Dry

Restin' Beside the Trail

Moonlight on the Painted Desert

We're Brandin' Today

Palomino Pal of Mine

I Only Want a Buddy Not a Sweetheart

I'll Be Back in a Year Little Darling

Green Pastures

So Long Old Pal

Twilight O'er My Cabin

Blued-Eyed Bonnie

Cowboy's Heaven

Moonlit Hours

Grieving Wind

I'll Take You Home Again, Kathleen

Whispering Sands

Goodnight, Little Cowboy

Old Chuck Wagon

I Wonder Where You Are Tonight

Molly McGee

An Old Enchanted Mesa

Notes

Introduction

1. "The Cowboy Code" comes from the Gene Autry Survivors Trust of 1994 as was featured in Delta Airlines *Sky* magazine, August 1998.

2. Dorinson, Patrick. "Why the Cowboy Code Is Not Frivolous." Published February 10, 2011, by FoxNews.com.

3. Owen, James P. *Cowboy Ethics: What Wall Street Can Learn From the Code of the West.* Ketchum, Idaho: Stoecklein Publishing, 2005.

4. Cronbaugh, Craig (April 1996). "The 'Golden Stars' Are Dying; No One Can Replace Them." "Record Scratches" opinion column, *North English Record,* North English, Iowa.

Chapter 1

1. King, Edward Fillingham. *Ten Thousand Wonderful Things: Comprising Whatever is Marvelous and Rare, Curious, Eccentric and Extraordinary.* New York: Ulan Press, 1923. p. 315.

2. Eddie Dean transcribed interview from April 1986.

3. Eddie Dean audio taped interview from December 21, 1997.

4. United States Census, County of Hopkins, Texas, 1910.

5. United States Census, County of Lauderdale, Alabama, November 6, 1850.

6. Familysearch.org, 35th Regiment, Alabama Infantry.

7. Eddie Dean transcribed interview from April 1986.

8. Ibid.

9.   Adams, Florence Chapman. *Hopkins County and Our Heritage*. Sulphur Springs, Texas, p. 197.

10. Ibid.

11. Eddie Dean transcribed interview from April 1986.

12. Ibid.

13. Eddie Dean audio taped interview from December 21, 1997.

Chapter 2

1.   Gee, Wilson. *The Place of Agriculture in American Life*. New York: The Macmillan Company, 1930, Online edition.

2.   Ibid.

3.   Eddie Dean transcribed interview from April 1986.

4.   United States Census, County of Hopkins, Texas, 1920.

5.   Sulphur Springs, Texas website at Sulphursspringstx.org.

6.   Ibid.

7.   Gilbert, Bob and Michelle. "Hopkins County," *Handbook of Texas Online*. Published by the Texas State Historical Association. http://www.tshaonline.org/handbook/online/articles/hch18

8.   Eddie Dean transcribed interview from April 1986.

9.   *The Hi Lander*, Sulphur Springs High School annual from 1926.

10. Russell, Tony. *Country Music Originals: The Legends and the Lost*. Oxford University Press, 2007.

11. "Radio," *Handbook of Texas Online*. Published by the Texas State Historical Association. http://www.tshaonline.org/handbook/online/articles/ebr01

12. "Jimmie Rodgers Biography," *Songwriters Hall of Fame*.

13. Jimmie Rodgers died on May 26, 1933, from a pulmonary hemorrhage while staying at the Taft Hotel in New York City.

14. Eddie Dean transcribed interview from April 1986.

15. *Gospel Music Hi-Lites*, August 1966, page 12. This ephemeral publication is available in microform at the library of the Indiana University School of Music, Blooming-

ton, Indiana.

16. Blackwell, Lois. *The Wings of a Dove: The Story of Gospel Music in America*. Norfolk, Virginia: Donning Publishing, 1978, pp. 49-50.

17. Eddie Dean transcribed interview from 1974.

Chapter 3

1. Turner, George Kibbe. "The City of Chicago, A Study of the Great Immoralities," *McClure's Magazine* 28 (April 1907); pp. 576-579. Turner's article from this gentlemen's magazine at the time features Prohibitionist rhetoric. It also provides a number of facts as to the extent of the bootlegging operations during Prohibition.

2. Piersen, Joe (2004). "Chicago and North Western: A Capsule History." Chicago and North Western Historical Society. http://www.cnwhs.org

3. Childers, Scott. "The Beginning." *The History of WLS Radio* (2010). http://www.wlshistory.com

4. Ibid.

5. Eddie Dean audio taped interview from April 1986.

6. WBBM radio. http://www.wbbmradio.org

7. Bradley Kincaid. Nashville Songwriters Foundation Hall of Fame website at nashvillesongwritersfoundation.com.

8. KMA website at kmaland.com

9. Earl May website at earlmay.com

10. United States Census, County of Yankton, South Dakota, 1920 and 2010.

11. WNAX website at wnax.com

Chapter 4

1. Eddie Dean audio taped interview from April 1986.

2. South Dakota Official State Homepage at sd.gov.

3. Mount Rushmore website mountrushmoreinfo.com

4. Corn Palace website at cornpalace.org.

Chapter 5

1. United States Census, County of Yankton, South Dakota, 2010.

2.   Kansas State Historical Society website at kshs.org.

3.   Eddie Dean audio taped interview from December 21, 1997.

Chapter 6

1.   PBS: *The Hayloft Gang: The Story of the National Barn Dance,* August 2011.

2.   WLS website on wls.com

3.   Ibid.

4.   Oshkosh website at oshkosh.com

5.   Gene Autry Official website at autry.com

6.   *Billboard* Magazine, August 28, 1954. A special edition of *Billboard* commemorating the twentieth anniversary of Decca Records.

7.   Campbell, Al, Biography on Arthur Satherley for Allmusic.com

Chapter 7

1.   Art Rush died from heart failure at age eighty-one on January 1, 1989, in Burbank, California.

2.   George-Warren, Holly. *Public Cowboy No. 1: The Life and Times of Gene Autry.* Oxford: Oxford University Press. 2007, pp. 170-171.

3.   Magers, Boyd. *Gene Autry Westerns.* Madison, NC: Empire Publishing, Inc. 2007, p. 124.

4.   Mathis, Jack. *Valley of the Cliffhangers Supplement.* Jack Mathis Advertising (1995). p. 10.

5.   Pop Sherman died in 1952 just as he was getting back in to production.

6.   According to a Les Adams review of *Harmony Trail* for the Internet Movie Database (IMDb).

7.   According to a signed contract by Eddie dated September 25, 1944.

8.   Eddie's Employee Earnings Statements from *The Lone Ranger* radio show.

Chapter 8

1.   United States Census, County of Los Angeles, California, 1940.

2. Realtor.com

3. Rumble, John. "Fred Rose: Biography at the Country Music Hall of Fame and Museum." Country Music Hall of Fame.org

4. Eddie's Employee Earnings statements from Gene Autry's Flying "A" Ranch Rodeo dated from February 1942.

5. Eddie Dean appeared as a guest on *All-Star Western Theatre* in September and December 1946.

6. Eddie Dean transcribed interview from 1974.

7. "Pan American and Bel-Tone Newest Indie Disk Labels," *Billboard* Magazine, July 28, 1945, p. 19.

8. *Billboard* announcement on August 24, 1946.

9. "Bel-Tone Folds: 40G Deficit," *Billboard* Magazine, December 7, 1946, p. 16.

10. International Association of Jazz Record Collectors (IAJRC), *IAJRC Journal*, Vol. 29, p. 33 (1996).

11. Eddie Dean audio taped interview from September 1997.

Chapter 9

1. "Cinecolor Photography." Widescreenmuseum.com

2. Fernett, Gene. *Hollywood's Poverty Row 1930-1950*. Florida: Coral Reef Publications. 1973, pp. 15-19.

3. Ibid.

4. Ibid.

5. Ibid.

6. B-Westerns.com website, Robert Emmett Tansey.

7. B-Westerns.com website, Al 'Lash' LaRue.

8. May-June 1999 #29 issue of *Western Clippings*, a Western-film magazine website on the Internet that is also published in print edition six times a year by Boyd Magers, (pronounced MAJORS), an authority on B-Western films who resides in Albuquerque, New Mexico.

9. Emmett Lynn, Biography, IMDb (Internet Movie Data Base).

10. According to the Internet Movie Database, Forrest Taylor is identified in about four hundred films, including three hundred twenty-five sound era films. Two hundred one are Westerns and thirty-six are chapter plays. His credits at Republic Pictures number about seventy-five between 1937-1953 (most of those are B-Westerns and serials).

11. Eddie Dean audio taped interview from January 1986.

12. B-Westerns.com website, Charles King

13. *Western Clippings* # 29, May/June 1999.

14. Charles King died on May 7, 1957, at John Wesley County Hospital in Los Angeles, CA. He was sixty-two years old.

15. *Western Clippings* # 29, May/June 1999, p. 15.

16. Ibid.

17. Roscoe Ates died on March 1, 1962.

18. Ed Wallace interview on B-Westerns.com, The Sunshine Boys

19. Ibid.

20. Ibid.

21. B-Westerns.com website, David Sharpe.

22. Telephone interview with Boyd Magers from August 2013, his home in Albuquerque, New Mexico.

23. Wierzbicki, Eugene. *Music, Sound and Filmmakers: Sonic Style in Cinema.* Oxford, England: Routledge, 2012.

24. B-Western.com website, Dennis Moore

25. Telephone interview with Boyd Magers from August 2013, his home in Albuquerque, New Mexico.

26. According to Richard Smith III, a contributing writer for *Western Clippings* # 29, May/June 1999, p. 24.

27. Ibid.

28. Louise Currie interview in *Western Clippings* # 29, May/June 1999, pp. 15-16.

Chapter 10

1. B-Westerns.com website, Ladies, Shirley Patterson.

2. B-Westerns.com, Eddie Dean.

3. *Western Clippings*.com website, Heavies, William Fawcett.

4. Ibid.

5. According to Richard Smith III, a contributing writer for *Western Clippings* # 29, May/June1999, p. 24.

6. Eddie Dean audio taped interview from January 1986.

7. *Los Angeles Daily News*, March 14, 1967.

8. Eddie Dean audio taped interview from September 1997.

Chapter 11

1. Ray Taylor, Biography, Wikipedia.org

2. Ibid.

3. Pitts, Michael R. *Western Movies: A Guide to 5,105 Feature Films,* 2nd Edition. Jefferson, NC: McFarland and Company, 2012, p. 58.

4. B-Westerns.com website, Villains, I. Stafford Jolley.

5. Patricia Harper, Biography, IMDb (Internet Movie Data Base).

6. Walter Greene, Biography, IMDb (Internet Movie Data Base).

7. Helen Mowery, Biography, IMDb (Internet Movie Data Base).

8. Elmer Clifton, Biography, IMDb (Internet Movie Data Base).

9. Ibid.

10. Robert B. Churchill, Biography, IMDb (Internet Movie Data Base).

11. Eddie Dean audio taped interview from September 1997.

12. Gregg Barton quote in *Western Clippings* # 29, May/June1999, p. 15.

13. Delores Castle, Biography, IMDb (Internet Movie Data Base).

14. Joseph Poland, Biography, IMDb (Internet Movie Data Base).

15. B-Westerns.com website, Eddie Dean.

16. *Andy Parker's Songs of the Plainsmen,* Vanguard Songs Music Publishers, Hollywood,

CA, 1947.

17. *Western Clippings* # 29, May/June 1999, p. 14.

18. Telephone interview with Joe Parker from August 2013, from his home in Chandler, Arizona.

19. Ibid.

20. Ibid.

21. *River of No Return*, IMDb (Internet Movie Data Base).

22. *Andy Parker's Songs of the Plainsmen*, Vanguard Songs Music Publishers, Hollywood, CA, 1947.

23. Ibid.

24. Ibid.

25. According to Paul Wadey of *The Independent*, a news source originating from the United Kingdom, March 9, 1999.

26. *Andy Parker's Songs of the Plainsmen*, Vanguard Songs Music Publishers, Hollywood, CA, 1947.

27. Corrigan, Tom. "I Remember Corriganville," as told to Don Creacy.

28. Ibid.

29. B-Westerns.com website, George Chesebro.

30. Eddie Dean audio taped interview from January 1986.

31. Joseph O'Donnell, Biography, IMDb (Internet Movie Data Base)

32. Nancy Gates website at nancygates.com

33. Russell Arms quote in *Western Clippings* # 29, May/June 1999, p. 15.

34. B-Westerns.com website, Eddie Dean.

35. William Edison Lively, Biography, IMDb (Internet Movie Data Base).

36. Brad Slaven quote in *Western Clippings* #29, May-June 1999, p. 15.

37. B-Westerns.com website, Terry Frost.

38.   Ibid.

39.   Ibid.

40.   Phyllis Planchard, Biography, IMDb (Internet Movie Data Base).

41.   *Los Angeles Times*, April 11, 2008.

42.   Young Actors website, Steve Drake, youngactors.org

43.   *Los Angeles Daily News*, December 20, 1948.

44.   Jennifer Holt, Biography, IMDb (Internet Movie Data Base).

45.   B-Westerns.com, Heroines, Jennifer Holt.

46.   Edward Earl Repp, Biography, IMDb (Internet Movie Data Base).

47.   Eddie Dean audio taped interview from September 1997.

48.   Classic TV Archive http://ctva.biz/US/Western.htm

49.   McNeil, Alex. *Total Television*, New York: Penguin Books, 1996, 4th ed., p. 311.

50.   Classic TV Archive http://ctva.biz/US/Western.htm

51.   IMDb (Internet Movie Data Base), *The Beverly Hillbillies*, Season One, Episode 19.

52.   Actors Television Motion Picture Day Players Contract from Filmways TV Productions, Inc., which Eddie signed.

53.   IMDb (Internet Movie Data Base), *The Beverly Hillbillies*, Season One, Episode 21.

54.   Eddie Dean transcribed interview from 1974.

55.   Ibid.

56.   *Your Cheatin' Heart*, IMDb (Internet Movie Data Base).

Chapter 12

1.   Majestic Records, Wikipedia.org

2.   Majestic Records Numerical Listing, http://www.78discography.com/Majestic.htm

3.   Ibid.

4. Eddie Dean audio taped interview from September 1997.

5. Eddie Dean transcribed interview from 1974.

6. According to music composer and publisher Dean Kay on his website, www.dean-kay.com

7. Whitburn, Joel (2006). *The Billboard Book of Top Country Hits: 1944-2006, Second Edition.* Record Research, p. 200.

8. Ibid., p. 367.

9. According to music composer and publisher Dean Kay on his website, www.dean-kay.com

10. Eddie Dean transcribed interview from 1974.

11. "Eddie Dean Obituary," Allbusiness.com, March 1999.

12. Eddie Dean transcribed interview from 1974.

13. Patsy Cline Biography at Allmusic.com.

14. Wikipedia.org, Eddie Dean.

Chapter 13

1. Signed contract from the American Federation of Musicians of the United States and Canada dated January 2, 1970,

2. Copeland, Bobby J. (May-June 1999). "Cowboy Commentary." *Western Clippings* #29, p. 28.

3. Lee, Cynthia (June 1985). "Ex-Film Cowboy Sets Sights on Sidewalk Star." *Daily News* (Los Angeles, CA).

4. "Eddie Dean Day" by the Los Angeles City Council in 1994 on You Tube (www.youtube.com)

5. Music Corporation of America (MCA) contracts.

6. Victor, Adam (2008). *The Elvis Encyclopedia.* Gerald Duckworth & Co. Ltd., p. 385.

7. Ibid.

8. Ibid., p. 148.

9. Dixon, Chris (September 4, 2005). "A Rhinestone Cowboy Who Grabbed Cars by the Horns." *The New York Times.*

10.   Beard, Tyler (2001). *100 Years of Western Wear*, p. 72. Gibbs Smith, Salt Lake City.

11.   Dixon, Chris (September 4, 2005). "A Rhinestone Cowboy Who Grabbed Cars by the Horns." *The New York Times.*

12.   According to a signed contract dated June 2, 1976, with the American Federation of Musicians of the United States and Canada, Local 47.

13.   Lee, Cynthia (June 1985). "Ex-Film Cowboy Sets Sights on Sidewalk Star." *Daily News* (Los Angeles, CA).

14.   Ibid.

Chapter 14

1.   *Western Clippings* # 29, May/June 1999, p. 14.

2.   "Eddie Dean Obituary." Allbusiness.com. March 1999.

3.   Ibid.

4.   Eddie Dean audio taped interview from September 1997.

Sources

Adams, Florence Chapman. *Hopkins County and Our Heritage*. Sulphur Springs, Texas, 2006.

Beard, Tyler (2001). *100 Years of Western Wear*, p. 72. Gibbs Smith, Salt Lake City.

Blackwell, Lois. *The Wings of a Dove: The Story of Gospel Music in America*. Norfolk, Virginia: Donning Publishing, 1978.

Gee, Wilson. *The Place of Agriculture in American Life*. New York: The Macmillan Company, 1930.

George-Warren, Holly. *Public Cowboy No. 1: The Life and Times of Gene Autry*. Oxford: Oxford University Press, 2007.

Everson, William K. *A Pictorial History of the Western Film*. Secaucus, NJ: Citadel Press, 1969.

Fernett, Gene. *Hollywood's Poverty Row 1930-1950*. Florida: Coral Reef Publications. 1973.

Gilbert, Bob and Michelle. "Hopkins County," *Handbook of Texas Online*. Published by the Texas State Historical Association.

King, Edward Fillingham. *Ten Thousand Wonderful Things: Comprising Whatever is Marvelous and Rare, Curious, Eccentric and Extraordinary*. New York: Ulan Press, 1923.

Lahue, Kalton C. *Riders of the Range: The Sagebrush Heroes of the Sound and Screen*. New York: Castle Books, 1973.

Mathis, Jack. *Valley of the Cliffhangers Supplement*. Jack Mathis Advertising (1995).

Magers, Boyd. *Gene Autry Westerns*. Madison, NC: Empire Publishing, Inc. 2007.

Owen, James P. *Cowboy Ethics: What Wall Street Can Learn From the Code of the West*. Ketchum, Idaho: Stoecklein Publishing, 2005.

Russell, Tony. *Country Music Originals: The Legends and the Lost*. Oxford: Oxford University Press, 2007.

Shaughnessy, Mary Alice. *Les Paul: An American Original*. New York: Morrow, 1993.

Whitburn, Joel. *The Billboard Book of Top Country Hits: 1944-2006, Second Edition*. Record Research, 2006.

Wierzbicki, Eugene. *Music, Sound and Filmmakers: Sonic Style in Cinema*. Oxford, England: Routledge, 2012.

Wolfe, Charles K. *Classic Country: Legends of Country Music*. New York: Routledge, 2001.

CPSIA information can be obtained at www.ICGtesting.com
Printed in the USA
BVOW02s1825160115

383682BV00010B/99/P